THE BIRD FARM

CARRIER AVIATION AND NAVAL AVIATORS
A HISTORY AND CELEBRATION

PHILIP KAPLAN

Skyhorse Publishing

Skyhorse Publishing books may be purchased in bulk at special discounts for sales promotion, corporate gifts, fund-raising, or educational purposes. Special editions can also be created to specifications. For details, contact the Special Sales Department, Skyhorse Publishing, 307 West 36th Street, 11th Floor, New York, NY 10018 or info@skyhorsepublishing.com.

Skyhorse® and Skyhorse Publishing® are registered trademarks of Skyhorse Publishing, Inc.®, a Delaware corporation.

Visit our website at www.skyhorsepublishing.com.

10 9 8 7 6 5 4 3 2 1

Library of Congress Cataloging-in-Publication Data is available on file.

Cover design by Tom Lau
Cover photographs courtesy of (clockwise from top) Philip Kaplan, the U.S. Navy, the U.S. National Archives, and HMS *Illustrious*

Print ISBN: 978-1-63450-482-9
Ebook ISBN: 978-1-63450-555-0

Printed in China

CONTENTS

Over the years, the aircraft carrier has come to be known to many American naval aviators as "the bird farm."

ON 2 DECEMBER 1908, REAR-ADMIRAL W.S. Cowles, Chief of the U.S. Navy Bureau of Equipment, recommended to the Secretary of the Navy that "a number of airplanes be purchased to operate from a ship's deck, carry a wireless telegraph, operate in weather other than a dead calm, maintain a high rate of speed, and be of such design as to permit convenient stowage on board ship." Thus began the history of the aircraft carrier and naval aviation.

At the advent of the aircraft carrier, the major navies of the world were battleship forces. These great vessels were the largest, most heavily-armed and armored warships afloat, and their very presence had, on occasion, seen them prevail without even engaging the enemy, so intimidating were they. Why, then, did the aircraft carrier virtually scuttle the venerable battlewagon as the new capital ship of the world's great sea powers? To begin with, it was her versatility. The aircraft carrier is at once a self-propelled mobile airbase that is essentially self-sufficient, as well as being a wholly effective servicing facility. Into the twenty-first century, the modern U.S. supercarrier operates as the spearhead of an awesome force called a carrier battle group. The other types of ships in carrier battle groups—destroyers, frigates, cruisers, replenishment tankers, and fast attack submarines—are there to protect "mother," the CVN or nuclear-powered aircraft carrier.

The carrier weapon has another edge over the battleship. It gives a fleet the ability to fight and win a naval battle at arm's length, out of sight of the enemy. At the start of the new millenium, the twelve operational carrier battle groups of the U.S. fleet, and its assault carriers, were capable of covering immense areas of ocean, sending massive air strikes at inshore as well as ocean targets, providing air support for amphibious landings, helicopter troop ferrying, search-and-rescue, and conducting highly sophisticated anti-submarine warfare. While perhaps less than totally invulnerable to enemy attack, the CVN, within the protective shelter of her battle group, is the biggest, widest-ranging, most powerful and fearsome threat that has ever put to sea. In just a quarter of a century her capabilities have utterly eclipsed those of her battleship predecessor. According to the late United States Senator John C. Stennis (namesake of the USS John C. Stennis, CVN-74), Chairman of the U.S. Senate Armed Services Committee from 1969 to 1980, and a strong supporter of a powerful, well-trained and well-equipped military, "The best way to avoid war is to be fully prepared, have the tools of war in abundance, and have them ready." Of the modern nuclear-powered aircraft carrier, Stennis said: "It carries everything and goes full-strength and is ready to fight or go into action within minutes after it arrives at its destination. There is nothing that compares with it when it comes to deterrence."

Clement Ader, a less than successful early French aviator, made the world's first "flight" in a powered airplane from level ground on 9 October 1890. He did the hop in a steam-powered monoplane, the Eole, a large bat-like craft. Ader was then asked by the French Minister of War to design, build, and test a two-seat plane to carry a light bomb-load for the military. The result was a failure, crashing at Satorg on 14 October 1891, and the contract for the warplane was cancelled. Ader, however, had an unshakeable faith in his personal vision of the future of aviation. He accurately forecasted that land warfare would be transformed by the practice of reconnaissance from aircraft, and that it would also revolutionize the methods of war fleets at sea. He predicted that they would carry their aircraft to sea with them. He coined the term porte-avions (aircraft carrier) and wrote that such ships would be unlike any other, with clear, unimpeded flight decks, elevators to take aircraft (with their wings folded) from the flight deck to stowage below for servicing and repairs and bring them back again, and the ability to operate at a high rate of speed. His foresight was amazing.

The world's first reasonably successful take-off by a fixed-wing aircraft from the deck of a ship was made by Eugene Ely, an exhibition pilot for aircraft designer and builder Glenn Curtiss, achieved in a Curtiss Pusher in November 1910. Ely flew the craft down a gently sloping wooden platform on the forecastle of the U.S. light cruiser Birmingham in the afternoon of 14 November as the ship steamed slowly in Chesapeake Bay. In the attempt, Ely's aircraft actually hit the water once, but he retained control and managed to land safely on the shore.

In another equally significant trial held at San Francisco in January 1911, Ely successfully landed a Curtiss aircraft on a specially-built platform over the quarter deck of the cruiser USS Pennsylvania. He used undercarriage hooks to engage one of twenty-two transverse wires that were stretched across the platform and anchored at the sides with sandbags. Within months of this second successful carrier trial, Eugene Ely was dead, killed in an air crash.

In the month prior to Ely's landing trial, Curtiss offered at his own

HMS *Illustrious* is the fifth Royal Navy ship to bear that name. The 20,000-ton *Invincible*-class aircraft carrier supported a mix of up to twenty-two aircraft. She was a sister ship to *Invincible* and *Ark Royal*.

Take-off from the flight deck of the USS *Lexington* in February 1929.

expense, "to instruct an officer of the U.S. Navy in the operation and construction of a Curtiss aeroplane." On 23 December Lieutenant T.G. Ellyson reported to North Island in San Diego bay, and four months later was "graduated" by Curtiss who wrote to the Secretary of the Navy: "Lt. Ellyson is now competent to care for and operate Curtiss aeroplanes."

Within eight years of the Wright brothers' initial powered flight at Kitty Hawk on the North Carolina coast, the capability to take off from and recover an aircraft to a carrier deck (using arresting wires) was proven. Gradually the American Navy became convinced of the value and importance of aviation for patrol and reconnaissance in its future. It concluded that floating airports—aircraft carriers—would have to be developed and acquired to support and exploit its combat airplanes. However,

it was the British who, by the occasion of the Royal Navy's 1913 Naval Maneuvers, had identified and defined nearly all the fundamental requirements for carrier-borne operation, aircraft, and equipment. Wing-folding to facilitate the improved stowage of otherwise bulky aircraft on the limited space of a ship deck, the testing and evaluation of bomb-dropping, gun mounting and firing, and the successful launch of a fourteen-inch torpedo from early British-built carrier-borne aircraft propelled the Royal Navy to the forefront of such development. They also concluded that the purpose-built aircraft carrier must be developed and, by the end of World War I, had achieved that goal. The way to this achievement led to the 1914 conversions of the bulk carrier *Ark Royal* and the large light cruiser *Furious* to aircraft carriers, *Ark Royal* being designed almost from scratch to meet the needs of

naval air operations as they were then perceived. At the same time, the Japanese began work converting the merchant ship *Wakamiya* to carry seaplanes. The French were actually the first to make such a conversion when, in 1912, they changed a torpedo depot ship to an operational seaplane carrier.

The American Navy followed the British lead and converted the collier *Jupiter* into an experimental aircraft carrier, recommissioning it as the USS *Langley* on 20 March 1922. On 22 December of that year, Japan commissioned its first aircraft carrier, the *Hosho*, and the first take-off from its deck was performed in a Mitsubishi IMFI by a British pilot named William Jordan, formerly of the Royal Naval Air Service. *Hosho* was one of the most significant aircraft carriers ever built. Quite small, displacing only 7,470 tons, she was so well designed, with her spaces so well planned, that she could operate up to twenty-six aircraft—a remarkable capability for her size. Even more remarkable, however, was her pioneering installation of an experimental light-and-mirror system for aiding pilots in their landing approaches to her flight deck. It was a concept far ahead of its time, as the approach speeds of the carrier aircraft of the day—and for many years to come—were far slower than those which were to require the eventual design and refinement of the ultimate mirror-light landing system. It is ironic that *Hosho* should be the only one of the ten principal Japanese carriers to survive the Second World War.

During the First World War, the Royal Navy, motivated by German airship bombing raids on East Coast Britain and reconnaissance activity over the North Sea, leaned toward development of sea-borne aircraft in an early warning / interception role: floatplanes operating from carrier vessels in the North Sea. But the concept was flawed. The seaplanes were simply too slow and lacked an adequate rate of climb, preventing them from a timely closure with the German aircraft. The drag created by the floats on the underpowered British planes was just too great. Still, the German airship campaign compelled the Britons to stick with the ineffectual concept.

A Royal Navy pilot, Squadron-Commander E.H. Dunning, was operating aboard HMS *Furious* in the summer of 1917. The ship was extremely fast and Dunning was convinced that her speed would provide the key to developing a routinely safe landing procedure for his pilots, who were flying the agile Sopwith Pup. He soon discovered that the Pup could be easily and gently coaxed over the flight deck of *Furious* to an acceptable landing. The ship had no arrestor wires, but Dunning had rope handles fitted to his Sopwith aircraft and

instructed the deck hands to grip the handles once he had landed, to hold the little plane firmly on the deck. On 2 August 1917 he approached *Furious* and made the first successful carrier deck landing on a ship that was steaming into wind. In a similar landing attempt two days later, Dunning touched down on the deck, a tire on the Sopwith burst, and the aircraft cartwheeled off the edge and into the sea before the deck party could stop it. Dunning was drowned. It was soon accepted that, for an aircraft carrier to operate its aircraft effectively and with relative safety for the pilots and aircrew, a much larger hull would have to be utilized to provide a far greater deck area—an area closer in size to that of a conventional airfield.

The warship designers had to rethink their approach to planning the layout of an aircraft carrier deck and the necessary bridge, funnel, and other external structures. Consensus finally led to acceptance of a full-length flight deck, as free of obstructions to the safe launch and recovery of the ship's aircraft as could be achieved. Safety and practicality required that take-offs be made from the forward end of the ship, and landings onto the aft end. Naval architects had to wrestle with the considerable challenge of positioning the ship's funnel in such a way as to at least minimize the hazard to aviators caused by the smoke of the ship's boiler gases, which reduced visibility for the airmen on landing. Various ideas were tried over many years of carrier development, including a system of ducting to take the smoke discharge toward the stern rather than allowing it eminate from amidships, as was the norm in island superstructure placement. The problem of smoke from a carrier funnel flowing across the flight deck, as it sometimes did, was never fully resolved until the advent of the (smokeless) nuclear powerplant for aircraft carriers in the 1960s. Logic

and pilot preference eventually dictated the starboard placement of the island superstructure, adopted by most of the world's navies for their carriers. The verticality of the narrow island structure which became a standard, and the funnel positioned behind and in line with it, stems from the need to put the bridge, and especially the navigation platform, relatively high and to discharge the smoke conveniently, if not always to the advantage of landing aviators.

I remember the jokes about sabotage and Dublin,
The noisy jungle of cranes and sheerlegs, the clangour,
The draft in February of a thousand matelots from Devonport,
Surveying anxiously my enormous flight-deck and hangar.
—from "HMS *Glory*" by Charles Causley

We sail the ocean blue and our saucy ship's a beauty, we're sober men and true and attentive to our duty.
—from HMS *Pinafore* by William S. Gilbert and Arthur Sullivan

In 1927, the new U.S. Navy carriers *Lexington* and *Saratoga* became the platforms on which the transverse arrestor wire-landing technique was perfected. Their thirty-four knot high speed and other features fulfilled Clement Ader's prophecy.

The period from 1928 through the decade of the 1930s was, despite the economic depression and the drastic restrictions on most nation's economies, one of important development of carriers and their aircraft and tactics. Britain got to grips with the threat posed by Germany rearming, and began a radical reevaluation of the needs of her armed forces. The Fleet Air Arm had been operated under the control of the Air Ministry and had not been well managed under these auspices. It lacked state-of-the-art aircraft and had lost many of its Royal Naval Air Service pilots through absorption into the newly formed Royal Air Force in 1918. Interservice rivalry between the Royal Navy and the RAF finally caused the British government in 1937 to return the responsibility for British naval aviation to the Royal Navy.

Among the most important contributing factors in the development of the aircraft carrier by the great naval powers of the world during the 1930s was the Washington Naval Treaty of 1922. The agenda at Washington was clearly to redefine the sea power of the signatories, in part by imposing a strict rationing on heavy warship construction in a blatant attempt to minimize battleship building. That ultimately worked, though not through the honorable adherence of the treaty participants to the type and tonnage limitations they had imposed on themselves. Rather, future development of battleships was largely curtailed owing to a clause in the treaty which allowed the signatories to opt for converting their unfinished battleship hulls to completion as aircraft carriers. Britain opted to complete her unfinished battleships *Nelson* and *Rodney* as battleships, which later proved to be a mistake as they were unable to achieve more than a twenty-three-knot top speed in a time when aircraft carriers were already capable of speeds in excess of thirty knots. The United States and Japan elected to take up the carrier option, and in so doing were able to launch fast new carriers in the same year that *Nelson* and *Rodney* were launched.

In another controversial decision, the British chose to convert *Furious*

to a proper aircraft carrier, but in the effort they chose to give her a flush-deck in combination with a short bow flying-off deck, for reasons of economy as much as utility. They gave the same design to her sister ships *Glorious* and *Courageous*.

The Japanese, who for several years had been heavily influenced by British carrier design and innovation, promptly based the design of their newest carriers *Akagi* and *Kaga* on that of *Furious*. The mistake here lay mainly in not recognizing that carrier-borne aircraft, both of the future and those about to come on stream, were becoming larger, heavier, and faster, and were certainly going to require considerably more flight deck for take-offs and landings, and more stowage space. The bow flying-off deck would quickly become obsolete. After many years of leading the field in aircraft carrier design and innovation, the British were suddenly no longer on the same page as the Americans.

Like many pilots who have flown for airlines since the Second World War, Frank Furbish came from a military aviation background. He was on the USS *Constellation* (CV-64) from 1984 through to 1986, flying the F-14A Tomcat with VF-21. "Life on an aircraft carrier is like no other. More than 5,000 men (and women now) are packed tightly within the floating city. As large as the ship is, the spaces are generally small and are separated by watertight doors. Only two levels allow continuous fore and aft access—the second deck and the 03 level. And even those levels have 'knee knockers' every few yards.

"On the *Constellation* there were two stores with sundry items, a barber shop, and a small gym. Room

accommodations were directly related to one's rank. Enlisted personnel were in large bunk rooms. Junior officers were in smaller bunk rooms, and senior officers either had their own rooms or shared a room with another officer. I had eight roommates. Our junior officer bunk room was about the size of a large hotel room, with three sets of three-deep bunks which were nothing more than metal frames and foam pads. The spacing between the bunks was so restrictive that big-shouldered guys could not roll over without first jutting out of their bunks. We had a desk/locker combination, a few stand-up gym lockers, and one sink. Privacy was obtained by hanging a curtain around your bunk. Your room was not only your rest area, but also your office. There was little air conditioning and plenty of noise. Rest was constantly interrupted by the needs of fellow roommates to report for watches at all hours of the night. Rest and paperwork was also affected by the location of the berthing. Aircrews were required to be on the 03 level, just below the flight deck. The noise level there is quite high during flight ops, with thirty-ton aircraft landing just above your head. Additional noise was provided by the 'chock chuckers' throwing heavy metal chocks and tie-down chains, and by 'paint chippers.' It always amazed me that there was a constant need for someone to chip paint somewhere on the ship.

"The bathroom or 'head' was another unique feature. On a conventional (non-nuclear) carrier like the *Constellation*, the water always had the aftertaste of fuel oil. The showerhead was a hose with a knob. The knob had a button that had to be held in for the 'mist' to dispense, in order to save water, which fluctuated between scalding and ice cold. At times it would just quit. This usually happened after you had covered yourself with soapy lather. It seems trivial, but after six months of such showers the desire for a long, warm shower with uninterrupted water is enormous.

"On another deployment, I graduated to a four-man bunk room located forward on the port side just under a catapult and abeam of the water-break. The water-break was the device that stopped the catapult shuttle, which travelled at 150 mph as it tossed a multi-ton aircraft into the sky. Imagine, if you will, that your cot is inside a dumpster and someone is randomly crashing a large sledge hammer into the side of it. You simply cannot sleep, period. Some people believed that if you could manage to sleep twelve hours a day the cruise would be only half as long. Some of them tried."

Royal Navy Rear Admiral Dennis Campbell's career as a Fleet Air Arm aviator exposed him to many near misses and close calls. He realized early on that one of the greatest hazards faced by a naval aviator was the probability of a collision with parked aircraft—or a barrier placed in front of such aircraft to protect them—if he should fail to catch an arresting cable in his deck landing. He came up with an amazingly simple solution . . . the angled flight deck, which allowed carrier pilots to approach the deck at a slight angle to the ship itself. Should the pilot fail to catch one of the arresting cables, he could "bolt" and go around again for another landing approach by applying full power on touch-down and flying off the clear port bow. The idea was so successful that both the Royal and U.S. navies adopted it immediately and most large aircraft

Chance Vought F4U Corsair fighters on the flight deck of the USS *Badoeng Strait* during the Korean War in the early 1950s.

Routine maintenance aboard HMS *Illustrious*.
The BAE Sea Harrier was the principal fighter
aircraft operated from *Illustrious* and her sister ships until the plane's retirement in 2006.

carriers now have an angled deck for recovering aircraft. Thanks to Dennis Campbell (and to the gyro-stabilized mirror landing system which continuously signals glide path corrections), today's naval aviator is able to make a landing approach on a constant speed and direction, and with a clear escape route should his tailhook fail to engage an arresting cable.

During the Korean War, Bill Hannan served aboard the USS *Kearsarge* as a jet engine mechanic. "It would be difficult to imagine a more hazardous place to be than an aircraft carrier. Apart from the airplanes landing, and sometimes crashing, on our roof, the ship carried millions of gallons of flammables, including fuel oil, high-octane gasoline, jet fuel, paints, thinner, as well as tons of bombs, rockets, and assorted ammunition. And scuttlebutt had it that we were being shadowed by submarines.

"Although much of our maintenance work was performed on the hangar deck, some of it was topside, often under incredibly harrowing conditions. Imagine working on a wintry night, on a frosty deck in rough seas, close to the edge of the ship. Only dim, red-lens flashlights could be employed under blackout conditions. If a man happened to slip over the side into the ocean, about eighty feet below, there was little chance of him being missed, let alone rescued. Being assigned to plane-pushing meant long hours of physically hard work in particularly dangerous circumstances. Once during my turn on this dreaded duty, I was well forward on the wet flight deck during a launch operation when I was suddenly blown to the deck. I went sliding toward the propeller planes poised aft with their engines running. I was desperately clawing at the wooden deck, hoping to grab on to one of the numerous metal tie-down strips,

when a huge bruiser of a fellow spotted my predicament and, at considerable risk to himself, literally tackled me and dragged me over the edge of the deck into a catwalk. Probably no one else had even seen me. I was speechless, and didn't even have a chance to thank him before he rushed back to his post . . . a hero in my view, but probably all in a day's work on the flight deck for him.

"Oral communication was usually difficult on the flight deck, even without aircraft engines running. With jet and prop-plane run-ups, it was almost impossible. The ship's powerful 'bull horn' public address system could sometimes be heard over the din, but even in the absence of noise, the bull horn messages were sometimes garbled or distorted like old-time railroad station announcements. So an elaborate system of hand signals evolved that worked to make a point.

"The *Kearsarge* converted sea water into fresh quite efficiently, but it had to serve many purposes, the first of which was feeding the ship's thirsty boilers. Conservation measures had to be strictly observed. The shower protocol, for example, was to wet down, turn off the water, soap up, turn on the water, rinse, and turn off the water. Once I had just finished soaping up and was covered with suds when 'general quarters' was sounded (loud horns over the intercom system, meaning 'Get to your duty station immediately!'). I grabbed a pair of shower sandals and my jockey shorts and rushed up to the hangar deck. A 'red alert' was in effect and we could not leave our stations for any reason until the 'all clear' was sounded. Still covered in soap suds, I was very cold and beginning to itch all over. But it could have been worse. At least I wasn't up on the flight deck.

"Field Days were clean-up times, and

meant hard work for anyone involved. The worst thing about them was the closure of the heads (toilet facilities) for cleaning. Time on the ship for 'pit stops' was at a premium, and often there was little margin for delay in attending to such bodily functions. How frustrating then, after climbing down a deck or two, to find a HEAD SECURED FOR CLEANING sign on the entrance, and, either by coincidence or design, any nearby heads were also frequently out of service.

"We headed home at a leisurely pace, probably to reduce wear and tear on the ship's machinery. As keeping idle hands out of mischief was a foremost consideration in the Navy, all sorts of chores, such as chipping paint from decks and then repainting them, were assigned to anyone who appeared to be unoccupied. In our squadron, the most unsavory of our F9F Panther jet fighters was selected to have its paint stripped, a dirty, tedious job at best, especially when it was freely admitted that the job didn't really need doing."

An aircraft carrier is a noble thing. It lacks almost everything that seems to denote nobility, yet deep nobility is there. A carrier has no poise. It has no grace. It is top-heavy and lopsided. It has the lines of a well-fed cow. It doesn't cut through the water like a cruiser, knifing romantically along. It doesn't dance and cavort like a destroyer. It just plows. You feel it should be carrying a hod, rather than wearing a red sash. Yet a carrier is a ferocious thing, and out of its heritage of action has grown nobility. I believe that today every navy in the world has as its number one priority the destruction of enemy carriers. That's a precarious honor, but it's a proud one.
—Ernie Pyle, war correspondent

Believe me, my young friend, there is nothing—absolutely nothing—half so much worth doing as simply messing about in boats.
—from *The Wind in the Willows* by Kenneth Grahame

left: A converted ocean liner, HMS *Argus* served in the Royal Navy from 1918 to 1944; below: The Royal Navy escort carrier HMS *Pursuer*, one of many such American-built ships in the British inventory during the war.

HMS *Illustrious* driving through a squall in the Bay of Biscay in 1999. After the Falklands War of 1982, the *Illustrious* and her sister ships *Invincible* and *Ark Royal* evolved into strike-fighter platforms.

A McDonnell Douglas F-4 Phantom twin-engine, all-weather, long-range supersonic jet interceptor / fighter-bomber originally developed for the U.S. Navy. Entering service in 1960, the Phantom was the primary air superiority fighter of the the Navy and the U.S. Air Force in the Vietnam War. This one is being prepared for launch from the aircraft carrier USS *Kitty Hawk* on Yankee Station in the Gulf of Tonkin off the coast of Vietnam.

THE AIRCRAFT

SHE WAS THE "STRINGBAG" TO ALL WHO flew in her or were associated with her. The Fairey Swordfish was a remarkably successful aircraft in its principal role as a carrier-based torpedo bomber of the 1930s and 1940s, and she performed creditably in other roles as well. She resulted from specifications for a naval torpedo bomber issued in July 1932 to the Fairey Aviation Technical Department. The requirement called for an aircraft to perform: 1) fleet reconnaissance with a crew of three; 2) torpedo attacks with a crew of two and of limited range; and 3) bombing attacks with two or three crew according to the bomb load.

Trials of several early models of the plane resulted in the specification S.38/34, calling for three developmental aircraft to be built. The subsequent production machines based on these craft became the final Swordfish.

John W.G. Wellham flew the Swordfish in the Fleet Air Arm attack on the Italian port of Taranto in November 1940. "It was astonishingly easy to fly. It was never used as a trainer because it was too easy to learn on. It had a very low take-off speed, a very low landing speed, and was incredibly robust. You could thump it down on a carrier deck, you could knock bits off it, you could bend it, and it still went on flying. It would carry almost anything you put on it. It was originally supposed to carry torpedos and a few bombs. Gradually, they added more and more: a modern radio, radar, later the homing torpedo, depth charges, and, if we were travelling somewhere, as when the squadron made a sudden move, we even tied motor bikes to the torpedo rack, spare propellers to the wings, and stuffed everyone's luggage into the back. It still took off and flew. Technically it wasn't allowed, but you could do aerobatics in it. I once did a loop with a roll off the top, and it did it perfectly happily."

"A venomous-looking little bumblebee of a fighter, the Wildcat—destined to be the progenitor of a dynasty of Cats—made up for its lack of aesthetic appeal in purposefulness of appearance . . . " wrote Royal Navy test pilot Eric Brown of the Grumman plane that fought against the best the enemy had in 1942. The Japanese Zero could easily outperform the F4F Wildcat in a turn, climb, or dash, and was only at a disadvantage against the Grumman fighter when the Wildcat had both height and surprise on its side. In a fight, the Wildcat had one other thing going for it. Though outgunned by the Zero, the Grumman was better able to absorb damage than the Japanese plane, and the Wildcat pilot was far better protected by armor and a bullet-proof windscreen.

In the Atlantic, the Royal Navy operated the Wildcat, which they called the Martlet (though later in the war they came to accept the U.S. nickname), from small escort carriers which sailed with Allied convoys and provided essential air cover protecting against enemy aircraft and U-boat attacks. Among the best-known achievements employing the Wildcat is that of Lieutenant Edward H. O'Hare of VF-42, flying from the USS *Lexington* (CV-2) on 20 February 1942. The *Lexington* had launched the Wildcat squadron to intercept inbound Japanese aircraft and Lt. O'Hare managed to down five Betty bombers that day, for which he was awarded the Congressional Medal of Honor.

Bob Croman flew the SBD Douglas Dauntless, referred to by some of its crews as "the clunk" or "the barge."

In its role as a dive-bomber, Croman recalled: "We dropped bombs, diving from up to 15,000 feet. We pulled out at about 1,500 feet and in this performance, the SBD4 never failed me. The only minor fault I found was that the landing flap handle and dive flap handle were next to each other and occasionally one could move the dive flaps when landing. This resulted in many accidents. The SBD was very capable in carrier landings and I very seldom received a wave-off from the LSO (landing signal officer)." Eric Brown: "Mundane by contemporary performance standards, the Dauntless was underpowered, painfully slow, short on range, woefully vulnerable to fighters, and uncomfortable and fatiguing to fly for any length of time, being inherently noisy and drafty. But it did possess certain invaluable assets that mitigated these shortcomings. Its handling characteristics were, for the most part, innocuous and it was responsive; it was dependable and extremely sturdy, capable of absorbing considerable battle damage and remaining airborne and, most important, it was an accurate dive-bomber.

"Throughout the Pacific War, it remained the principal shipboard dive-bomber available to the U.S. Navy; it was the only U.S. aircraft to participate in all five naval engagements fought exclusively between carriers, and, deficiencies notwithstanding, it emerged with an almost legendary reputation as the most successful shipboard dive-bomber of all time—albeit success that perhaps owed more to the crews that flew it in truly dauntless fashion than to the intrinsic qualities of the aeroplane itself."

The Curtiss SB2C Helldiver was the third in a line of Curtiss planes to carry that name. The SB2C was purpose-built to be both a bomber

Grumman F6F Hellcats on the USS *Yorktown,* circa 1944.

and dive-bomber, and was a sturdy, two-man, low-wing, all-metal monoplane which had a production run of 7,200. Flown by both the U.S. Navy and Marines, the later versions of the Helldiver were armed with either four 12.7mm wing-mounted machine-guns or two 20mm cannon. Late variants were also produced by both Fairchild, and Canadian Car & Foundry, which was a manufacturer of later marks of the Hawker Hurricane fighter as well.

Problem: Aircraft handles funny. Solution: Aircraft warned to straighten up and fly right.

The Imperial Japanese Navy sent its requirements for a new front-line fighter to both the Nakajima and Mitsubishi aircraft companies in 1937. It wanted a top speed of at least 310 mph, the ability to climb to 10,000 feet in 3.5 minutes, exceptional maneuverability, and greater range than that of any existing fighter. It had to be armed with two cannon and two machine-guns, a requirement thought to be unrealistic by both manufacturers, and Nakajima pulled out of the competition to design and build it. Although Mitsubishi agreed to solve the problem of the plane's armament, the requirement was eventually modified. In their determination to keep the weight of the new fighter to a minimum, thus enhancing its overall performance, a new lightweight alloy that the manufacturers called Extra-Super Duralumin (ESD) was used. The new carrier fighter was called Zero-Sen, and designated A6M1. It was accepted by the Imperial Navy on 14 September 1939. Later, when the Navy accepted a new 925 hp aero engine built by Nakajima, the NK1C Sakae 12, the next Zero variant carried the new powerplant and was designated A6M2. It was this

greatly improved aircraft that Allied fighter pilots in the Pacific had to contend with in 1943 prior to the arrival in that theater of their own new and highly capable Corsair and Hellcat fighters.

Among Japan's principal performers in their surprise attack on the U.S. battleships in Pearl Harbor, Hawaii, which brought America into World War Two, was the Aichi D3A Val naval dive-bomber. A successor to Aichi's D1A, the Val was prominent in Japan's strikes throughout Southeast Asia and the South Pacific until late in 1942 when the quality and performance of the U.S. carrier fighters improved dramatically. After that, the Val was no longer in the game and was utilized in secondary roles, including training, land-based attack and, finally, in the desperate kamikaze suicide attacks of 1945 against the American fleet.

No one has flown and evaluated more military aircraft types than Eric Brown, the extraordinary British test pilot who became the first naval officer to head the elite Aerodynamics Flight at the Royal Aircraft Establishment, Farnborough, England: "As a result of a brilliant piece of improvisation, the Navy had been presented with the Sea Hurricane, which had proved that a high-performance shore-based fighter could be operated with relative safety from a carrier, but the Hawker fighter's chances of survival against a Bf 109G or Fw 190 were anything but good. Nevertheless, its successful adaptation for the shipboard role had at least brought about something of a revolution in naval thinking, and logically enough in 1941 the Admiralty began to demand a similar adaptation of what was then the highest performing fighter available—the Spitfire.

"This scheme was received with mixed feelings by those naval pilots in the know. Everyone admired the Spitfire and itched to fly it—but from an aircraft carrier? That was a horse of a very different color! No one needed convincing of the performance or handling attributes of this magnificent fighter which was surely one of the greatest warplanes ever conceived, but there was a certain air of fragility about the aeroplane: a ballerina-like delicacy that seemed inconsistent with the demanding, muscle-taxing scenario of shipboard operations. Could that slender fuselage stand the harsh deceleration of an arrested landing? Would that frail undercarriage absorb the shock of 15 ft/sec (4.7 m/sec) vertical velocity, and could those wafer-like wings take the acceleration forces of a catapult launch? What of the Spitfire's high landing speed? Above all, would the pilot ever be able to see the carrier deck on the approach?

"I had been selected to undertake the first Seafire deck trials on an escort carrier. At 1330 hours on 11 September 1942 I was flying a Seafire towards HMS *Biter*—the time being significant as it turned out. As I approached *Biter*, I confidently assumed that all would be breached up for this momentous occasion—the first landing of a Seafire on one of these postage stamp-sized platforms—and I did a quick circuit at 400 feet and settled into my approach. Contrary to earlier recommendations, I adopted a straight final approach with the aircraft crabbed to starboard so that I had a good, clear view to port of both the deck and, supposedly, the batsman of whom, in the event, I saw no sign.

"Nevertheless, all went smoothly and I touched down on *Biter*, picking up the second wire. I came to a stop somewhat smartly and cut the engine, and it was only then that

North American T-2 Buckeye trainers at NAS Pensacola, Florida, with Naval Flight Officer students in flight training.

I realized that the deck was completely deserted! Then striding from the island came a lone figure—the Captain. He stepped up on the wing and said, with a pleasant smile, 'I say, old boy, you were not expected so early and everyone's at lunch!' It was only then that the truth dawned on me: I had landed with the carrier 25 degrees out of wind, only 13 knots windspeed over the deck, the arrester wires lying flat and unsupported, and no batsman!"

"Deck-landing the Seafire was not too difficult if everything was done properly. The aircraft handled well at low speeds, but I found it necessary to stick my head out over the edge of the cockpit coaming and peer under the exhaust stubs in order to see the batsman's signals. If you handled the aircraft as directed by the batsman, if the batsman gave you the correct signals (as they usually did), and if the

flight deck did not duck or dive, then the landing was usually OK."
—Alan Leahy, former Royal Navy fighter pilot

Problem: Dead bugs on windshield. Solution: Live bugs on order.

In World War Two, Grumman Aircraft Engineering Corporation of Bethpage, New York, quickly established itself as the premier designer and manufacturer of high-quality, dependable and effective carrier-borne aircraft. The tradition continued with the coming of the TBF / TBM Avenger torpedo-bomber to the American fleet in 1942, and to the British Fleet Air Arm early in 1943. Well-armed and quite capable of defending itself, the structurally rugged Avenger proved to be a superb warplane. Operating primarily from escort carriers, FAA Avengers flew anti-submarine patrol missions and mine-laying

sorties over the waters surrounding Britain, and worked well in the campaign to deny the use of the English Channel to enemy shipping in the run-up to the Normandy landings. FAA Avengers were extremely effective against the Japanese in the Pacific War, flying from the carriers Illustrious, Victorious, Indefatigable, Indomitable, and Formidable, and attacking enemy airfields and oil refineries. The big Grumman performed magnificently and inspired confidence in its crews. It is regarded as one of the best shipboard aircraft of World War Two.

Of what may have been the most effective U.S. Navy fighter of that war, Eric Brown wrote: "No more outstanding example of skill and luck joining forces to produce just the right aeroplane is to be found than that provided by the Grumman Hellcat, unquestionably the most important Allied shipboard fighter of World

A rare moment of down-time on the flight deck of a U.S. Navy carrier off the coast of Vietnam in the 1960s.

War Two. U.S. Navy observers . . . had learned that speed, climb rate, adequate firepower and armour protection, pilot visibility and manoeuvrability were primary requirements in that order. In the case of the shipboard fighter, these desirable qualities had to be augmented by ample fuel and ammunition capacity, and the structural sturdiness that was a prerequisite in any aeroplane intended for the naval environment. The Grumman team had . . . formulated its own ideas on the primary requirements in a Wildcat successor, these having been arrived at by consensus: the opinions of U.S. Navy pilots had been canvassed and the results equated with analyses of European combat reports.

". . . so spacious was the cockpit that when I first lowered myself into the seat, I thought I would have to stand up if I was to see through the windscreen for take-off! There was a great deal of engine ahead, but in spite of the bulk of the Double Wasp, the view was not unreasonable, thanks to the Hellcat's slightly hump-backed profile. The take-off was straight forward, with a tendency to swing to port requiring gentle application of rudder. Final approach to the deck was at 80 knots and the Hellcat was as steady as a rock, with precise attitude and speed control. I always used a curved approach to get a better view of the deck.

"The Hellcat had twice the power of the Zero-Sen in a tight loop and U.S. Navy Hellcat pilots soon learned to avoid any attempt to dogfight with the Japanese fighter, and turn the superior speed, dive and altitude characteristics of the American fighter to advantage. The Hellcat had not been the fastest shipboard fighter of World War II, nor the most manoeuvrable, but it was certainly the most efficacious, and one of its virtues was

its versatility. Conceived primarily as an air superiority weapon with the range to seek out the enemy so that he could be brought to battle, as emphasis switched to offensive capability, the Hellcat competently offered the strike potential that the U.S. Navy neeeded to offset the reduced number of bombers aboard the service's fleet carriers. The Hellcat was certainly the most important Allied shipboard aircraft in the Pacific in 1943–44, for it turned the tide of the conflict, and although Japanese fighters of superior performance made their appearance, they were too late to wrest the aerial ascendancy that had been established largely by this one aircraft type."

In the Second World War era, the American Navy had a pronounced preference for powering its fighter aircraft with air-cooled radial engines, while the American Army preferred liquid-cooled inline engines for its fighters. The Navy put its money on what it perceived as the ruggedness and reliability of the radial engine and saw it as better suited to long over-water flights. It was natural then that Chance-Vought selected the big Pratt & Whitney R-2800 to power their impressive and unusual new fighter, the F4U Corsair. U.S. Navy personnel referred to it as the "bent-winged bird," and the Japanese would call it "whistling death."

The Corsair came from the drawing board with many inherent flaws that would require more than a hundred separate modifications relating to lateral stability and aileron control alone. But when the XF4U-1 prototype flew on 29 May 1940, the Navy knew it was on course toward the special air superiority fighter it so desperately needed. The prototype surpassed 400 mph in level flight, the first American combat airplane to do that.

Teething troubles with the engine challenged Pratt & Whitney for a while, but the marriage of the R-2800 to the F4U airframe was a good one and would ultimately produce one of the finest propeller-driven airplanes of all time.

The radical gull-wing design of the Corsair was Chance-Vought's solution to the problem of propeller clearance brought about by the huge 13' 4" prop needed to transfer power from the R-2800. With a conventional wing design, the airplane would have an unacceptably high angle of attack when landing or taking off. The gull-wing design also provided the pilot increased visibility across the wing at the "bend," as well as an improved drag factor which added to the performance, and the folding-point of the wing aided in the stowage problem on board carriers.

According to Eric Brown, "The incipient bounce during landing resulting from overly stiff oleo action . . . was found to be most disconcerting by pilots fresh to the F4U-1, but not so disconcerting as the virtually unheralded torque stall that occurred all too frequently in landing condition. Compounded by a serious directional instability immediately after touchdown—and coupled with the frightful visibility from the cockpit during the landing approach—it was small wonder that the U.S. Navy concluded that the average carrier pilot was unlikely to possess the necessary skill to master these unpleasant idiosyncrasies, and that committing the Corsair to shipboard operations until these quirks had been at least alleviated would be the height of foolhardiness.

"Oddly enough, the Royal Navy was not quite so fastidious as the U.S. Navy regarding deck-landing characteristics, and cleared the Corsair for shipboard operation some nine

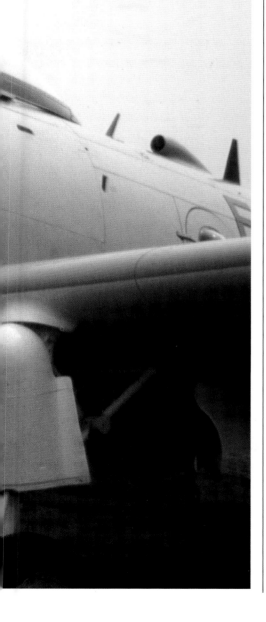

The Douglas A-1 Skyraider attack aircraft, notable for its impressive performance during the Vietnam War. By the end of its production run in 1957, the Douglas design by Ed Heinemann had seen nearly 4,000 examples delivered for service with the U.S. Navy, U.S. Air Force, the British Royal Navy, and the South Vietnamese Air Force.

months before its American counterpart. The obstacles to the Corsair's shipboard use were admittedly not insurmountable, but I can only surmise that the apparently ready acceptance by their Lordships of the Admiralty of the Chance-Vought fighter for carrier operation must have been solely due to the exigencies of the times, for the landing behaviour of the Corsair really was bad, a fact to which I was able to attest after the briefest acquaintance with the aircraft.

"I was well aware that the U.S. Navy had found the Corsair's deck-landing characteristics so disappointing in trials that it had been assigned for shore duties while an attempt was being made to iron out the problems, and although the Fleet Air Arm was deck-landing the aircraft, I knew that, by consensus, it had been pronounced a brute and assumed that shipboard operations with the Corsair were something of a case of needs must when the devil drives. The fact that experienced U.S. Navy pilots could deck-land the Corsair had been demonstrated a couple of months earlier. I was most anxious to discover for myself if the Corsair was the deck-landing dog that it was reputed to be. It was!

"In the deck-landing configuration with approach power, the Corsair could demonstrate a very nasty incipient torque stall with dangerously little warning, the starboard wing usually dropping sharply. With the large flaps fully extended the descent rate was rapid, and a simulated deck-landing at 80 knots gave very poor view and sluggish aileron and elevator control. A curved approach was very necessary if the pilot was to have any chance of seeing the carrier, let alone the batsman! When the throttle was cut the nose dropped so that the aircraft bounced on its main wheels and

once the tail wheel made contact the aircraft proved very unstable directionally, despite the tail wheel lock, swinging either to port or starboard, and this swing had to be checked immediately with the brakes. Oh yes, the Corsair could be landed on a deck without undue difficulty by an experienced pilot in ideal conditions, but with pilots of average capability, really pitching decks and marginal weather conditions, attrition simply had to be of serious proportions."

Eventually, most of the negative characteristics of the Corsair were overcome and her pilots came to appreciate her excellent performance. In World War II, Corsair pilots destroyed 2,140 enemy aircraft for a loss of 935 Corsairs (190 in aerial combat, 350 due to anti-aircraft fire, 230 from other causes, and 165 in crash landings). A further 692 were lost on non-operational flights.

Just too late for World War Two, the Douglas A-1 Skyraider joined the U.S. military inventories in 1946 and really began to show what it could do when the Korean War broke out in 1950. The Skyraider is easily the most unique, versatile, and utilitarian single-engined propeller-driven combat plane in aviation history. Able to carry a bomb load greater in weight than its own empty weight, it was operated very successfully by several U.S. Navy, U.S. Marine, and U.S. Air Force squadrons, as well as the South Vietnamese Air Force during the Vietnam conflict. It has also been in the service of Britain, France, Cambodia, Chad, and the Central African Republic. In Vietnam it was referred to as "Spad" or "Sandy." The big 318 mph plane could carry 8,000 pounds of ordnance on sixteen underwing pylons, considerably more than the bomb load of a four-engined B-17 bomber in WWII.

A Douglas A-4 Skyhawk on the catapult for launch.

Among the many wonderful aircraft of the Duxford, England-based Fighter Collection is, arguably, the ultimate piston-engined air superiority fighter of the Second World War era, the Grumman F8F Bearcat. Stephen Grey, the man behind the superb Fighter Collection, has flown his Bearcat spectacularly (as well as several other splendid fighter types) in major air shows like Flying Legends at Duxford for years. He probably knows the Bearcat at least as well as anyone who has ever had anything to do with it. "One approaches the Bear with care. On the deck, it looks exactly as it was intended—the smallest airframe that could be mated to the Pratt & Whitney 2800 engine, while swinging that huge Aeroproducts propeller, 12' 7" in diameter, with the broadest blades you ever did see and just 6" ground clearance, without the oleos depressed. The whole thing is achieved by sitting it on extraordinarily long mainwheel legs. They have, of necessity, been attached to the extremities of the wing center section and an ingenious double hinge system is adopted to fold the upper portion outwards as the main portion folds in. Difficult to describe but, believe me, an amazing amount of ironmongery folds away into a small hole. Somehow, they also found space for a 150-gallon centerline droptank.

"The wingspan is only 35' 6", the length an exceptionally short 27' 8", but it sits 13' 8" high. A mean, muscular-looking, long-legged Bulldog. The cockpit is tiny, European style, with controls well placed but with canopy rails so tight against my shoulders that I have to be helped in—damn that apple pie.

"I am in it, so fly it. Those early days were quite educational. The only piston-engined fighter I had then flown was the Mustang. While

the P-51 has bags of torque, no one would complain that it was overpowered—rather, slightly overweight, like certain pilots I know. The briefing was pretty exhaustive: 'Do not exceed 54", and get the gear up before 140 knots.'

"Having been used to the long throttle travel on the 51, and needing all of it on take-off, I was surprised that an inch of throttle movement gave me 50" and a very rapid view of the side of the runway. I pulled up the nose to avoid exceeding the gear speed and the runway lights, to find myself in what seemed like the vertical. Finally cleaned up, I looked down to see this major Florida airfield as a tiny model, thousands of feet below. Out over the Everglades, even back at 1,900 r.p.m. and 29.5", I was still several miles behind the aircraft. Within a few more minutes I had a sensation of familiarity and increasing exhilaration. The Bearcat is a joy to throw around. Harmony of control, aided by its spring tab ailerons, is outstanding; the controls delightfully light and very responsive. It demonstrates all the hallmarks of a great day fighter in that it has poor stability, which translates into rapid divergence and, with its high power / thrust-to-weight ratio, outstanding agility. The Bearcat manual says this is not an instrument airplane. Believe it.

"Clean stalls are under the book figure of 100 knots, as the Fighter Collection aircraft is unarmed and lighter. The onset has little warning, excepting a very brief stick shudder prior to an immediate wing drop. With everything down, the stall comes at 70 knots, the nose dropping hard and violently off to the left after the same brief shudder. A rapid application of power will torque you around the prop. Potentially disastrous on the approach.

"Accelerated stalls are straightforward, until you try them while reducing or, still worse, adding coarse power. The resulting snap rolls have to be experienced to be believed. The aircraft is so short coupled, you need the draught over the tail at any time you go for high Alphas.

"Another cute trick, which took me some time to work out, is aileron reversal. Induced by simultaneously pulling hard and rolling at very high speeds at low altitude, I first put in hard left aileron and found myself rolling right. Then, just as you have considered what the hell is happening and the speed is backing off, the Bear rolls hard left. We went right through the geometry, the rigging, the spring tabs, the lot, before I flew it again.

"Subsequent, deep examination of the manual showed a max deflection aileron limit of 4.5g. An experienced old salt confirmed that the wing was first twisting unloaded, then the ailerons work. This was, apparently, a 'design feature' of all Bearcats. Whoever said wing warping was ineffective? Needless to say, we now do no barrel-like manouvers at high speed in the Fighter Collection Bearcat.

"Another part of the early education was during practice for the first air show. I pulled up for the first Cuban and while inverted looked for the rollout target on the airfield, only to find it twice as small as the same in a 51. Yippee, I will do a one-and-a-half downward instead of a half. Through 360 degrees and back to inverted, the Bear was oscillating longitudinally and beginning to tuck under. A quick glance at the airspeed indicator showed I had hit the Candy bar, 435 knots and still accelerating. Fortunately I was unladen and still rolling (the correct way) when I hit the compressibility dive brakes. The oscillation stopped and I now had the problem of avoiding the increasingly large airfield. We thoroughly inspected the airframe and my underwear after that one.

"I do not wish to leave you with the impression of an impossible roaring monster. The airplane is a beautiful, well domesticated 'Pussycat' (but still with teeth and claws) when flown well within its envelope—as we have done since those early 'hooligan' days. The Bearcat was the end of an era, the end of a technology. The ultimate piston-engined air superiority fighter? The Spitfire XIV or the Sea Fury could give it a run, but different fun."

Hawker's World War II Typhoon ground attack fighter led to their Tempest which, in turn, led to Sydney Camm's Project F.2/43, resulting in a great naval fighter, the Sea Fury, with deliveries of Sea Fury F Mk Xs to the Fleet Air Arm beginning in February 1947.

With the invasion of South Korea by the North Korean army in June 1950, the British Government contributed the services of the British Eastern Fleet headed by the carrier HMS *Triumph*. The *Triumph* was to operate off Korea together with the ships of the U.S. Navy. HMS *Theseus* replaced *Triumph* in October, bringing with her No. 807 Squadron and its twenty-one Sea Fury FB Mk 11s. Subsequently, *Theseus* gave way to HMS *Glory*, as British carriers continued to operate off the Korean coast in six-month cycles. The Sea Fury proved highly successful as a fighter bomber in the demanding conditions of the Korean conflict. Perhaps its finest hour came on 9 August 1952 when four of the piston-engined fighters of 802 Squadron were intercepted by eight MiG-15 jets, resulting in a spectacular air fight and the downing of one MiG, with two oth-

ers severely damaged. None of the Sea Furys were hit.

Since the 1960s, the Sea Fury has become popular with warbird enthusiasts, air show and air racing participants, and spectators, being among the fastest propeller-driven fighters of all time.

The U.S. Navy was able to field the highly effective Grumman F9F Panther fighter on more than 78,000 combat sorties in the Korean War because in Britain Rolls-Royce had developed an excellent jet engine in its Nene. The U.S. Navy became interested in the Nene in the summer of 1946 when looking for an engine to power its new Grumman-designed, radar-equipped, all-weather day and night fighter, the XF9F. Two Nenes were brought from England to the Philadelphia Navy Yard where, in December, the Rolls product became the first jet to pass the extremely demanding Navy test schedule. Rights were acquired for American aircraft engine manufacturer Pratt & Whitney to redesign and build a version of the Nene to be designated J42, which was developed and refined to power the F9F2, the Panther that, together with the McDonnell F2H Banshee, did the primary day fighter job in Korean skies. The design evolved into the F9F-8 Cougar which, while not arriving in Korea in time to have an impact on the conflict, was to become the primary fighter of the U.S. Navy in the fifteen years after World War II.

The McDonnell Douglas A-4 Skyhawk was rugged, reliable and quite agile, so much so that its carrier-based U.S. pilots referred to it as "Scooter." It was almost always ready to work, and in the Vietnam War the nimble delta-winged jet could carry and deliver nearly its own weight in bombs and

rockets. The little Skyhawk was one of the many brilliant designs of Douglas Aircraft's Ed Heinemann, and was initially a private venture by Douglas to be a successor to their extraordinary Skyraider. At the time the U.S. Navy had in mind an aircraft of similar capabilities to those of the Skyraider, but powered by a turboprop engine. Heinemann had a better idea, and designed a relatively small airframe to be powered by a Pratt & Whitney turbojet and capable of the payload and range requirements of the Navy, with a far-greater-than-specified performance, and about half the specified maximum take-off weight. The result performed impressively for decades as a primary strike fighter for the U.S. Navy, U.S. Marines, Argentina, and Israel.

The British Aerospace / Blackburn Buccaneer S. Mk 2B was rushed to the Persian Gulf in 1991 to provide laser designation for the missiles of RAF Tornados as they struck at Iraqi targets. The two-seat, low-level strike plane originally served with Nos. 800, 801, and 809 Squadrons, Royal Navy, in the S Mk 1 version. The brilliant, long-lived Buccaneer had been mobilized and was in actual combat in just ten days. The Bucs utilized an American system called the AVQ-23E Pave Spike system to help the Tornados accurately deliver laser-guided bombs from medium altitude. As the Gulf air war progressed, Buccaneers were also used to drop Portsmouth Aviation CPU-123/B 1,000-pound Paveway II laser-guided bombs, mainly attacking bridges and airfields. The Buccaneer was among the most important contributions of the British to the coalition effort in the Gulf. Armed with AIM-91 Sidewinders for self-defense until the missiles were declared unnecessary,

A Royal Navy aviator arriving at his Sea Harrier for departure on a combat air patrol from HMS *Illustrious.*

the Bucs alone made it possible for the RAF Tornado bomber force to hit its targets with unparalleled precision and efficiency. The Tornado crews had never dropped laser-guided bombs before, and had to undergo a quick and very intensive training program with their Buccaneer laser buddies prior to their first LGB mission on 2 February. From the start, the Buccaneer-Tornado operating procedure was a great success. For the thirty-year-old Buccaneer, fighting what would probably be its last action, it was an impressive performance.

Known as the "airborne eyes of the fleet," the Grumman E-2 Hawkeye has for five decades carried the primary responsibility for airborne early warning and operational coordination in the U.S. Navy. It is expected to continue as the front-line AEW and control platform for the American fleet well into the twenty-first century. Like so many naval aircraft designed and brought into manufacture in the 1950s and 1960s, the Hawkeye has been continually revised electronically to keep it technologically current. Subject to a prolonged early development phase owing to its complexity, the plane finally reached the Pacific and Atlantic fleets in quantity between 1964 and 1966.

The Hawkeye flies with a crew of five including a pilot, co-pilot, and three radar operators, as a shipboard early warning and fighter control aircraft. Its two Allison turboprop engines power it to a maximum speed of 397 mph and a typical cruising speed of 315 mph with a ceiling of 31,700 feet and a ferry range of 1,905 miles. The Hawkeye first went to war aboard the USS Kitty Hawk (CVA-63) in the South China Sea off Vietnam in 1965 where it began its high-achieving career controlling air strikes, warning of enemy aircraft in the vicinity, and guiding friendly aircraft around ground defense installations.

Plagued with problems from the outset, the Grumman F-14 Tomcat first flew in late 1970 and first went to sea on deployment aboard the carrier USS *Enterprise* (CVN-65) in 1974. It was finally retired from U.S. Navy service in September 2006. During that service the big twin-engined interceptor offered and provided a unique threat to potential enemies of the American fleet. It could destroy multiple targets at extreme distances and was capable of bringing down enemy fighters before they could attack, as well as missile-launching aircraft before they could launch their weapons. The Tomcat was the largest and heaviest of the American Navy's strike aircraft prior to being replaced by the excellent F/A-18 Hornet family of multi-role strike fighters.

far left: An F4U Corsair traps on the deck of the USS *Tarawa* in 1946; above: A Royal Navy Grumman Martlet (Wildcat) suffers a crash on deck; below: A Curtiss SB2C Helldiver preparing for take-off.

A BAE Sea Harrier is airborne from the ski
launch ramp of HMS *Illustrious*.

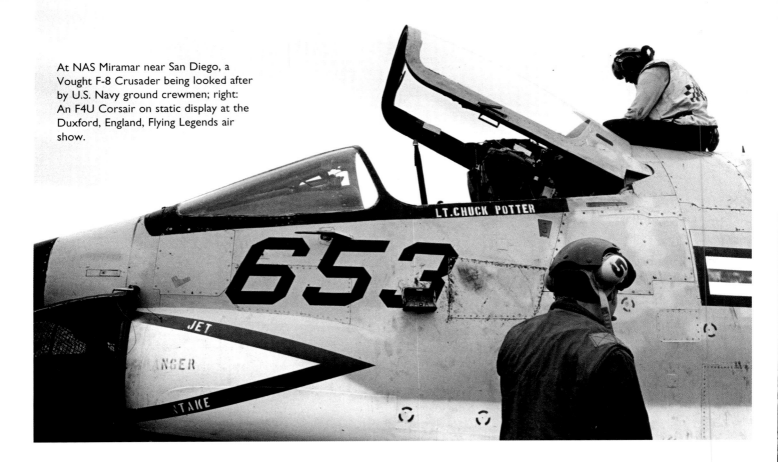

At NAS Miramar near San Diego, a Vought F-8 Crusader being looked after by U.S. Navy ground crewmen; right: An F4U Corsair on static display at the Duxford, England, Flying Legends air show.

Not the most agile of combat planes, the Tomcat was designed to defeat the Soviet MiG-21 and MiG-23 fighters, but was not a match for the MiG-29 or the Su-27. In its long career the Tomcat suffered upwards of forty losses through spinning accidents, a slew of engine compressor blade failures resulting in many more losses, and a growing lack of trust by its pilots in the planes's engines, bringing with it a collective attitude of excessive caution. But with production of the F-14A, B, and D models, the Tomcat gained a new lease of life in the 1990s. However, the collapse of the Soviet Union and the end of the Cold War, and resultant cutbacks in U.S. military spending, then brought a major contraction in the Tomcat community, as well as the disestablishment of many historic squadrons which were equipped with the plane.

Lieutenant Jennifer Brattle was a Naval Flight Officer with VF-211

aboard the USS *John C. Stennis* (CVN-74), flying in the F-14A Tomcat as a Radar Intercept Officer (RIO)—a backseater. In her squadron she also functioned as Public Affairs Officer, Assistant Personnel Officer, Coffee Mess Officer, Educational Service Officer, and Morale, Welfare, and Recreation Officer. She flew as a RIO in Tomcats from May 1998 and by November 1999 had accumulated about 300 flight hours in the plane: "Basically, I help the pilot in his duties. I help with navigation and I'm in charge of the radar and the weapons systems. If the mission we are on is bombs, I set up all the stations for the bombing, I work the radar and back up the pilot in his work."

Dating from the 1950s, the original Dassault-Breguet Etendard transonic strike fighter was planned to be a land-based strike plane for NATO and

the French Air Force, but in the end it was the French Navy that maintained an interest and took it on board for carrier operations. Eventually the plane went through further development and a more powerful, high-performance version emerged. The Super Etendard is, in fact, quite different from the standard model, with a modified high-performance wing, as well as significantly improved avionics and armament. The Super entered fleet service in 1978, with the French Navy accepting a total of seventy-one aircraft. Five were leased to Iraq, while fourteen went to Argentina where they were operated against the British in the 1982 Falkland Islands campaign from the Argentine carrier *Veinticinco de Mayo* (originally a *Colossus*-class carrier of the Royal Navy). It was an Argentine Super Etendard naval strike fighter which launched a French Exocet missile to sink the

British destroyer HMS *Sheffield* in the Falklands campaign.

In the 1960s the Royal Navy and the Royal Air Force were told by the British Air Ministry to study the possible commonality of their requirements regarding a new aircraft type; a short-take-off-landing fighter, to be based on the Hawker P1127 VSTOL prototype. The Navy wanted an air superiority, catapult-launched fighter, while the Air Force was more interested in a supersonic ground attack plane. Nearly every time the British and American services are asked by those on high to put aside their differences and find a way to make the same aircraft work for them both, the result is months or even years of pulling and pushing until the concept is finally declared unacceptable by both branches. It happened just that way with this VSTOL attempt.

The Navy opted instead to buy the McDonnell F4K Phantom, while the Air Force went on with its feasibility studies until 1965, when the British government cancelled further work on a P1154 supersonic VSTOL variant. By special agreement, the government, together with the U.S. and Germany, continued development on the P1127 version which evolved into the Pegasus 3-powered Kestrel. In early tests aboard HMS *Ark Royal* at Lyme Bay in 1963, the Royal Navy showed but minor interest in what it regarded then as little more than a novelty. By 1965 the RAF requirement for such a front-line VSTOL plane, primarily in Germany, finally meshed with the ongoing development of the Kestrel. It had been almost totally redesigned to incorporate the avionics of the cancelled P1154, and utilized an uprated Pegasus engine of 19,000 pounds thrust. It entered service with the

RAF in 1969 as the Harrier. By April 1973 a new class of ship, a sort of combined anti-submarine and VSTOL carrier, was at last agreed on and the first of the class, HMS *Invincible*, was ordered on 17 April.

In 1971, No 1 Squadron RAF had deployed to HMS *Eagle* in an exercise to test their Harrier GR1s in "emergency deployment" to RN helicopter carriers. The exercise was of more than casual interest to the Royal Navy at that point, and they immediately began pursuit of a navalized version: the Sea Harrier. This variant required many major changes, not least being the employment of an uprated 21,500 pound thrust Pegasus 104 engine.

In the 1982 Falklands War, the Sea Harrier, armed with the American AIM-9L Sidewinder missile, provided a wake-up call that the Argentine Air Force, who referred to the plane as "the black death," could not ignore.

No Sea Harriers were lost in air combat there, though several were destroyed by enemy action or were casualties of the terrible South Atlantic weather. In 166 days at sea during the conflict, the Sea Harriers of HMS *Invincible* had a 95 percent serviceability rate. The airplane certainly proved itself, along with the Fleet Air Arm case for the continued operation of fixed-wing aircraft from its carriers.

The Grumman A-6 Intruder joined the U.S. Fleet in February 1963 and served there with distinction until the late 1990s. The Intruder stemmed from a Navy requirement in the late 1950s for a carrier-borne day-night medium attack jet capable of delivering a range of weaponry, including nuclear. It was to be a very sophisticated plane with amazing electronic capability and great flexibility of

function. The Intruder could carry a massive 18,000 pound load of ordnance on five external store stations under the wing and fuselage, which ranged from conventional iron bombs through such smart weapons as the HARM and Harpoon and the AIM-9 Sidewinder for self-defense. It carried a radar package enabling it to perform virtually "blind" at low level. Operated by a crew of two, the pilot and the

The formidable U.S. Navy F4U Corsair, sometimes referred to by the Japanese as "whistling death" during the Pacific campaign of the Second World War.

bombardier / navigator sat side-by-side. In the Vietnam War the A-6 often flew in company with other U.S. Navy aircraft, such as the A-4 Skyhawk, and provided bomb-release commands to these less sophisticated planes.

Both U.S. Navy and U.S. Marine front-line units flew the A-6 for more than three decades, including considerable duty in Southeast Asia. After a period of "de-bugging" common to most new, and nearly all complex aircraft, the A-6A became fully operational and demonstrated that it was more than capable of effectively replacing the very best propeller-driven medium bomber to date, the Douglas A-1 Skyraider. The Intruder was formidable and could operate independently in the worst weather conditions, something it had to do frequently during the Vietnam War. When no other aircraft could do the work, the A-6 was invariably a reliable performer, putting its bombs precisely on target. With greatly improved avionics, it became better and better over the years and, while not quite as versatile as the Skyraider, the Intruder delivered an overall level of performance without parallel.

It came to the U.S. Navy in 1961, the big, noisy, smoke-dirty McDonnell F-4

Phantom, seven years after the Saint Louis airplane builder had been commissioned to design the twin-engined strike fighter-interceptor. Its requirement was changed early in the design stage when the Navy decided that the new plane should be purely a missile fighter. Evidently both the service and the builder had become convinced that the days of close-in dogfighting were over forever, and that there was no need to carry a gun on the Phantom, a view that found little favor among Phantom crews who were to fly it in air combat. Still, it was the finest aircraft of its type for more than ten years . . . the fastest, highest-climbing aircraft then operating.

The two-man crew of the Navy F-4 sat in tandem, with the pilot doing the flying from the front seat while the RIO (Radar Intercept Officer) operated the powerful long-range acquisition radar from the rear cockpit. The method worked well and both crew members appreciated the second pair of eyes on board in the unforgiving aerial combat arena.

Two missile types were carried as fundamental ordnance on the Phantom. The short-range heat-seeking Sidewinder for use in distances up to two miles, and the radar-guided Sparrow with a range of thirteen miles. When the airplane entered into air combat during the Vietnam War, it became clear that the lack of an internal gun put the crew at a distinct disadvantage. Early in that war U.S. rules of engagement required Phantom crews to make visual identification of every target, perfectly reasonable in that most aircraft in Vietnamese skies then were American. The practice virtually eliminated the standoff capability of the Sparrow missile, compounding the F-4 crews' disadvantage in not having a gun, but was overcome with the development of a special radar

receiver. Eventually, in May 1967, crew complaints about the armament of the plane were rewarded with the arrival in Vietnam of the F-4D model, which accommodated a pod-mounted 20mm Vulcan cannon. The installation was later modified to be fully internal in the F-4E variant. The powerful Gatling gun gave the Phantom the ability to dogfight on more even terms than its pilots and RIOs had ever known.

The Royal Navy's Fleet Air Arm operated the FG Mk 1 Phantom with 892 Squadron at RNAS Yeovilton in March 1969. With the cancellation of CVA-01, the new British aircraft carrier intended to replace HMS *Ark Royal* by the late 1970s, the Royal Navy requirement for Phantoms was reduced and a number from its order were transferred to the RAF. These were used to equip 43 Squadron at RAF Leuchars near Saint Andrews, Scotland. In July 1972 all of the 892 Squadron Phantoms were relocated to Leuchars which became home to all Royal Navy and Royal Air Force FG Mk 1s in Britain. Powered by Rolls-Royce Spey engines, the FG Mk 1 was slightly faster than the U.S. airplane. It was deployed at sea on *Ark Royal* the only Royal Navy carrier then capable of operating the Phantom.

Another excellent effort from the designers at Grumman was the EA-6 Prowler, a carrier-borne, all-weather electronic warfare plane. The Prowler came into the U.S. Navy inventory in 1971 and served as the only dedicated electronic warfare aircraft for the use of the Navy, the U.S. Marine Corps, and the U.S. Air Force for nearly four decades, until the arrival in the fleet of the EA-18G Growler in 2009.

The Prowler came about in the development of the Intruder strike aircraft, when it became clear that a specialized electronics-based support

version of the aircraft was needed to help the Intruders get in and out of enemy airspace. To some extent the EA-6 evolved from the Intruder, but the ultimate EA variant had a very special and distinctive electronic counter-measure stand-off jamming capability. In addition to its highly sophisticated electronic warning systems, the Prowler, which is operated by a crew of four, carries HARM missiles. It has a range of 1,100 miles.

The principal strike fighter of the U.S. Navy from the 1990s has been the Boeing McDonnell Douglas FA/18 Hornet. It first flew in 1978 and entered service in 1980 and is probably the most capable and versatile fighter-bomber in the entire history of the American Navy. In the Iraq and Bosnian conflicts the Hornet showed its worth in both the air-to-air and air-to-ground missions. It is a twin-engined, light-weight, relatively low-cost fighter offering both rapid acceleration and economical performance. Being fairly small and easily accommodated in the limited space of an aircraft carrier, it has a rather small fuel capacity, and its operations generally involve aerial refuelling. It was designated primarily as a naval plane to operate from aircraft carriers, but in the inventories of the Canadian, Spanish, and Australian air arms, it operates from land bases. It is a highly automated machine whose computers signficantly reduce the flying workload of the pilot, freeing him or her to fight the enemy. Its electronic offensive and defensive systems make it an extremely potent adversary. U.S. Marine Corps F/A-18Ds are two-seat versions in which the back-seater participates in the combat role and can also act as a forward air controller for other aircraft.

The Hornet has a gun, the M61 20mm cannon, an electric Gatling gun with a 540-round magazine. It can also carry a combination of very capable weapons including the AIM-9M all-angle heat-seeking anti-aircraft missile, the AGM-88 anti-radar missile, and the 1,000-pound laser-guided bomb. Pilots and maintenance personnel share respect for the F/A-18's reliability and ease of maintenance, despite the complexity of its systems. In the Gulf War and over Bosnia, the Hornet force had an amazing availability rate of better than 90 pecent, reaching a peak of 95 percent in the Gulf. No other naval fighter has inspired such admiration and high regard from those who fly it.

U.S. Navy aviator jacket patches.

IN THE NIGHT OF 11 / 12 NOVEMBER 1940, two waves of British Royal Navy Fleet Air Arm Fairey Swordfish biplanes launched from the newly operational RN aircraft carrier HMS *Illustrious* to attack warships of the Italian fleet at anchor in the harbor of Taranto. A major sea port, Taranto lies in the arch of the Italian boot, about 250 miles southeast of Rome. Taranto had been founded in 706 BC as a Spartan Greek trading post called Taras, and was known as Tarantum in the time of the Roman Empire.

The Royal Navy had been attempting to provide cover and protection for Allied convoys of merchant ships from the constant threat of land-based air attack, from U-boats, and from many sorties by the capital ships of the Italian fleet. The convoys were carrying vitally needed supplies to the island of Malta, whose survival was crucial in the effort to defeat German and Italian forces in North Africa during this early phase of the Second World War.

British Admiral Sir Andrew Cunningham was the Royal Navy Commander-in-Chief in the Mediterranean from 1939 to 1943. To ease the pressure on his forces in their role of shepherding the convoys, Cunningham ordered a two-carrier strike in the autumn of 1940 on key Italian warships in the Taranto base. The carriers *Eagle* and *Illustrious* were assigned the mission, but various mishaps and a problem with the fuel system of *Eagle* caused her to be withdrawn from the task. Before her withdrawal, five of her Swordfish aircraft and eight air crews were transferred to *Illustrious* for the raid.

A reconnaissance flight by an RAF aircraft on 11 November identified six battleships of the Italian fleet in harbor at Taranto, and the raid was scheduled for that evening. In the late afternoon, *Illustrious*, together with her escort of four cruisers and four destroyers, was steaming toward the launch point for the mission. The first wave of twelve Swordfish, fitted with internal auxiliary fuel tanks to augment their range, was being armed. Six of them were to carry torpedos, four carried bombs, and two were taking flares and bombs. The striking force would have to contend with some twenty-two Italian anti-aircraft gun positions, as well as barrage balloons and torpedo nets guarding the harbor.

The British plan for the operation called for the torpedo-armed Swordfish to launch their missiles at the battleships anchored in the outer harbor. Meanwhile, in a synchronized diversion, the other aircraft would attack cruisers and destroyers moored along the harbor quay. It was thought that the small-warhead eighteen-inch British aircraft torpedos could be launched at low-level into the shallow waters of the harbor to good effect against the Italian capital ships. It was hoped that the bomb and flare-dropping Swordfish would distract the local defenses while the torpedo planes utilized their ultra-low seventy-five knot cruising speed to weave around and between the barrage balloon cables toward their targets.

The strike force of British aircraft formed up several miles from *Illustrious* and proceeded along the 170-mile route to Taranto harbor by 8:57 pm, with Lieutenant Commander M.W. Williamson in command. At 9:15 pm, however, the flying conditions had deteriorated and the squadron became separated in heavy cloud. The planes were compelled to make their attacks independently.

At 10:56 pm the aircraft carrying flares and bombs laid an illuminating pattern of flares along the eastern

ATTACK
ON TARANTO

A Fairey Swordfish torpedo bomber of the Royal Navy Historic Flight based at RNAS Yeovilton, Somerset, England.

Royal Navy deck handlers.

edge of the harbor. They then went on to dive-bomb a nearby oil tank farm which they set afire. At about this time, three of the torpedo Swordfish, with Lt. Cdr. Williamson in the lead, had positioned themselves for a diving run on the battleship *Cavour.* They descended from 4,000 feet to 400 feet where they released their torpedos. One of the three torpedos struck *Cavour,* causing such substantial damage that the ship was never able to be repaired. Return fire from the battleship hit and downed Williamson's plane, but he and his observer survived to become prisoners of war.

Now the second lot of the first wave of Swordfish arrived led by Lt. N. Kemp, and their torpedo aircraft attacked the battleship *Littorio.* Their

bombing aircraft struck at the cruisers and destroyers and the seaplane base in the harbor, severely damaging one hangar.

At 11:23 pm the second wave of Swordfish began taking off from *Illustrious,* led by Lt. Cdr. J.W. Hale. This force included five torpedo aircraft, two bombers and two planes with flares and bombs. The flare and bomber aircraft made additional strikes on the oil storage facility as the five torpedo-carrying Swordfish assumed a line-astern approach to the battleships. By this time the Italians had begun to put up a fearsome box barrage of anti-aircraft fire from their many shore and ship-based gun positions, and Hale's planes had to fly through the worst of the flak. One of the aircraft was shot down.

While the British striking force lost two aircraft in the raid, they managed to score four hits on the battleship *Littorio,* and one each on the battleships *Cavour* and *Duilio. Littorio* was left listing heavily, her deck awash. The following day she settled on the bottom of the harbor. Other ships received some damage, including two *Trento*-class cruisers and two fleet auxiliaries. The oil storage facility and the seaplane base were significantly damaged. The raid was considered to be highly successful. The Italians were left with only two operational battleships. Within six months of the attack, one-third of the Fleet Air Arm air crewmen who had flown it were dead . . . killed in other actions.

It has often been claimed by historians and others that the Japanese drew the inspiration for their low-level torpedo attack on battleships of the U.S. fleet at Pearl Harbor on 7 December 1941, from the Taranto raid. In fact, the Pearl Harbor attack had been thoroughly planned before the British raid was conducted. Still, the method and results of the Taranto raid certainly served to influence and motivate the Japanese forces when the time came to execute their attack.

John Wellham, Royal Navy Fleet Air Arm pilot: "I was serving in HMS *Eagle*, a very old carrier which had been in the fleet for some years. We came to the Mediterranean at a time when it was obvious that Mussolini was going to come into the war on the side of the Germans. He'd been sitting on the sidelines, waiting to see which side was likely to produce the most glory for him. As the Germans were sweeping through Europe, it was clearly going to be their side that he wanted to join. We, therefore, were sent to join the Mediterranean fleet, which we did but a few weeks before Mussolini came into the war.

"Led by Sir Andrew Cunningham, a wildly enthusiastic chap, we tore around the Med looking for someone with whom to be hostile, and actually only found the Italian fleet at sea once. We attacked them twice in four hours with our Swordfish torpedo bombers. Unfortunately, there were only nine of us making the attacks, quite inadequate against their fast-moving fleet. So it was necessary for us to catch them in harbor. Our admiral did his homework and found that attacking enemy ships in harbor had been quite successful right back to 300 BC.

"The RAF had a squadron of Bristol Blenheims in the area which they were using for reconnaissance of the various North African harbours

including Bomba. One day they told us about a submarine depot ship at Bomba with a submarine alongside it. They did a recce for us the next morning and discovered another submarine coming into the harbour, so the three of us went off in our Swordfish and, at Bomba, spotted the large submarine on the surface, obviously recharging its batteries. Our leader put his torpedo into it and the sub blew up and sank very satisfactorily. The other chap and I went on and as we got closer we found that, not only was there a depot ship and a submarine, there was a destroyer between the two of them. I let my torpedo go towards the depot ship. My colleague dropped his from the other side and it went underneath the submarine and hit the destroyer. I was very excited and was shouting. Things were going up in the air and we discovered that all four ships had sunk, which was confirmed later by aerial reconnaissance. That night the Italians admitted on the radio that they had lost four ships in the harbour. However, they said that the loss was due to an overwhelming force of motor torpedo boats and torpedo bombers which had attacked them during the night. If I had been commanding officer of that base, I would have reported something along those same lines. I certainly wouldn't have been prepared to admit that three elderly Swordfish biplanes had sunk four of my ships.

"The attack on the ships in harbour at Bomba had confirmed for us, and for Cunningham, that the best way to attack ships was when they were in harbour. He had then decided that an attack on the main Italian fleet in their base at Taranto was imperative. This was all very well, but we in *Eagle* had a limited number of aircraft and no long-range fuel tanks to get us there

and back. We also needed absolutely up-to-date reconnaissance to do an attack like that. Then the new carrier *Illustrious* came to join us, bringing us the long-range tanks we needed. The Royal Air Force provided a flight of three Martin Maryland bombers for the reconnaissance work, and they were very good for that. They had the speed, the training, and the ability, and each day at dawn and dusk they gave us reports on the positions of ships in Taranto. We couldn't have done the job without them.

"The go-ahead was given for the raid because both *Illustrious* and *Eagle* were fully prepared to do it—but then complications arose. *Illustrious* had a fire in the hangar deck which caused a delay. Meanwhile, *Eagle*, which had been bombed repeatedly by the aircraft of the Reggia Aeronautica, had developed plumbing problems. When we tried to fuel our aircraft we weren't quite sure what we were fuelling them with, and so *Eagle* was scrubbed from the operation. We went on with the plan, however, and transferred five aircraft and eight crews over to *Illustrious*.

"The attack was called Operation Judgement and it was set for 11 November 1940. Diversionary actions involving merchant navy convoys elsewhere in the Med were organised and worked well, disguising the fact that we were going to hit Taranto.

"We went off in two waves, some of us with bombs, some with torpedos. The Martin recce flights had shown us that the Italian battleships were in the Mar Grande, the largest part of Taranto Harbour, while destroyers, cruisers, submarines and various auxiliary vessels were in the inner harbour, Mar Piccolo.

"At Taranto, I had to dodge a barrage balloon and in doing so I was hit by flak which broke the aileron

The Fairey Swordfish biplane torpedo bomber was operational with the Royal Navy from 1934 to 1945. Given the nickname "Stringbag," the Swordfish was particularly effective against the capital ships of the Italian fleet in Taranto and against the mighty German battleship *Bismarck.*; right: The Fairey Albacore was developed from the design of the Swordfish; bottom right: The crew of a Royal Navy Swordfish.

control spar, and I couldn't move the control column, which is very embarrassing in the middle of a dive. So, using brute force and ignorance, I cleared the column enough to get it fully over to the right. While this was going on and I was trying to get the thing to fly properly, I suddenly appreciated that I was diving right into the middle of Taranto City, which was obviously not a good thing. So I hauled the plane out of the dive, found the target and attacked it. But when you drop 2,000 pounds off an aircraft of that weight, it rises. There is nothing you can do about it, and it rose into the flak from the battleship I was attacking. I was hit again and got a hole about a metre long by at least a half-metre wide. The Swordfish still flew and we got back 200 miles over the sea with the aircraft in that condition. It was very painful because, to fly straight, I had to keep left rudder on all the time, which is bad for your ankle, but we got home."

You were throwing the aircraft about like a madman, half the time, and every time I tried to look over the side, the slipstream nearly whipped off my goggles! The harbour was blanked out by ack-ack and I had to check with the compass to see which way we were facing!
—from *To War in a Stringbag* by Commander Charles Lamb, Royal Navy

Bill Sarra and his observer, Jack Bowker, were flying in the diversionary bombing element of the first strike of Swordfish on the harbor at Taranto. They had been briefed to drop their bombs on the cruisers, destroyers, or oil storage tanks in the inner harbor, the Mar Piccolo. Sarra was unable to discern the specified targets and crossed over the dock-

yard. It was then that he spotted the hangars of the Italian seaplane base just ahead. He released his bombs from an altitude of 500 feet and watched as one made a direct hit on a hangar, with the others blasting the slipways. The anti-aircraft fire was intense, but Sarra and Bowker returned safely to the carrier *Illustrious*. The Royal Navy victory at

Taranto that night meant that the balance of capital ship power in the Mediterranean had been shifted in favor of the Allies. The first awards made to participants in the Taranto strike were few indeed. And six months later, in a supplementary list, Sarra and Bowker were "mentioned in despatches," but by then they were both prisoners-of-war.

Pearl Harbor, Hawaii, before the Japanese surprise attack of 7 December 1941. The bulk of the U.S. Pacific Fleet battleships are shown anchored in pairs near Ford Island at center.

INFAMY

SPARKED BY HER EXPANSIONIST POLICY in the late 1930s, the armies of the Empire of Japan moved first into Manchuria and then were fighting on the Chinese mainland in pursuit of their conquest of Southeast Asia. They called their plan the Great East Asia Co-Existence Sphere.

By September 1940 the United States had reacted to Japan's incursions by imposing an embargo on her which covered war materials, including scrap iron, steel, and aviation spirit, as well as by freezing all Japanese assets in the U.S.

In a country with few natural resources, Japan's military government knew that they would not survive long without new sources of strategic commodities. They had become persuaded that to win in China they must have the rubber, tin, bauxite, and most importantly, the oil of the Dutch East Indies and Malaya. To get their hands on these resources, Japan's leaders knew that they would have to go to war with the British Empire as well as the Dutch government in exile. And they concluded that war with the United States would also be inevitable, as the Americans had a significant military presence in the Philippines and were not likely to tolerate such an adventure on the part of the Japanese. To achieve their goal, the Japanese militarists planned attacks that would destroy the U.S. bomber bases in the Philippines, as well as the U.S. Pacific Fleet at Pearl Harbor, Hawaii. They believed that these targets would have to be hit and wiped out to clear the way for Japanese forces to take Malaya, the East Indies and, ultimately, China.

Harvard-educated Admiral Isoroku Yamamoto, Commander-in-Chief of the Japanese Combined Fleet, had

Admiral Isoroku Yamamoto planned the surprise attack by Japan's naval air forces on the warships of the American Pacific fleet in Pearl Harbor on 7 December 1941; right: Aircraft about to take off from one of the Japanese carriers near the Hawaiian islands.

once served as a naval attaché in Washington. A brilliant tactician, he knew the military strengths of the United States and had no illusions about America as an adversary. He opposed war with the U.S. but came to accept its inevitability and was quick to warn that when the war came it would be absolutely essential "to give a fatal blow to the enemy fleet at the outset, when it was least expected." He believed that anything less than the total destruction of the American fleet would "awaken a sleeping giant."

In 1921 a new book called *Sea Power in the Pacific* by Hector C. Bywater, a British naval authority, was attracting considerable interest, not least in Japan where by 1922 it had become required reading at the Imperial Naval Academy and the Japanese Naval War College. Bywater took the view that the Japanese home islands were fundamentally protected from direct assault by U.S. forces owing to distance and the secondary fuel and supply consumption involved in such an effort. He proposed that the key to American success against

Japan (in the Pacific War) would be by means of an island-hopping campaign through the Marianas, to Guam and the Philippines. In 1925, Bywater published a second book, *The Great Pacific War*. In it his premise was that Japan could develop a virtually invulnerable empire by making a surprise attack on the U.S. Pacific Fleet, invading Guam and the Philippines, and fortifying its mandate islands. During a 1934 trip to London, Yamamoto met and spent an evening with Bywater in the admiral's hotel suite. He was fascinated by Bywater's theories and their implications for Japanese and American strategy.

It was Yamamoto who would conceive, plan, and direct the breathtaking surprise attack on the capital ships of the U.S. Navy at Pearl Harbor in the early morning of Sunday 7 December 1941. It was clear to him that it might not be possible to achieve the complete elimination of the U.S. Pacific Fleet in one blow. He knew that many American warships were stationed on the U.S. west coast, were undergoing refit, or were in transit between the west coast and Hawaii. His master plan called for a vital second and final strike on what would remain of the enemy fleet, to be staged six months after the Pearl Harbor attack. With only two U.S. aircraft carriers, *Enterprise* and *Lexington*, then operating in the Pacific (*Saratoga* was in port on the west coast), Yamamoto liked the odds as he was able to field six Japanese carriers for the Pearl Harbor strike.

In May 1941 senior officers of the Imperial Japanese Navy called on their Italian counterparts at the southern port of Taranto where, in a bold raid on 11 November 1940, two waves of Fairey Swordfish bombing and torpedo aircraft from the Royal Navy carrier HMS *Illustrious* had attacked and done major damage to capital ships of the Italian fleet. Meeting on the deck of the crippled battleship *Littorio*, the Japanese were fascinated by the methods and achievement of the British in putting half of the Italian fleet out of action in one cleverly planned and executed blow. At a cost to them of only two Swordfish, the RN Fleet Air Arm, it seemed, had solved the problem of how to effectively deliver torpedos against warship targets at anchor in a relatively shallow harbor. While historians often disagree about the extent to which the Japanese, and

Yamamoto in particular, were influenced by the techniques and results of the Taranto raid in the planning and execution of their Pearl Harbor attack, it seems certain that they were inspired and highly motivated by the British example. Thus encouraged, Admiral Yamamoto proceeded with his planning of the attack on the important forward base of the U.S. Pacific Fleet.

In 1940, both Pearl and Taranto harbors were thought by their warship fleet occupants to be safe and proper anchorages. Both adjoined cit-

ies, Honolulu and Taranto, with populations of about 200,000, and both ports were well defended and considered powerful threats to the fleet of any opponent. The U.S. facility and presence at Pearl Harbor was a major impediment to Japan's designs on Southeast Asia, while the Italian fleet at Taranto threatened the sea lanes that linked Britain with her interests in Gibraltar, Egypt, Singapore, and India.

The British carrier pilots, in their effort to dispose of the Italian fleet at Taranto, had to approach the port from the Mediterranean without being

The battleship USS *Nevada*, damaged in the December 1941 raid by Japanese carrier-borne aircraft; right: A metal plaque embedded in the decking of the American battleship USS *Missouri* commemorating the signing of the formal surrender of Japan the Allied powers in 1945.

discovered by multitudes of Italian reconnaissance aircraft, and evade the fire of fifty-four enemy warships and twenty-two shore batteries. This they had to accomplish while avoiding the steel cables of more than fifty barrage balloons, and the attentions of several squadrons of Italian fighter planes. The matter of overcoming these barriers to success at Pearl and Taranto was shared by Yamamoto and British Admiral Sir Andrew Cunningham, respectively, but the course of history compelled Cunningham to act first, in November 1940, and set the historic precedent. For the Japanese Navy to successfully mount a surprise raid on Pearl Harbor, it would first have to assemble a thirty-two-ship task force,

including six aircraft carriers, *Akagi*, *Hiryu*, *Kaga*, *Shokaku*, *Soryu*, *Zuikaku*, in the Kurile Islands north of Japan, and proceed undetected some 4,000 miles, without resupply, to within 200 miles of the Hawaiian Islands. From that point the aircraft of its carriers would have to approach and face the defensive fire of shore batteries, the guns of up to sixty-eight warships, and upwards of a hundred enemy fighter planes.

The shallow harbor at Pearl adjoins the present-day Honolulu airport. The harbor is a basin which surrounds a small airfield facility called Ford Island, and is linked to the sea by a single narrow channel. The eastern side of the harbor was the site of oil storage

U.S.S. MISSOURI

OVER THIS SPOT
ON 2 SEPTEMBER 1945
THE INSTRUMENT
OF FORMAL SURRENDER
OF JAPAN TO THE ALLIED POWERS
WAS SIGNED
THUS BRINGING TO A CLOSE
THE SECOND WORLD WAR
———
THE SHIP AT THAT TIME
WAS AT ANCHOR
IN TOKYO BAY

LATITUDE 35° 21' 17" NORTH ~ LONGITUDE 139° 45' 36" EAST

Upper left: The Japanese surrender party aboard the USS *Missouri* in September, 1945; left: Visitors at the USS *Arizona* war memorial in Pearl Harbor, Hawaii; right: The battleship USS *Missouri* being towed to her new berth alongside Ford Island in Pearl Harbor.

General Douglas MacArthur signing the document of surrender aboard the USS *Missouri* on 2 September 1945.

tanks, drydocks, and a submarine base. On the morning or 7 December 1941, eight battleships of the U.S. fleet, *Arizona*, *California*, *Maryland*, *Nevada*, *Oklahoma*, *Tennessee*, *Utah*, and *West Virginia,* lay at anchor southeast of Ford Island. A ninth such vessel, *Pennsylvania*, was in a nearby drydock.

Probably the greatest challenge faced by the Japanese in their preparations for the Pearl Harbor strike was that of how to successfully deliver torpedos by aircraft into a shallow basin. The technology of the time, at least prior to the Taranto attack, dictated that a torpedo would virtually always sink to a depth of at least seventy feet before levelling and proceeding to its target. Such weapons would certainly be hopelessly mired in the mud bottom of the target waters. Impressed by the successes of the British Navy in their raid on the Italian fleet the year before, munitions engineers of the Mitsubishi company near Nagasaki labored overtime to perfect a missile with a newly designed stabilizer fin. If properly dropped, the redesigned torpedo would sink less than the forty-foot depth of Pearl Harbor and continue on to the target. By 17 November, 180 of the special weapons had been completed and delivered to the Japanese carriers.

Negotiations in Washington with Japan's special envoys there, Saburo Kurusu and Kichisaburo Nomura, to resolve the differences between the two nations by diplomatic means, were clearly failing by 22 November when, on orders from the Japanese government, the fleet that would attack Pearl Harbor was being assembled. The Japanese believed that the time for talking had run out and their task force headed east from Hitokappu Bay in the Kuriles toward Hawaii on 25 November. The six carriers, escorted by battleships, heavy cruisers,

destroyers, and submarines, observed strict radio silence as they crossed the western Pacific, in the hope that they would reach the area north of the Hawaiian Islands undiscovered.

On 2 December, Task Force Commander Vice Admiral Chiuchi Nagumo received the coded radio signal from Yamamoto: Nitaka Yama Nabora (Climb Mount Nitaka), authorizing him to commence the attack operation.

By 7 December the force had reached their launch position approximately 200 miles north of the island of Oahu and at 6 am the initial wave of planes rose from the carrier *Akagi*. In minutes the aircraft—dive-bombers, horizontal bombers, torpedo bombers, and fighters—had launched and were climbing en route to their target. Led by Lieutenant Commander Mitsuo Fuchida, the first wave of 183 rounded Barber's Point southwest of Pearl at 7:53 am. The calligraphic characters on the hachimaki scarf tied round Fuchida's leather flying helmet translated as "Certain Victory." Using the coded phrase "Tora, Tora, Tora" (Tiger, Tiger, Tiger), he alerted the carrier force that his planes had reached the objective and were commencing their attack.

AIR RAID PEARL HARBOR. THIS IS NOT A DRILL was the radio message emanating from the command center at Ford Island a few minutes before 8 am as the Japanese torpedo bombers began their strikes on the sleeping ships in the harbor. The first to receive torpedos were a minelayer, a light cruiser, and the battleship *Arizona*, which was literally blown from the water, her bottom ripped out. *California* and *Oklahoma* each took three torpedos, ruining them. Then a fourth torpedo struck *Oklahoma*, capsizing her. *Arizona* was hit by a bomb which exploded in her forward magazine, tearing her

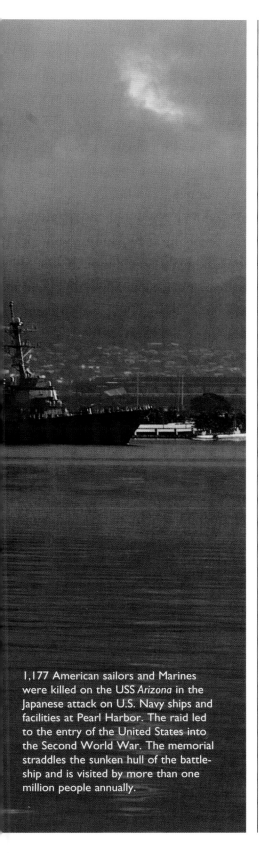

1,177 American sailors and Marines were killed on the USS *Arizona* in the Japanese attack on U.S. Navy ships and facilities at Pearl Harbor. The raid led to the entry of the United States into the Second World War. The memorial straddles the sunken hull of the battleship and is visited by more than one million people annually.

apart. More than a thousand of her crew died.

At Ewa, Wheeler, and Hickam airfields, Japanese bombers and fighters appeared while their colleagues were wrecking the U.S. capital ships in Pearl, and began bombing and strafing the parked aircraft exposed on the aprons. American marines and soldiers were strafed as they ran from their barracks at the Hickam base. The attack was followed an hour later by one from a second wave of Japanese carrier aircraft, 167 this time, to further pound the U.S. facilities.

A total of 2,403 military and civilian Americans died in the raids at Pearl and the other U.S. bases on Oahu. Another 1,178 were wounded; 292 American planes were destroyed or damaged, and the eight U.S. battleships in the harbor were sunk or massively damaged.

In the afternoon of 8 December the American president, Franklin D. Roosevelt, addressed a joint session of the Congress in Washington DC and asked for a declaration of war against the Empire of Japan. Similar declarations against Japan's Axis allies Germany and Italy followed.

Richard "Mac" McCutcheon was a powder carman in the number two turret aboard the battleship USS *West Virginia* on 7 December 1941. At just before 8 am, dive-bombing and torpedo aircraft of the Imperial Japanese Navy appeared over the battleships of the U.S. Navy that lay at anchor in Pearl Harbor near Honolulu, Hawaii. The *West Virginia* was struck and severely damaged in the attack that followed. Her crew was ordered to abandon ship. Mac McCutcheon jumped into the water and swam for the nearby shore where he found himself but a short distance from the home of a woman who had been witnessing the Japanese aerial attack.

She acted quickly when she saw sailors swimming to shore. She gathered clothing from her husband's closet and began distributing it to Mac and the other seamen who had made their way to the shelter of her home.

In the aftermath of the Japanese raid on the American ships and facilities at Pearl Harbor, it became clear that the results might have been far more favorable for the Japanese had they been more efficient in the effort.

Certain of the key targets at Pearl, the U.S. Navy machine shops and the large oil storage tank farm were mainly unaffected by the attack, and most significantly, the Japanese failed to block the narrow and shallow single entrance to the harbor. Had they been able to sink a ship in that tiny channel, they would have denied the U.S. Navy access to Pearl for some time. In failing to destroy the machine shops, they allowed essential repair work to begin immediately on the U.S. warships heavily damaged in the raid. The U.S. ships at Pearl that were still seaworthy, and those that had avoided the attack through being elsewhere, were left able to function and fight owing to the fuel available from the intact tank farm.

In time, nearly eighty percent of the U.S. aircraft that had been damaged, seemingly beyond repair, at Pearl and other American airfields in Hawaii were repaired and made fully operational again.

Flushed with success, Admiral Nagumo's Fast Carrier Striking Force sailed back to Japan where it was made ready for the action to come in the escalating Pacific War. What occupied Yamamoto's thoughts in the wake of the Pearl attack, though, was not the recent naval triumph, but rather the fact that not a single American aircraft carrier had been harmed in the execution of his plan.

THE TIDE HAD TURNED IN THE PACIFIC theater of World War II by early 1944. By then warships of the U.S. Navy were moving steadily westward in their island-hopping campaign, pounding Japanese shore defenses before landing masses of invading soldiers and marines whose job it was to re-take these islands from the occupying enemy forces. To take some of the strain from the pilots, air crews, and over-worked sailors of the U.S. fleet fast carriers, the Americans urgently needed the island airfields that the Japanese held. The stage was set for the greatest carrier battle in history, the First Battle of the Philippine Sea.

Admiral Chester W. Nimitz was Commander-in-Chief of the U.S. Pacific Fleet and in June his Task Force 58, under the command of Vice-Admiral Marc Mitscher, was sent to attack the Marianas and Bonin Islands. On 15 June, Nimitz's forces struck at Saipan in the Marianas, some 1,300 miles east of the Philippines and more than 3,000 miles west of Hawaii. Saipan was defended by Lieutenant General Yoshitsugu Saito and his 32,000 soldiers. They were to meet a U.S. force of 127,000 men, two-thirds of them marines from an assemblage of 535 U.S. Navy ships under the direct command of Vice-Admiral Raymond Spruance.

In raids on the Bonins, U.S. Navy carrier-based aircraft destroyed 300 Japanese planes for the loss of twenty-two of their own. The way was then clear for American troops to land on the other beaches of the Marianas, with the support of eight escort carriers and their 170 aircraft. In the Marianas campaign, the large U.S. carriers included the *Wasp*, *Lexington*, *Hornet*, *Yorktown*, *Essex*, *Bunker Hill*, and the *Enterprise*, as well

as the smaller escort carriers *Cabot*, *Cowpens*, *Bataan*, *Langley*, *Belleau Wood*, *Monterey*, *San Jacinto*, and *Princeton*.

In the months before the Marianas attacks, the Japanese suffered considerable losses among their most experienced air crew. Training standards for their replacements had fallen and the remaining Imperial Japanese Navy aircraft carriers were not at sea much owing to concern about the possibility of their being sunk by U.S. Navy submarines. Japan's carrier force in the Marianas included *Hiyo*, *Shokaku*, *Zuikaku*, *Junyo*, *Ryuho*, *Chitose*, *Chiyoda*, and the newly operational *Taiho*, the largest, fastest, and most sophisticated of her carrier fleet.

For the Marianas operation the American carriers had 900 aircraft available to launch, half of which were fighters, with 300 being newly-arrived Grumman F6F Hellcats. The Japanese Navy had but 430 aircraft ready for action, in addition to some shore-based naval and air force planes. The Americans had achieved air supremacy over Saipan. Now Vice-Admiral Spruance sought to deny the use of Iwo Jima to the Japanese as a staging platform for reinforcing aircraft coming from the home islands, by sending half of his carrier task group north to bomb Iwo.

Vice-Admiral Jisaburo Ozawa had brought the Japanese fleet to the east of Saipan, and in the morning of 19 June, intended to attack the fifteen fast carriers of the recently formed U.S. Fifth Fleet which was under the overall command of Spruance, who had ordered his two task group divisions to rendezvous with the balance of his fleet, 180 miles west of Tinian. His primary mission was to safeguard the U.S. invasion fleet and the Saipan beachhead, and he chose to maintain a defensive

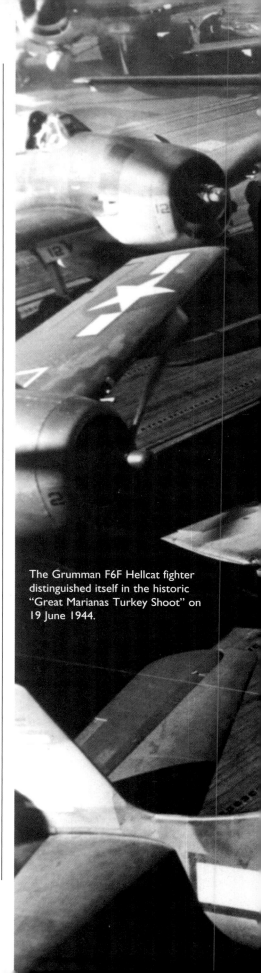

The Grumman F6F Hellcat fighter distinguished itself in the historic "Great Marianas Turkey Shoot" on 19 June 1944.

position between Saipan and the approaching Japanese fleet.

Ozawa's second-in-command, Vice-Admiral Takeo Kurita, planned to hit the American carrier force at a point between his own carriers and the Marianas so his fighters could then refuel and rearm at Japanese bases on Rota and Guam, and then carry out a second attack on the enemy planes as they returned to the U.S. carriers. Both the Americans and the Japanese had sent submarines into the Philippine Sea prior to the events of 19 June. Reconnaissance planes had pinpointed the position of the U.S. ships for Kurita a day earlier, giving him an advantage over Mitscher, who was still uncertain of the enemy fleet position. Mitscher had to protect his ships and did so by mounting constant combat air patrols over the American carriers.

A series of attacks by shore-based Japanese planes from Guam began at 10 am and lasted nearly five hours, during which 143 of their aircraft were downed. None of the Japanese planes in these attacks reached the U.S. carriers. In anticipation of further attacks, Admiral Mitscher directed many of his fighters some fifty miles beyond the American carriers where they met and engaged four additional waves of Japanese carrier-based aircraft which suffered grave losses by both U.S. fighter planes and the flak put up from U.S. warships. Of the Japanese striking force, only 100 aircraft returned to their carriers. Fewer than twenty of their planes got through to the American ships, making hits on the carriers *Wasp* and *Bunker Hill*, causing but minor damage.

Vice-Admiral Ozawa was using the carrier *Taiho* as his flagship on 19 June when it was hit by torpedos fired from the U.S. submarine *Albacore*, causing fuel leaks. Eight hours later, fumes caught fire and a gigantic explosion ripped the great ship apart. She

sank with the loss of approximately 1,650 of her 2,150-man crew. Four hours after *Taiho* was torpedoed, a similar fate befell *Shokaku*, the victim of another American submarine, the *Cavalla*. After three hours of explosions and spreading fires, *Shokaku* went to the bottom of the Philippine Sea. Vice-Admiral Ozawa had moved his flag to the cruiser *Haguro*.

The next day Ozawa could field but 100 serviceable aircraft. At dusk on 20 June Mitscher launched eighty-five fighters to escort 131 strike planes in an effort to destroy what remained of the Japanese carrier fleet. They attacked and sank *Hiyo* and damaged *Chiyoda* and *Zuikaku*, as well as the battleship *Haruna* and the cruiser *Maya*. In the action, the Japanese lost sixty-five aircraft against fourteen for the Americans. However, the U.S. pilots faced a 300-mile flight back to their carriers following the air battles of the 20th, and either a ditching at sea when their fuel ran out, or a treacherous deck landing at night. Mitscher, from his flagship, the *Lexington*, elected to illuminate the flight decks of his carriers to help his pilots through their ordeal, despite the possibility of alerting enemy submarines to the presence of his ships. Still, eighty of the returning U.S. planes were lost when they were forced to ditch or crash, taking the lives of forty-nine American airmen.

The Imperial Japanese Navy never again met the U.S. Navy in real strength in the remainder of World War Two. The First Battle of the Philippine Sea was the last major carrier-versus-carrier engagement of the war. Going into the battle with inferior numbers of warships, aircraft, and air crews, against a foe that was introducing a new aircraft in the Grumman F6F Hellcat, with superior performance to their own fighters, proved disastrous for Japan. Her air groups were wiped

out. The loss of three of her aircraft carriers and hundreds of aircraft and air crew in just two days all but ended her carrier striking capability. Japanese carrier forces would never again be a threat. The one-sided two-day air battle would forever be remembered by U.S. Navy pilots and air crew as the "Great Marianas Turkey Shoot."

"I was closing fast. Then I heard a very loud noise. Imagine being in a galvanized tin shed when someone throws a big handful of rocks against the outside. That is what is sounds and feels like when your plane is hit by machine-gun fire. It certainly got my attention. I looked back and 300 yards behind me was a pair of Zeros and a stream of red tracers coming at me from the 7.7mm machine-gun in the nose of the lead plane."
—Hamilton McWhorter, former U.S. Navy fighter pilot

Jack Glass served with Air Groups Six and Ten aboard the USS *Enterprise* in 1944: "On 20 June 1944 the pilots and radiomen of VB-10 were on the alert hoping the Japanese fleet would be found before the end of the day. At about 4:40 pm word came down to the ready room that the Jap fleet had indeed been located about 250 miles away. We were very worried about such a long mission so late in the day. If we somehow made it back to our carriers, it would mean night landings. All of our pilots were qualified for night landings but had made only a few in recent months. Despite the drawbacks we were all eager to take another crack at the Jap fleet. We sure weren't heroes, but this was what it was all about. With the climb-out and a full bomb load, the SBD [Douglas Dauntless dive-bomber] just wasn't supposed to make it there and back.

U.S. Navy deck personnel manhandle a Douglas SBD dive-bomber into position for take-off from this carrier deck.

"We were launched at about 5:30 and I remember looking into the sun low on the horizon when we took off. This had to be the most important strike for me personally, since we would be returning to the States after the Saipan invasion. I had been on the *Enterprise* off and on since July 1942, first with Air Group Six and later with AG-10, so I knew this would probably be the last crack at the enemy fleet before the invasion of Japan.

"The flight to the Japanese fleet took about two hours. The time was spent checking out our guns, looking for enemy fighters, and operating our radar, hoping to pick up our target. My pilot, Lt. Oliver Hubbard, was leading the second section in Skipper 'Jig Dog' Ramage's division. Hubbard had agreed that a hit was a must. The skipper sent Bangs and his division to one carrier, and our division took the *Ryuho*. The anti-aircraft fire was very strong, but we managed to get into our dive with no problem, with the exception of a half-hearted attack by several Zeros which were promptly taken care of by our fighters. In our dive we became twisted around trying to get on target. We had to settle for a port-to-starboard run and only scored a near miss. On our pull-out we were headed away from our return heading and had to do a 180 back through the entire fleet, skipping over ship after ship. The battleships were firing their main batteries as we went by. I was strafing everything in sight, mainly out of frustration.

"After leaving the enemy fleet, our main thought was finding our way back to our Task Force. Again it was about a two-hour flight. Our new radar worked fine and we picked up the *Enterprise* at about 100 miles. There were many frantic calls about fuel problems and going in the drink,

but the old faithful SBDs just kept chugging along. As I recall, Jig Dog made only one transmission: 'Land on any base.' We did just that, finding the *Wasp* right away. We had barely left the plane and entered the island hatch when a Hellcat crashed the barrier, putting the *Wasp* out of operation for about twenty-five minutes. The next morning I measured our fuel. We had less than three gallons remaining. Without the excellent landing by Lt. Hubbard, we would have taken a swim that night. A flight of over five and a half hours in a plane that wasn't supposed to fly more than about four hours. That's fuel management."

Jack Leaming was a radioman in SBD dive-bombers during World War Two. He was involved in attacks on the Marshall Islands of Roi and Taroa, Wake Island, and Marcus Island. In the latter, Leaming and his pilot completed their dive and were immediately bracketed by machine-gun fire. Flak then struck an outboard fuel tank setting their plane ablaze. They made a water landing and were taken prisoner by the Japanese. They survived their ordeal and were repatriated in September 1945. "Because there were no landmarks on our long, overwater scouting hops, the pilot had a tremendous navigation task. I always waited for him to initiate conversation . . . didn't want to interfere with his thought processes. In dive-bombing, you had to have complete confidence in your pilot and his expertise. In wartime, if he was hit, killed, or disabled, and you were still functioning, in all likelihood you were 'going in.' Gravity and speed were against you. There was no time to turn the seat around, put in the auxiliary stick and pull out."

When Larry Caudle left the American west coast aboard the jeep aircraft

carrier USS *Barnes* in February 1944, he could not have imagined the adventure that awaited him in the Southwestern Pacific. "The jeep carrier was built on a merchant ship hull and was smaller and slower than the fleet carriers. It was built utilizing the Kaiser shipyard assembly-line method, which took only about one-fifth of the time needed to build a fleet carrier. The ship was packed stem to stern and the hangar deck was full of aircraft being transported to the combat area to replace losses. There were about thirty of us ensigns going out as replacement pilots to squadrons in action. The number of additional officers made things very crowded on a ship of that size. We were travelling through the tropics and, of course, in those days there was no air-conditioning. Such niceties as sleeping spaces, cool ventilation, and water for showers were in short supply.

"It can be a little awkward, joining a squadron already in combat and replacing a pilot who has been killed or lost in action. The squadron members may tend to compare you with their missing friend and squadron mate. I have to say though that in both of the squadrons I joined and flew combat with, I was readily accepted and, after a few days of flying, was treated as a fully-fledged member.

"I was assigned to Fighting Squadron Five (VF-5) aboard the USS *Yorktown* (CV-10) when we arrived at Espiritu Santos in the New Hebrides. After a brief familiarization with the squadron, my first combat flight was to be an attack on airfields on the island of Peleliu. It was 30 March 1944, and I was so nervous and keyed up that I didn't see a lot of what was going on, including where my own .50 caliber rounds were hitting.

"As we circled back after strafing and sinking a small enemy freighter

Sturdy and reliable, the little Grumman F4F Wildcat held her own against Japanese fighters until the better performing Hellcats and Corsairs arrived in the Pacific War.

about five miles off the coast, we saw life boats in the water with uniformed soldiers in them. We knew that the Japanese were shipping replacement troops down from the home islands, so we attacked the life boats. The .50 caliber machine-guns really tear up wooden boats and human bodies. Between my section leader and myself, we were firing twelve .50s. Pieces of life boats and bodies were flying everywhere. What we didn't know when we opened fire was that,

in addition to the soldiers, there were women in the boats. What they were doing there, in an active combat area, I had no idea. Although it was an unpleasant and very graphic sight, if I had it to do over, I would not do the mission differently. We had, of course, read of terrible attrocities committed by the Japanese; Nanking, where some 300,000 Chinese civilians were raped and slaughtered, being just one example, and our squadron had lost three pilots the day before this mission, so

revenge was undoubtedly a factor too. Our marines were then having a difficult time in the ground fighting on Palau, and they certainly didn't need to face fresh enemy reinforcements. War is a messy business of killing people and breaking things. There is no nice way to do it. Obviously, I would have preferred that there had been no women in those life boats, but they were there so they were going to get the same treatment as the combat troops in that situation.

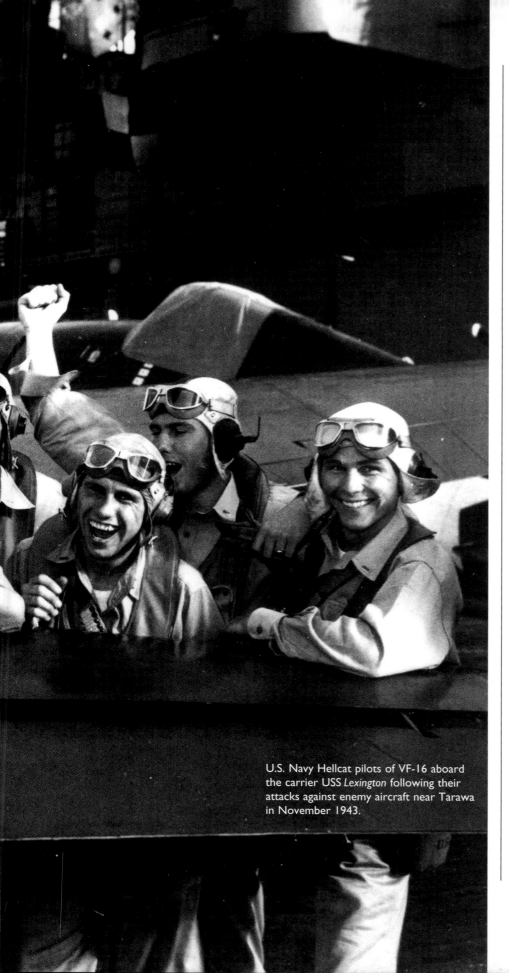

U.S. Navy Hellcat pilots of VF-16 aboard the carrier USS *Lexington* following their attacks against enemy aircraft near Tarawa in November 1943.

"I had only been with the squadron two months when it was ordered to return to the U.S. to be reformed and readied for another combat tour. I persuaded the CO to let me transfer to a training squadron so I would be sent out again as a replacement pilot. I was ordered to VF-1 and flew a brand new F6F Hellcat aboard the *Yorktown*. On my first day aboard, the commanding officer invited the eleven of us who had just reported in, to his stateroom. He told us that he didn't know why we were aboard, and that he didn't need us. He then chastized several officers for having non-regulation belts or other uniform infractions. That was the last time I had any direct contact with him. VF-1 had been out in the combat area for about five months when I joined them, and had been shore-based on the island of Tarawa before being transferred to the *Yorktown*. After our greeting from the skipper I had no desire to stay with VF-1, so when we got back to Hawaii I requested transfer to the replacement squadron at Barber's Point.

"The replacement squadron felt that our squadron had been out in combat for such a long time that we needed a rest, so they sent us to spend two weeks in a mansion right on Waikiki Beach for a little R and R. It was delightful . . . private beach, surf boards, food prepared by a Navy staff, and a hostess who mothered us and chaperoned when young ladies were brought out from town.

"After that pleasant interlude, I returned to the war, this time with VF-19 aboard the USS *Lexington*, and a great commanding officer. My fellow pilots there were most welcoming. Friendship and camaraderie develop quickly under combat conditions, not just between contemporaries, but between seniors and juniors, because each is dependent on the other in a tactical situation for protection from attack by enemy aircraft, and other mutual assistance.

"I was assigned as wingman to Lt. Bruce William, with Lt. JG Paul Gartland second section leader. I flew many combat flights with this tactical division, with the first five flights being combat air patrols over the fleet. These flights were in defense of the task group and we generally flew in thirty- to forty-mile circles at 20,000 to 25,000 feet, waiting for the ship's fighter director to send us to intercept attacking enemy aircraft.

"On 21 September 1944, I participated in the first attack of the war on Manila. We were part of a fighter sweep sent to get control of the air. It was to be the first time I had been fired at by another airplane. Tracer shells going by your wing can get your adrenaline going very quickly and some pilots lose control of one bodily function or another in such circumstances. It is a very frightening experience. Fortunately, another pilot behind our division shot the attacking plane down before its pilot had a chance to correct his aim. Over Manila one of our planes was badly shot up and the pilot had to bail out. We saw his parachute open, but as he was descending he was strafed by an enemy fighter. The bullets appeared to saw him in half. It was a gruesome sight and made us realize that there was no chivalry in this air war. That particular enemy fighter was then shot down by one of our squadron pilots.

"On 14 October I shot down a Zeke, my second kill. I shared it with "Willy" Williams since we had both fired at it simultaneously. The task force then headed south. Being so close to Japan, the Navy was concerned that the enemy could fly replacement aircraft down to rein-

force its units on Formosa, and for the next three days I flew combat air patrol over the fleet as we headed for an area to the east of the southern Philippines.

"Our division was sent out on 21 October to fly west across the Philippines and look for targets of opportunity. We found a wooden barge tied up at the island of San Isadore, and there was no anti-aircraft fire so Willy told us to get ready by sections for a strafing run. As Willy and I made our run in from 5,000 feet, we were scoring a lot of hits when the barge suddenly erupted in one massive explosion. Willy's plane was slightly ahead and about fifty feet lower than mine, and he caught the full force of the blast from what had obviously been an ammunition barge.

"Willy's canopy was shattered. His face was cut in so many places that blood was getting in his eyes. He thought he was losing his eyesight. We had been at full power for the strafing run and he was still at full power and heading west away from our ship. We were now 250 miles from the *Lexington* and were concerned about having enough fuel to get back to the ship. We had been out about two and a half hours. Leading the second section, Paul radioed for me to get Willy; that he (Paul) was heading back to the carrier. There was no response to my radio calls asking Willy to reduce power and turn back towards the ship. Finally, I caught up with him and could see that there were big chunks of wood protruding from his wings, pieces of flap and tail section were missing, and his canopy was broken.

"We were using fuel at an alarming rate and heading the wrong way. It took three or four minutes and seemed like an eternity until, with the use of hand signals, I was able to get him to give me the lead. I started

A Grumman F6F Hellcat departs the carrier on a combat air patrol in 1944.

reducing power to economic cruise and got us turned around and headed toward the *Lex*. We had a two and a half hour flight ahead of us, so we exchanged hand signals every few minutes as I wanted to keep Willy alert and informed about fuel management, the distance to go, and other flight information. Many of his instruments were shattered, so he could not navigate. When we were thirty miles out from the carrier, I contacted them about our situation. They instructed me to land first. They were concerned that Willy might crash-land and foul the deck if he landed first, leaving me no possibility of coming aboard. Willy seemed to understand my hand signals that he was to land last, but when he saw the carrier he headed straight in without flying a pattern, landed, and immediately ran out of fuel. I circled once while they pushed him out of the landing area. Then I landed and ran out of fuel. We had been in the air five hours and thirty-six minutes, a long flight for the Hellcat.

"On 28 October *Lexington* was ordered to the fleet anchorage at Majuro in preparation for her return to Hawaii and the U.S. As we were leaving the combat area, we were told to transfer some of our best airplanes to the USS *Franklin*. I was one of the pilots selected to fly a Hellcat over to the *Franklin*. We were to fly there, land and be returned by breeches buoy transfer to a destroyer, and then

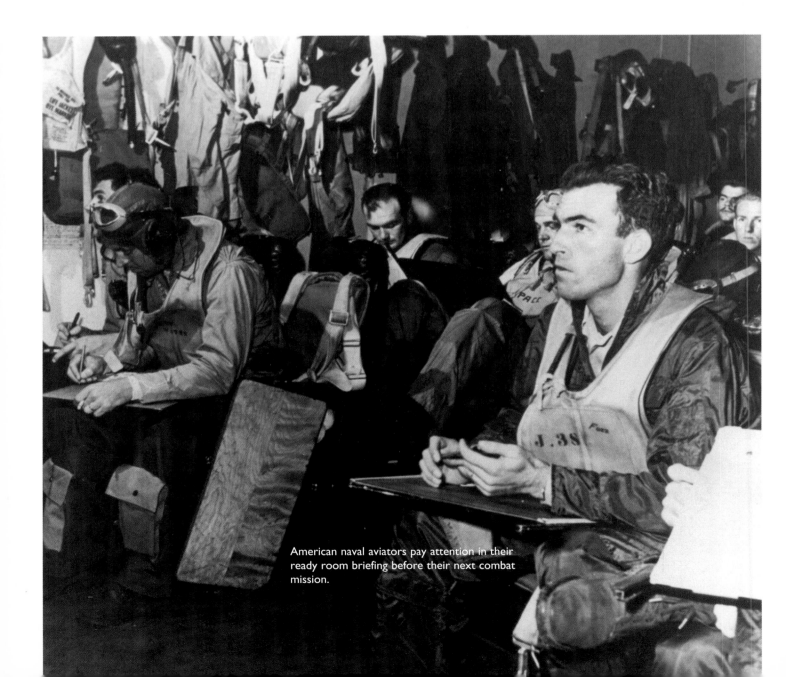

American naval aviators pay attention in their ready room briefing before their next combat mission.

transfer back to the *Lexington*. We were expected to be back aboard the *Lex* in two to three hours. It was late in the day and, as there was a slight chance that we might not be able to get back before dark, I decided to take a shaving kit and khaki uniform with me. We no sooner landed aboard *Franklin* when the fleet was attacked by Betty bombers out from Manila. Our transfer was cancelled, of course. The *Lexington* was hit by a kamikaze which did great damage to the island structure. *Lex* was ordered to leave the task force and proceed to the fleet anchorage at Majuro for emergency repairs. There I was on the *Franklin* with no way to get back to my clothes and possessions, my squadron mates and my ticket back to the States. Then things got worse.

"The next day the *Franklin* was hit by a kamikaze. Many people were killed, there was a lot of fire and the damage was considerable. I had no general quarters station so I joined one of the pilots from VF-13 in manning a fire hose on the flight deck. I knew several of the pilots there from training and replacement squadron days, and they helped me get a place to bunk. Owing to the extensive damage, there were to be no hot meals for the duration of my stay on board.

"*Franklin* survived (just) to return to Majuro for her emergency repairs, so she could get back to the Pearl Harbor shipyard for more complete repair. Luckily, Air Group 19 was being transferred from the *Lexington* to the *Enterprise*, for transportation back to Hawaii and on to the U.S., and I was able to get back to the *Lex* to pack my things and leave the war zone for the last time."

We were shooting three types of rounds: the incendiary, the tracer,
and the armor-piercing. The standard belting was 1-1-1, just repeating straight on through. I became convinced that this was not the most effective way to belt them. The armor-piercing would shoot through anything in the Zero. It might have been the preferable round if we were strafing barges with diesel engines in them, but it was an overkill on the Zero, totally unnecessary. The tracer burned out and was pretty much just an empty shell. But the incendiary got our kills for us; there was no question about it after shooting into drums filled with gasoline. The incendiary had enough impact to knock cylinders off of engines (the Zero had no armor plate at that time) and to shoot through anything. Probably nine out of ten Zeros shot down burned. It was very easy to burn the Zero.
—John Bolt, former U.S. Marine Corps fighter pilot

The U.S. Navy carrier *Hornet* (CV-8) was moving toward a large Japanese naval force near the Pacific island of Midway on the evening of 3 June 1942, when the pilots of Torpedo Eight filed into the ready room. Earlier in the day, B-17 bombers flying into Midway had attacked the Japanese ships, setting two afire.

The torpedo squadron pilots in *Hornet* had gathered to receive the plan that would be employed when the two opposing forces finally engaged. In addition, their skipper, Lieutenant Commander John C. Waldron, handed them mimeographed copies of his own final message to them, prior to what was to be the Battle of Midway. "Just a word to let you know that I feel we are all ready. We have had a very short time to train and we have worked under the most severe difficulties. But
we have truly done the best humanly possible. I actually believe that under these conditions we are the best in the world. My greatest hope is that we encounter a favorable tactical situation, but if we don't, and the worst comes to the worst, I want each of us to do his utmost to destroy our enemies. If there is only one plane left to make a final run-in, I want that man to go in and get a hit. May God be with us all. Good luck, happy landings, and give 'em hell."

Some of the men of Torpedo Eight then wrote letters to their loved ones. It was as if they had premonitions of what lay ahead:
Dear Mom, Dad and Mary,
This letter will be mailed only if I do not get through battle which we expect to come off any hour. I am making a request that this be mailed as soon as possible after I fail to return. As you know, I am the gunner and radioman in a plane and it is up to me to shoot first and best. I would not have it any different. I want you all to know that I am not the least bit worried, and Mom, you can be sure that I have been praying every day and am sure that I will see you 'up there.' Perhaps I have not always done the right thing. Only hope that you do not think too badly of my action. The best of luck to you all and be seeing you when life will be much different 'up there.' Be sure and remember I am only one of many and you are also one of many.
Love, Bill

Honey,
If anything happens to me, I wish you would keep on visiting the folks, for they love you just as much as they would if you were one of their own kids. And by all means, don't become an old maid. Find someone else and make a happy home. Don't be

worrying about me and I will be trying to write more often.
Pete

And from Commander Waldron:
Dear Adelaide,
There is not a bit of news that I can tell you now except that I am well. I have yours and the children's pictures here with me all the time, and I think of you all most of the time. I believe that we will be in battle very soon. I wish we were there today. But, as we are up to the very eve of serious business, I wish to record to you that I am feeling fine. My own morale is excellent and from my continued observation of the squadron, their morale is excellent also. You may rest assured that I will go in with the expectation of coming back in good shape. If I do not come back, well, you and the little girls can know that this squadron struck for the highest objective in naval warfare—to sink the enemy. I hope this letter will not scare you and, of course, if I have a chance to write another to be mailed at the same time as this, then I shall do so. I love you and the children very dearly and I long to be with you. But I could not be happy ashore at this time. My place is here with the fight. I could not be happy otherwise. I know you wish me luck and I believe I will have it. You know, Adelaide, in this business of the torpedo attack, I acknowledge we must have a break. I believe that I have the experience and enough Sioux in me to profit by and recognize the break when it comes, and it will come. I dislike having the censors read a letter from me such as this, however, at this time I felt I must record these thoughts. God bless you, dear. You are a wonderful wife and mother. Kiss and love the little girls for me and be of good cheer.
Love to all from
Daddy and Johnny

At 01:11 a message was flashed to *Hornet* telling of the attack by four U.S. Navy PBY Catalina patrol bombers on enemy ships to the southwest of Midway. A little over two hours later "general quarters" was sounded on the *Hornet* and the pilots of Torpedo Eight again assembled in their ready room, but it was a case of "hurry up and wait." The teleprinter was silent and the airmen reclined in their big leather chairs, some of them dozing off. The delay was due to Admiral Marc Mitscher and the *Hornet* skipper, Captain Mason, being uncertain of the Japanese fleet's exact position. Without that intelligence, they could not know if the U.S. carriers would be positioned close enough to the enemy ships for the American pilots to operate with a safe fuel margin. Secure from general quarters at 0600 Midway time, the Torpedo Eight pilots adjourned to the wardroom for breakfast. Just as they finished the meal, general quarters was sounded again, followed by "All pilots report to your ready rooms." Arriving at theirs, the torpedo plane pilots found the message: MIDWAY BEING ATTACKED BY JAPANESE AIRCRAFT.

Ensign George Gay, a TBD-1 Devastator pilot of Torpedo Eight recalled: "There was a real commotion as we hauled our plotting boards, helmets and goggles, gloves, pistols, hunting knives, and all our other gear. We took down the flight information.

"We had only six of our planes on the flight deck as there was no more room. And since we were to be alone anyhow, we were the last to be launched. The skipper had tried in vain to get us fighter protection. He even tried to get one fighter to go with us, or even to get one fighter

Eager young American sailors in their Second World War adventure.

plane and one of us would fly it even though we had never been up in one, but he could not swing it. The group commander and the captain felt that the SBDs needed more assistance than we did. They had caught hell in the Coral Sea and the torpedo planes had been lucky. However, the torpedo planes had made the hits in the Coral Sea, so the Japs were going to be looking for us.

"The TBD could not climb anywhere near as high as the dive-bombers needed to go, and the group commander and the fighter boys did not want us at two levels up there.

"Under these conditions, Commander Waldron reasoned, our best bet was to be right on the water so the Zeros could not get under us. Since it was obvious that we would be late getting away with nine of our planes still to be brought up from the hangar deck for launching, the problem would be overtaking to form a coordinated attack.

"As I went up to the flight deck, I suddenly ducked into a first aid station and got a tourniquet and put it in my pocket. When I got to the edge of the island, I met the skipper coming down from the bridge. 'I'm glad I caught you,' he said. 'I've been trying to convince them that the Japs will not be going toward Midway—especially if they find out we are here. The group commander is going to take the whole bunch down there. I'm going more to the north and maybe by the time they come north and find them, we can catch up and all go in together. Don't think I'm lost. Just track me so if anything happens to me, the boys can count on you to bring them back.'

"Each of us would be tracking, and the others all knew how to do it, but it would be my job since I was Navigation Officer. That is also the reason why I was the last man in the formation. It gave me more room to navigate instead of flying formation so closely.

"At a little before 0900, the planes started taking off, and it was 0915

Alex Vraciu became the fourth highest-scoring U.S. Navy fighter ace of World War Two.

when the signal man motioned me forward to the take-off position. He only had me move forward enough to that I could unfold my wings, and so I began my take-off with the tail of my plane sitting on the No. 3 elevator. I had more than enough room on the deck in front of me to take off, and I noticed as I came by the ship that the planes that were to follow me were being moved further up the deck with the hope of being able to bring the rest of the torpedo planes of Squadron 8 up the elevator from the hangar deck so they could get in take-off position.

"The rest of Torpedo Eight got off after what seemed an eternity. Then we all joined up and headed away from our fleet. After an uneasy and uneventful hour, the skipper's voice broke radio silence. 'There's a fighter on our tail.' What he saw proved to be a Jap scout plane flying at about 1,000 feet. It flew on past us, but I knew—and I'm sure the others did—that he had seen us and reported to the Japanese Navy that there were carrier planes approaching.

"We had been flying long enough now to find something, and I could almost see the wheels going around in Waldron's head. He did exactly what I had expected. He put the first section into a scouting line. Each of the eight planes was to move out into a line even with the skipper's wingtips. We had never done this before, only talked about it and, in spite of the warnings and dire threats, the fellows got too much distance between the planes. I knew immediately that this was wrong, as the planes on each end were nearly out of sight. The basic idea is OK, so that you can scan more ocean, but this was ridiculous.

"The skipper was upset, and he gave the join-up signal forcefully. We had just gotten together when smoke columns appeared on the horizon. In less time than it takes to tell, it became obvious that the old Indian had taken us as straight to the Japs as we could fly.

"The first capital ship I recognized as a carrier, the *Soryu*. Then I could make out the *Kaga* and the *Akagi*. There was another carrier further on screening ships all over the ocean. The smoke was from what looked like a battleship, and the carriers were landing planes. The small carrier off on the horizon had smoke coming out of her also. My first thought was, 'Oh, Christ! We're late!'

"The skipper gave the signal to spread out to bracket the biggest carrier for an attack, and that was when the Zeros swarmed all over us.

"Since we had flown straight to the enemy fleet, while everyone else was off looking for them, there was no one else for their air cover to worry about.

"Seeing immediately that the Zeros had us cold, the skipper signalled for us to join back together for mutual protection. We had not moved far apart, so we were back together almost immediately. The skipper broke radio silence again. 'We will go in. We won't turn back. Former strategy cannot be used. We will attack. Good luck.'

"I have never questioned the skipper's judgement or decisions. As it turned out, it didn't make any difference anyhow. We had run into a virtual trap, but we still had to do something to disrupt their landing planes, so he took us right in. We had calculated our fuel to be very short, even insufficient to get us back to *Hornet*, but this was not considered suicidal by any of us. We thought we had a fighting chance, and maybe after we dropped our fish we could make it to Midway. Things then started happening really fast.

"I cannot tell you the sequence in which the planes went down. Everything was happening at once, but I was consciously seeing it all. At least one plane blew up, and each would hit the water and seem to disappear,

"Zeros were coming in from all angles and from both sides at once. They would come in from abeam, pass each other just over our heads and turn around to make another attack. It was evident that they were trying to get our lead planes first. The planes of Torpedo Eight were falling at irregular intervals. Some were on fire and some did a half-roll and crashed on their backs, completely out of control. Machine-gun bullets ripped my armor plate a number of times. As they rose above it, the bullets would go over my shoulder into the instrument panel and through the windshield.

"Waldron was shot down very early. His plane burst into flames, and I saw him stand up to get out of the fire. He put his right leg outside the cockpit, and then hit the water and disappeared. His radioman, Dobbs, didn't have a chance. Good old Dobbs. When we had been leaving Pearl Harbor, Dobbs had orders back to the States to teach radio. But he had chosen to delay that assignment and stay with us.

"Much too early, it seemed, Bob Huntington, my radioman / gunner, said, 'They got me!' 'Are you hurt bad,' I asked. I looked back and Bob was slumped down almost out of sight. 'Can you move?' I asked. He said no more.

"It was while I was looking back at Bob that the plane to my left must have been shot down, because when I looked forward again it was not there. I think that was the only plane I did not actually see get hit.

"We were right on the water at full throttle and wide open which was about 180 knots. Anyone slamming into the sea had no chance of survival—at that speed the water is just like cement. That is why I was so sure that they were all dead.

"It's hard to explain, but I think Bob being put out of action so soon was one of the things that saved me. I no longer had to fly straight and level for him to shoot, so I started dodging. I even pulled up a few times, and took some shots at Zeros as they would go by. I am positive I hit one, knocking Plexiglas out of his canopy. I may have scared him, but I certainly did not hurt him personally, or even damage his plane much.

"The armor plate bucket seat was another thing that worked well for me. I could feel as well as hear and sometimes see, those tracer bullets. They would clunk into the airplane or clank against th armored seat, and I had to exercise considerable control over when to kick the rudder.

"About this time I felt something hit my left arm and felt it to see what it was. There was a hole in my sleeve and I got blood on my hand. I felt closer, and there was a lump under the skin of my arm. I squeezed the lump, just as you would pop a pimple, and a bullet popped out. I remember thinking, 'Well, what do you know—a souvenir.' So I put the bullet in my mouth, blood and all, thinking, 'What the hell—it's my blood.'

"We were now in a position, those of us still left, to turn west again to intercept the ship we had chosen to attack, but the Zeros were still intent on not letting us through, and our planes kept falling all around me. We were on the ship's starboard side, or to the right and ahead of our target, and as we closed range the big carrier began to turn toward us. I knew immediately from what the skipper had said so often in his lectures that if she got into a good turn she could

not straighten out right away, and I was glad that she had committed herself. At that moment there were only two planes left of our squadron besides my own. One was almost directly ahead of me, but off a bit to my left. I skidded to the left and avoided more 20mm slugs just in time to pull my nose up and fire at another Zero as he got in front of me. I only had one .30 caliber gun, and although I knew I hit this Zero also, it did little damage. When I turned back to the right, the plane that had been directly ahead of me was gone, and the other one was out of control.

"My target, which I think was the *Kaga,* was now in a hard turn to starboard and I was going toward her forward port quarter. I figured that by the time a torpedo could travel the distance it should be in the water, the ship would be broadside. I aimed about one-quarter of the ship's length ahead of her bow, and reached out with my left hand to pull back the throttle. It had been calculated that we should be at about eighty knots when we dropped these things, so I had to slow down.

"I had just got hold of the throttle, when something hit the back of my hand and it hurt like hell. My hand didn't seem to be working right, so I had to pull the throttle back mostly with my thumb. You can well imagine that I was not being exactly neat about all this. I was simply trying to do what I had come out to do. When I figured that I had things about as good as I was going to get them, I punched the torpedo release button.

"Nothing happened. 'Damn those tracers,' I thought. They've goofed up my electrical release and I'm getting inside my range. I had been told that the ideal drop was 1,000 yards range, eighty knots speed, and eighty feet or so of altitude. But by the time I got

Crash on deck! Chewed up wooden planking surrounds this Grumman Avenger torpedo bomber as its landing goes awry aboard the carrier USS *Philippine Sea*.

Making his post-mission strike report, Lt. JG Bill Adams aboard the USS *Lexington* in April 1944; far right: Ensign George Gay.

the control stick between my knees and put my left hand on top of it to fly the plane, and reached across to pull the cable release with my good right hand, I was into about 850 yards. The cable, or mechanical release, came out of the instrument panel on the left side, designed to be pulled with the left hand. But those damn Zeros had messed up my program. My left hand did not work. It was awkward, and I almost lost control of the plane trying to pull out that cable by the roots. I can't honestly say I got rid of that torpedo. It felt like it. I had never done it before so I couldn't be sure, and with the plane pitching like a bronco, I had to be content with trying my best.

"God but that ship looked big! I remember thinking, 'Why in the hell doesn't the *Hornet* look that big when I'm trying to land on her?'

"I remember that I did not want to fly out over the starboard side and let all those gunners have a chance at me, so I headed out over the stern.

"I thought, 'I could crash into all this and make one great big mess, maybe even get myself a whole carrier, but I'm feeling passably good, and my plane is still flying, so the hell with that—I'll keep going. Maybe I'll get another crack at them and do more damage in the long run.'

"Flying as low as I could, I went between a couple of cruisers and out past the destroyers. If you've ever seen movies of this sort of thing, you may wonder how anything could get through all of that gunfire. I am alive to tell you that it can be done. I think my plane was hit a few times . . .

"The Zeros had broken off me when I got into ack-ack, but they had no trouble going around to meet me on the other side. A 20mm cannon slug hit my left rudder pedal just outside my little toe, blew the pedal apart and knocked a hole in the firewall. This set the engine on fire, and it was burning my left leg through that hole.

"When the rudder pedal went, the control wire to the ailerons and the rudder went with it. I still had the elevators, so I could pull the nose up. Reaching over with my right hand, I cut the switch. That was also on the left side. I was able to hold the nose up and slow down to almost a decent ditching speed.

"Most airplanes will level out if you turn them loose, especially if they are properly trimmed. Mine was almost making it, but I was crosswind, so the right wing hit first. This slammed me into the water in a cartwheel fashion and banged the hood shut over me before it twisted the frame and jammed the hood tight.

"As I unbuckled, water was rising to my waist. The nose of the plane was down, so I turned around and sat on the instrument panel while trying to get that hood open. It wouldn't budge. When that water got up to my armpits and started lapping at my chin, I got scared—and I mean really scared. I knew the plane would dive as soon as it lost buoyancy and I didn't want to drown in there. I panicked, stood up and busted my way out.

"The Zeros were diving and shooting at me, but my first thought now was of Bob Huntington in the back seat. I was almost positive he was dead. I think he took at least one of those cannon slugs in the chest, but

I thought that the water might revive him and I had to try and help him. I got back to him just as the plane took that dive, and I went down with it, trying to unbuckle his straps and get him out.

"The beautiful water exploded into a deep red and I lost sight of everything. What I had seen confirmed my opinion of his condition and I had to let Bob go. The tail took a gentle swipe at me as if to say goodbye, and I came up choking. I lost the bullet from my mouth and as I watched it sink in that blue, clear water, I grabbed for it but missed. Zeros were still strafing me and I ducked under a couple of times as those thwacking slugs came close. As I came up for air once, I bumped my head on my life raft out of the plane."

George Gay was the only member of Torpedo Eight to survive their attack that day. With his wits and luck, he evaded capture by the ships of the enemy fleet that drove past him as he floated near them, his head covered by a thin black seat cushion that had emerged from his sinking plane, along with a four-man life raft. That entire afternoon, in the presence of the Japanese warships, he "rode" that uninflated raft like a horse, concealing it and himself from his foes, having to wait until nightfall to inflate it. From his vantage point, he watched the destruction of three great carriers of the enemy fleet by the dive-bombers of Hornet and other U.S. flattops. After about thirty hours in the water, Gay was saved when he was sighted by a PBY crew who landed nearby to pick him up. He was flown to Midway and later to Pearl Harbor where a doctor examined him and noted that the ensign had lost roughly a pound an hour in body weight during his time in the sea. While recovering, George was visited in his hospital room by Admiral Chester W. Nimitz, Commander-in-Chief of the U.S. Pacific Fleet. The admiral had a more than casual interest in the ensign's account of what he had observed in the course of his amazing adventure. Gay later received the Navy Cross and the Purple Heart.

George Blair was a U.S. Navy fighter pilot aboard the USS Essex: "In mid-February 1944 our air group was involved in the first strike against the Japanese at Truk. We were expecting fierce opposition, but it did not occur. After destroying the few enemy aircraft there, our main objective was the bombing and strafing of shipping and shore installations. While engaged in strafing I was hit by anti-aircraft fire at about 400 feet and had to ditch in the lagoon. Fortunately, others in my flight remained over me for a while and were able to intercept an enemy destroyer that was coming to pick me up. They set it afire and caused it to beach on the reef. When I had landed, my F6F Hellcat sank so fast that I was unable to deploy my raft, and was floating about in my life jacket for three hours after my companions were forced to leave me due to fuel shortage. Then I looked to the north and saw an OS2U float plane from the USS Baltimore. It had been dispatched to retrieve me. The pilot, Lieutenant Denver Baxter, made a landing in very rough water, and the rescue was complete." This was one of the first rescues of a downed U.S. pilot from the midst of a Japanese stronghold in the Second World War.

Don McMillan, former U.S. Navy torpedo bomber pilot: "My day began with breakfast, getting into flight gear, a navigation and intelligence briefing. Along with a complement of fighters and dive-bombers, we took off into a good weather day. Lieutenant Prater brought us into the Jap fleet area and the fighter escort kept what few enemy fighters there were at bay as we approached the carrier Zuikaku which was at full speed and fleeing north, trying to get to safety with the rest of the Japanese diversionary force. Prater put us into our standard torpedo plane attack formation, a 'cut-the-pie' attack which, despite intensive manouvering by the intended victims, still resulted in some attackers getting hits. I was one of the last in, as my assigned approach was to have been a port beam shot. As Zuikaku manouvered in an S-shaped path, I was to have a bow shot. After releasing my torpedo at about 1,500 yards and an altitude of about 300 feet, I barreled on in and flew down the starboard side of the ship. We flew through falling streams of phosphorus shot at us as we reformed to head back to the Lexington. Our group had made several hits on the Japanese carrier, leaving her smoking. Later, another attack finished her off and by later in the afternoon she was no more."

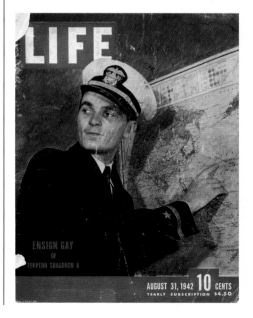

It is absolutely out of the question for you to return alive. Your mission involves certain death. Your bodies will be dead, but not your spirits. The death of a single one of you will be the birth of a million others. Neglect nothing that may affect your training or your health. You must not leave behind any cause for regret, which would follow you into eternity. And, lastly: do not be in too much of a hurry to die. If you cannot find your target, turn back; next time you may find a more favorable opportunity. Choose a death which brings about a maximum result.
—from *The First Order to the Kamikaze*

IN WHAT MAY HAVE BEEN AN INCIDENT created by the Japanese military as an excuse for mounting an offensive campaign against the Chinese, an explosive device damaged a vital Japanese rail link in 1931, leading to their incursion into Manchuria, the taking of Peking, and the sacking and burning of Nanking. By 1936 the Japanese Cabinet was dominated by military figures and several senior government officials had been assasinated. A new order had taken control in Japan and the Japanese Imperial Army was on the march through Indo-China. It proceeded to drive the British from Shanghai and the Dutch from the East Indies as the Great East Asia Co-Existence Sphere, the Japanese euphemism for their newly-occupied territories, was being formed.

By early December 1941 Japanese militarists had decided that the time had come to implement a bold surprise attack on warships of the U.S. Navy at anchor around Ford Island in Pearl Harbor, Hawaii. The raid came in the early hours of 7 December in an attack by carrier-based aircraft of the Imperial Japanese Navy.

Their bombs and torpedos sank the U.S. battleships *Arizona*, *California*, *Oklahoma*, *Utah*, and *West Virginia*, and damaged the *Maryland*, *Nevada*, *Pennsylvania,* and *Tennessee*. Of these *California*, *Nevada*, and *West Virginia* were later salvaged. In a great irony, the Japanese had unwittingly committed an act which would lead to their ultimate destruction as a military power and to their defeat in World War Two. Their attack at Pearl Harbor came at a moment when the principal battleships of the U.S. fleet lay at anchor there, but none of the American aircraft carriers were present. Thus the Japanese virtually forced the U.S. Navy to rely heavily on its aircraft carriers throughout the course of the war, the majority of its battleships being unserviceable. Traditionally, the U.S. Navy had led with its big stick, the battleship, but now it would be the aircraft carrier that would form the nucleus of its task force groups.

The Pearl Harbor attack brought the U.S. into the war when President Franklin Roosevelt addressed the Congress a day later to ask for a declaration of war against the Empire of Japan. In the months to follow, Japanese troops moved to capture the Philippines, Burma, and Singapore.

In 1942 the U.S. Navy maintained an airfield and a refuelling station on the island of Midway located 1,136 miles west of Hawaii. In June of that year Japanese Admiral Isoroku Yamamoto made a plan to eliminate the U.S. carrier threat by drawing the big American ships out for battle at Midway. The Japanese naval force of eight carriers, eleven battleships, eighteen cruisers, and sixty-five destroyers significantly outnumbered the American fleet of just three carriers, no battleships, eight cruisers, and fifteen destroyers. Still,

the Japanese were defeated in the Battle of Midway, 4–6 June (their first naval defeat since 1592), owing largely to the Americans having cracked the Japanese naval codes. The Japanese Navy's failure at Midway marked the turning point of naval power in the Pacific War. Japanese carriers would never again pose quite the threat to the U.S. fleet, and the U.S. Navy was, from that point, able to go on the offensive. In the Battle of Midway no gunfire was exchanged between the warships. It was an air battle between planes of the two carrier forces, and the Japanese lost four of their carriers, *Akagi*, *Kaga*, *Hiryu*, and *Soryu*, while the Americans lost the carrier *Yorktown*.

I was walking across the flight deck in the still half-dark dawn to man my plane. I had reached the middle of the deck when I heard the very loud sound of 20mm cannon fire coming from astern the *Randolph*. Almost immediately, huge red tracers began coming up from astern, from below the port edge of the flight deck and parallel to the ship. As I hastily dropped to the deck wishing I could dig a foxhole, a kamikaze Zero arced up alongside the flight deck with its guns still firing, and flashed by less than fifty feet from me. The Zero then nosed down and turned in an attempt to crash into the carrier. Fortunately, he had misjudged his speed and passed just in front of, and under the bow of the ship, crashing and exploding in the water on the starboard side. The carrier got quite a jolt from the bomb explosion and lots of shrapnel on the flight deck, with little damage.
—Hamilton McWhorter, former U.S. Navy fighter pilot.

In the final months of 1944, Imperial Japan was losing the war, and some of its military leaders began to express the belief that desperate times called for desperate measures. The notion of self-sacrifice for Emperor and country was commonly accepted among the Japanese, and suicide per se was not alien, and was honored for its purity by many who had been raised on tales of samurai warriors. Thus, it was a short step to the concept of suicide as a weapon, i.e. the *kaiten* (turning the tide) human torpedo. The kaiten, fifty-four feet long, carrying a 3,000-pound warhead, had a range of thirty miles at slow speed or twelve miles at a top speed of forty knots. It was designed around the Japanese Type 93 torpedo, primarily by naval architect Hiroshi Suzukawa. Launching the kaiten meant a one-way trip for the crew, who could not get out. Only one U.S. ship was sunk by a kaiten, the tanker USS *Mississinewa*, and most kaitens proved unstable, killing their "pilots" before reaching their targets.

General Yashida of the Japanese Army Air Force, meanwhile, was advocating suicidal air attacks, and ramming techniques were being secretly included in the pilot training syllabus. Army General Yoshiroko, in command of units in the Solomon Islands, was particularly frustrated by the ineffective anti-tank weapons in his arsenal, and called upon his troops to make the supreme sacrifice by strapping satchels of explosives to their bodies and diving under the tanks of the American enemy. The effort was mostly without result and the general was the subject of severe criticism from Tokyo before being transferred to another post. The concept and use of "human bullets" by the Japanese continued, however.

On 15 June an invasion force of U.S. Marines landed on the island of Saipan in the Marianas chain, as long-range American B-29 Superfortress

A miscalculated final plunge and this kamikaze aircraft narrowly misses the crowded flight deck of the escort carrier USS *Sangamon* in the spring of 1945.

DIVINE WIND

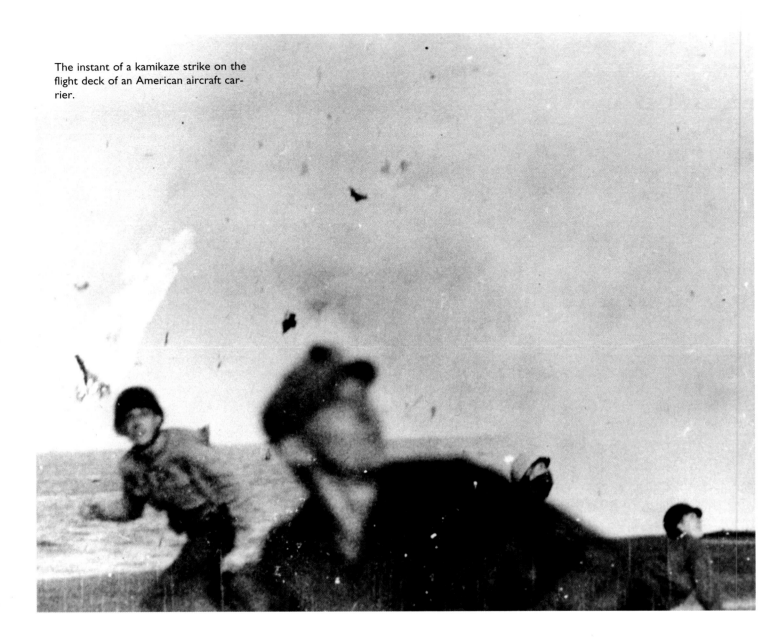

The instant of a kamikaze strike on the flight deck of an American aircraft carrier.

bombers were attacking the Japanese mainland. The bombers frequently flew well beyond the range of both anti-aircraft and defending fighters, further frustrating the Japanese High Command who were shocked to witness the enemy planes operating, seemingly with impunity, over their sacred homeland.

The First Battle of the Philippine Sea took place on 19 June with Japanese carriers and battleships engaging U.S. naval forces off Saipan. Within this pivotal clash, aircraft of both sides met in what has ever since been referred to by U.S. naval aviators as "The Great Marianas Turkey Shoot." When it was over, the Japanese had lost 328 carrier-based planes, 50 land-based planes, three more carriers, and the last of their best pilots. The Americans lost just twenty-nine aircraft. After this engagement Japanese naval power was largely neutralized for the remainder of the war.

Vice-Admiral Takejiro Onishi, Imperial Japanese Navy, Chief of the Ministry of Munitions, Arms, and Air Control Bureau, was a principal advocate of the kamikaze idea. It was he who originated the name kamikaze, which means "divine wind" and is believed to be a reference to the ancient winds that sank the threatening Mongol fleet in the late thirteenth century. Kamikaze pilots were members of special attack units.

Their mission was to become human bombs, one with their airplanes, and sacrifice themselves by diving their planes into enemy ships with the goal of sinking them. In an effort to instill high morale among his airmen, the vice-admiral introduced some ceremonial aspects to the kamikaze units, including the pre-flight toast of sacred water, later changed to sake, and the wearing of a decorated white headband called a *hachimaki*, a touch of samurai indicating that the warrior was prepared to fight to the death. The majority also wore a *sennin-bari*, a silk cloth band stitched with red threads that was said to have the power of a bullet-proof vest. Most kamikaze pilots carried a personal flag, usually a small square of white cloth with a red *hinomaru* circle in the center and calligraphy encouraging "a suicide spirit." Kamikaze pilots and their families received privileges, including extra food rations, as well as "very honorable" status. By some, the kamikaze were referred to as "the black-edged cherry blossoms."

Admiral Onishi was painfully aware of the shortage of truly skilled Japanese pilots, but he still believed that his aircraft were a potent weapon. "If a pilot facing a ship or plane exhausts all his resources, he still has his plane left as a part of himself. What greater glory than to give his life for emperor and country?"

In his book *Kamikaze—Japan's Suicide Samurai*, Raymond Lamont-Brown states that "the Kamikaze pilots evolved from four main sources of recruitment. First came the 'patriotic crusaders' who were all volunteers, usually from *daimyo* or *samurai* families; they were motivated by nationalistic fervour, military ideals and the concept of chivalry upon which their ancestors had based personal sacrifice to fulfil perceived duties to the State.

From this group evolved the ritualization of the kamikaze before suicide flights (i.e. the wearing of samurai symbols, singing patriotic songs, writing poetry glorifying kamikaze action, composing testamentary last letters home, distributing personal effects, and so on).

"Next came the 'nation's face savers.' These were recruits who did volunteer, but often for negative reasons, to avoid personal shame in not emulating the deaths of the patriotic crusaders, or to espouse military heroism in order to save the Kami land of Japan from humiliating defeat. Like the patriotic crusaders, they too were conformists to the traditions of Japanese society. As the kamikaze Susumu Kitjitsu (1923–1945) wrote to his parents: 'I live quite a normal life. Death does not frighten me; my only care is to know if I am going to be able to sink an aircraft carrier by crashing into it.'

"By the last few months of the war the third category of recruits emerged: these were the 'young nationalists.' They came mostly straight from higher education, went through hurried training and died to sustain the war effort and to keep Japan free from foreign taint. As Bernard Millot wrote: 'With a very few rare exceptions, they were the most affectionate, well-educated, least troublesome sons who gave their parents the greatest satisfaction.'

"The last group of recruits were also mostly young, the 'appointed daredevils,' who emerged right at the end of the war. It may be noted that among their numbers were do-or-die delinquents, hell-raisers, and those of shady moral reputation and social deviation who, through the drastic measure of suicide, were escaping the legal, civic and social consequences of their behavior."

In his official code of ethics of January 1941, then Army Minister of Japan Hideki Tojo stated: "Do not think of death as you use up every ounce of your strength to fulfil your duties. Make it your joy to use every last bit of your physical and spiritual strength in what you do. Do not fear to die for the cause of ever-lasting justice. Do not stay alive in dishonor. Do not die in such a way as to leave a bad name behind you."

Dear Parents,
Please congratulate me. I have been given a splendid opportunity to die. This is my last day. The destiny of our homeland hinges on the decisive battle in the seas to the south where I shall fall like a blossom from a radiant cherry tree.
—from a last letter home of a kamikaze, in *The Divine Wind* by Captain Rikihei Inoguchi and Commander Tadashi Nakajima, with Roger Pineau

In pre-war Japan, naval pilots were required to log a minimum of 400 flying hours before they qualified to train for carrier operations. They then had to accrue an additional 400 hours on carriers before being considered combat ready. As the war situation worsened for Japan, its pilot training was reduced to a maximum of 200 hours with virtually no navigation, aerobatics, or combat technique included. These poorly-trained student pilots quickly became easy prey for U.S. carrier aviators.

Now the American B-29s were based on Saipan, posing a far greater threat to the Japanese home islands. Japanese High Command, in a progressively more desperate mindset, ordered a dramatic, large-scale, three-pronged battleship and cruiser attack (which did not involve its own carriers) against the U.S. fleet. The plan called for a diversionary force to draw the U.S. carrier-based planes far away from the U.S. fleet. When it failed, the High Command immediately dispatched Vice-Admiral Onishi to the Philippines to take command of the First Air Fleet. U.S. carrier planes, meanwhile, were busy bombing the Japanese airfields there—Clark, Negros, and Cebu—causing extensive damage.

Onishi could not actually order his pilots to fly the special suicide attacks—they had to volunteer, and with no expectation of survival, they did so almost unanimously. On 20 October 1944 he addressed twenty-six fighter pilot volunteers who were to comprise the *Shimpu* (God and wind) force. "My sons, who can raise our country from the desperate situation in which she finds herself? Japan is in grave danger. The salvation of our country is now beyond the power of the Ministers of State, the General Staff, and lowly commanders like myself. It can come only from spirited young men such as you. Thus on behalf of your hundred million countrymen, I ask you this sacrifice, and pray for your success. You are already gods, without earthly desires. But one thing you want to know is that your own crash-dive is not in vain. Regrettably, we will not be able to tell you the results. But I shall watch your efforts to the end and report your deeds to the Throne. You may all rest assured on this point. I ask you to do your best."

Soon after Onishi's address, 201st Air Group Chusa Tadashi Nakajima was sent to Cebu in the central Philippines to organize a new kamikaze unit, and told the pilots on his arrival: "I have come here to organize another Special Attack Unit. Others will want to follow in the footsteps of the first pilots charged with this mission. Any non-commissioned officer or

enlisted flyer who wishes to volunteer will so signify by writing his name and rate on a piece of paper. Each piece of paper is to be placed in an envelope which will be delivered to me by 2100 hours today. It is not expected, however, that everyone should volunteer. We know that you are all willing to die in defence of your country. We also realize that some of you, because of your family situation, cannot be expected to offer your life in this way. You should understand also that the number of volunteers required is limited by the small number of planes available. Whether a man volunteers or not will be known only to me. I ask that each man, within the next three hours, come to a decision based entirely upon his own situation. Special attack operations will be ready to start tomorrow. Because secrecy in this operation is of utmost importance, there must be no discussion about it." All of the pilots volunteered.

The vice-admiral began launching his kamikaze missions against U.S. Navy ships on 21 October. That day his pilots failed to locate their targets and returned to their Philippine base, where they had to watch helplessly as many of their precious aircraft were destroyed in a U.S. bombing attack. The outcome was different, though certainly not all good, for Japanese forces the next day. Conventional bombing aircraft of Japan's Second Air Fleet struck at U.S. ships in a massive raid, sinking one carrier and three smaller ships. For the day though, Japan had to endure the loss of three battleships, six cruisers, seven destroyers, and more than a hundred aircraft. And by this time, most Imperial Japanese Navy pilots were dead and the role of the kamikaze had to be carried on by Army Air Force pilots, the *Tokko Tai*. On 25

October kamikaze pilots succeeded in sinking a U.S. carrier and damaging several others. In Japan, the Emperor sent his congratulations to the suicide unit on its latest achievement, but disquieting rumors were circulating that the kamikaze claims of destruction and damage of U.S. ships were wildly exaggerated and that perhaps fewer than ten percent of such claims were actually valid. A belief seemed to prevail that the pilots of the Divine Wind were reluctant to admit to any sacrifices that had been in vain.

Onishi launched a frenzy of kamikaze activity in November. On the 5th of the month a group of his aircraft was en route to strike at a U.S. landing force at Leyte when it encountered a stream of U.S. bombers. All of the Japanese pilots rammed their American adversaries. Then, in an attempt to stave off the U.S. invasion of Luzon, Onishi diverted his pilots from primary attacks on U.S. carriers to hitting transport ships. He also began employing heavy bombers loaded with explosives in his suicide units. His most important achievement of the period came in the third week of November, when his forces flew against the U.S. carriers again, seriously damaging four and causing them to be withdrawn for repairs. The U.S. naval command was then compelled to add many new destroyers as pickets around the carriers, and to double the number of fighters in the carrier air wings for greatly increased combat air patrols. Sailors given shore leave were ordered not to discuss the kamikaze attacks. U.S. saturation bombing of Japanese airfields on Luzon was intensified, leading to the grounding of all locally-operating Japanese aircraft for several days. At this point the weather became a crucial factor, as a typhoon struck the Philippines on 15

A kamikaze suicide attack of 25 October 1944, in which the U.S. Navy escort carrier *St Lo* was lost when torpedoes stored on the hangar deck exploded, blowing the stern off the ship.

December, damaging many ships from the U.S. fleet. Three destroyers were lost and much of the fleet was forced to withdraw for repairs.

The fortunes of Onishi's kamikaze units continued to dwindle too. He now had fewer planes than pilots and decided that, when the enemy forces landed on Luzon, he would order all pilots without planes to fight on as infantry.

On 9 January, "Mike One," the U.S. invasion of Luzon, began. The Americans met stiff resistance, including a lot of attention from suicide motor boats as well as the kamikazes. For the crews of the U.S. ships, the only option was to bring maximum concentrated gunfire on the incoming suicide planes. By 13 January the kamikaze campaign had cost the lives of 1,208 Japanese pilots. Vice Admiral Onishi was shifted to Formosa where he quickly organized new kamikaze units. These units were soon to engage a U.S. fleet which had gathered off Formosa as a part of the American effort to take the island of Iwo Jima where it needed to establish a base for Mustang fighters to put them within a range to escort B-29s on their Japan raids.

Japan's urgent goal now was to destroy the U.S. fleet in order to force some sort of honorable peace settlement, and the kamikaze were key to this objective. In retaliation for the huge B-29 strike on Tokyo of 9 March, which took nearly 100,000 lives and made more than one million people homeless, the Japanese launched Operation Tan, a bomber and kamikaze strike on U.S. Navy ships anchored in the harbor at Ulithi. It too failed.

At this point the Japanese position was truly desperate. After the fall of Iwo Jima, most in the Japanese military believed that they had but two choices left—surrender or fight to the death utilizing the suicide weapon to the fullest extent. Their anger and frustration at the relentless B-29 fire raids over their homeland reinforced their determination to win the war that they had clearly already lost. They refocused on the kamikaze concept with a grim new dedication. But they were rapidly running out of time, aircraft, and fuel, and the forced restrictions on pilot training had resulted in a relatively small corps of airmen who were barely able to fly at all. On 17 March, with the U.S. fleet only 100 miles south of the Japanese mainland, Admiral Yugaki ordered his diminished force of kamikaze and conventional bombers up to strike at the enemy with the greatest intensity. In the attack fifty-two of his aircraft were lost. The U.S. carrier *Franklin* was badly hit and the Americans suffered more than 1,000 casualties. Yugaki, however, saw the attack as yet another failure and levelled blame on inferior training practices.

In a display of unusual enmity within the ranks, some kamikaze airmen began referring to their conventional bomber colleagues as "lechers" who seemed to prefer earthly delights over those of the spiritual resting place of their dead heroes. The bomber types, in turn, called the kamikaze madmen.

On 21 March another new development in the Tokko Tai program appeared. Ships of the U.S. fleet were about to be attacked by Japanese bombers carrying manned flying bombs called *Ohka*s (suicide attack aircraft). Before they could release the ohkas, the bombers were spotted by U.S. Navy combat air patrol aircraft and all of the Japanese planes were shot down.

The island of Okinawa was of major importance to the Americans, as it would provide them with the closest base yet from which to strike with B-29s at the Japanese home islands.

As the U.S. fleet, minus some of its carriers that had been significantly damaged in the recent kamikaze attacks and had been withdrawn for major repair work, made its way toward Okinawa, the last major Japanese-held island, an odd thing happened. Japanese reconnaissance reports led them to conclude that the absence of a number of U.S. carriers from the current enemy fleet composition meant that the carriers had been sunk and the fleet was no longer on the offensive. They soon found, however, that this was not the case. The American invasion of Okinawa was moving ahead at full steam. On the morning of 1 April U.S. landing forces arrived on the Okinawan beaches. The Japanese defenders were well established in caves on the island and lay in wait for the enemy troops who were met with little initial resistance during the landings. In the afternoon, though, kamikaze attacks began and by 6 April the Japanese had launched what they called "the holy war" against the American enemy.

In 1956, Jean Larteguy's edited version of the George Blond description of a typical kamikaze attack in *Le Survivant du Pacifique* appeared in Larteguy's *The Sun Goes Down*: "On 14 May, at 6:50 am, the radar plotter reported an isolated 'blip,' bearing 200° at 8,000 feet, range about twenty miles. The rear guns were pointed in that direction, ready to fire as soon as the 'phantom' should appear. At 6:54 it came into sight, flying straight for the carrier. It disappeared for a moment in the clouds; then, after approximately three-and-a-half miles, it emerged again, losing altitude. It was a Zero. The 5-inch guns opened fire. The Japanese aircraft retreated into the clouds. The batteries continued to fire. The crew had been at action stations since four in the morning. All the air-

craft that were not in the air had been de-fuelled and parked below decks.

"The Japanese machine approached from the rear. It was still not to be seen, as it was hidden by the clouds. Guided by radar, the 5-inch guns continued to fire at it, and soon the 40mm guns began to fire as well. It was very strange to see all these guns firing relentlessly at an invisible enemy.

"The Japanese aircraft emerged from the clouds and began to dive. His angle of incidence was not more than 30°, his speed approximately 250 knots. There could be no doubt—it was a suicide plane. It was approaching quite slowly and deliberately, and manoeuvring just enough not to be hit too soon.

"The pilot knew his job thoroughly and all those who watched him make his approach felt their mouths go dry. In less than a minute he would have attained his goal; there could be little doubt that this was to crash his machine on the deck [of the carrier *Enterprise*].

"All the batteries were firing: the 5-inch guns, the 40mm and the 20mm, even the rifles. The Japanese aircraft dived through a rain of steel. It had been hit in several places and seemed to be trailing a banner of flame and smoke, but it came on, clearly visible, hardly moving, the line of its wings as straight as a sword.

"The deck was deserted; every man, with the exception of the gunners, was lying flat on his face. Flaming and roaring, the fireball passed in front of the 'island' and crashed with a terrible impact just behind the for'ard lift.

"The entire vessel was shaken, some forty yards of the flight deck folded up like a banana-skin: an enormous piece of the lift, at least a third of the platform, was thrown over 300 feet into the air. The explosion killed fourteen men. The

last earthly impression they took with them was the picture of the kamikaze trailing his banner of flame and increasing in size with lightning rapidity.

"The mortal remains of the pilot had not disappeared. They had been laid out in a corner of the deck, next to the blackened debris of the machine. The entire crew marched past the corpse of the volunteer of death. The men were less interested in his finely modelled features, his wide-open eyes which were now glazed over, than in the buttons on his tunic, which were to become wonderful souvenirs of the war for a few privileged officers of high rank. These buttons, now black, were stamped in relief with the insignia of the kamikaze corps: a cherry blossom with three petals."

The men of the U.S. Navy ships off Okinawa were surprised and amazed by the numbers and ferocity of kamikaze and escort aircraft subjecting them to this new and greatly intensified attack. These American sailors who were fighting to live were up against Japanese airmen determined to die . . . a shocking realization that was repeatedly brought home to them during the incessant attacks. In addition to the efforts of the kamikaze, Japanese warships, including *Yamato*, the world's largest battleship, sailed to Okinawa in an attempt to destroy the U.S. transport ships. They then intended to deliberately run the *Yamato* aground and use her as a coastal fortress. The Japanese plan was foiled, however, when U.S. Navy PBY Catalina flying boats sighted the Japanese warships, and U.S. carriers launched air strikes sinking the *Yamato*, the *Yahagi*, and four smaller ships.

By 19 June the fight for Okinawa had reached a critical state for the Japanese defenders, and their commander ordered all of his troops to "go out and die." When Okinawa had fallen to the Americans after eighty-two days of fighting, they had suffered 12,500 casualties; the Japanese more than 100,000. A total of thirty U.S. ships had been sunk. In Japan the people were being told that every citizen was now considered a *Toko Gunjin*, or special attack soldier, for the defense of the homeland.

In the Marianas, the B-29s of General Curtis LeMay's 20th Air Force were continuing their campaign of fire raids against Tokyo and the sixty or so principal cities of Japan. It had begun in January when LeMay took command of the 20th and reorganized it for the task of efficiently bombing the Japanese into submission and, hopefully, bringing the Pacific War to an end.

The American raids were still going on in early August when U.S. President Harry S. Truman ordered the use of the first atomic bomb on a target city in Japan. This first use of a nuclear weapon in war took place on 6 August when a B-29 called *Enola Gay* (named after the mother of the pilot and airplane commander, Colonel Paul W. Tibbets, Jr.) released the bomb called Little Boy over the city of Hiroshima. Little Boy, together with the bomb called Fat Man which was dropped on Nagasaki three days later, led to Japan's capitulation, but not before Russia declared war on Japan on 8 August and launched its own offensive in Manchuria, completely overwhelming the Japanese there.

In what would be the final mission of the kamikaze airmen, Vice Admiral Matome Ugaki launched what remained of his force against the U.S. carriers on 15 August. On the way to the target he sent this radio message to his headquarters: "I

alone am to blame for our failure to defend the homeland and destroy the arrogant enemy. The valiant efforts of all officers and men of my command during the past six months have been greatly appreciated. I am going to make an attack at Okinawa where my men have fallen like cherry blossoms. There I will crash into and destroy the conceited enemy in the true spirit of Bushido, with firm conviction and faith in the eternity of Imperial Japan. I trust that the members of all units under my command will understand my motives and will overcome all hardships of the future and strive for the reconstruction of our great homeland that it may survive forever. *Tenno hai Ka, Banzai!*" That evening Vice Admiral Onishi took his own life.

The psychology behind the kamikaze attacks was too alien to us. Americans who fight to live, find it hard to realize that another people will fight to die.
—Admiral William F. Halsey, Commander, U.S. Third Fleet, after the attack on the USS *Intrepid*, 25 October 1944.

On Kudan Hill in the heart of Tokyo, near the Imperial Palace, stands the *Yasukuni-jinja*, or Shrine for Establishing Peace in the Empire. It is dedicated to Japan's war dead and is a controversial memorial because it contains personal effects of executed war criminals, including Hideki Tojo. According to Raymond Lamont-Brown: "Even today, any government minister who makes an official visit to the shrine would be technically liable to be stripped of his office." Displays in the Yasukuni include relics of the kamikaze pilots of the Great East Asian War, as the Japanese refer to World War II. Japanese war veterans groups, as well as representatives of the Bereaved Families Association, regularly visit the shrine

and petition the public to sign for the Yasukuni to be reinstated as the official Japanese war memorial. Lamont-Brown: "As time passes, according to some sections of the Japanese press, the spirits of the dead kamikaze 'cry out' for honourable, official recognition through the members of the 'Thunder Gods Association' who meet annually at the Yasukuni-jinja on 21 March (the day on which the first Ohka suicide attack was made)."

In the last days before their final attacks, the kamikaze pilots were mostly calmed by the Bushido philosophy. They were able to relax in a seeming detachment, spending their waiting time listening to gramophone records, playing cards, reading, writing their last letters home. They gave their belongings to comrades and friends, and they all carried three sen in copper coins, their fare to cross their religious equivalent of the River Styx.

If destruction be our lot we must ourselves be its author and finisher. As a nation of free men we must live through all time, or die by suicide.
—Abraham Lincoln, from a speech on 27 January 1838, Springfield, Illinois.

The question is whether suicide is the way out, or the way in.
—from *Journals*, Ralph Waldo Emerson

We cannot tear out a single page from our life, but we can throw the whole book into the fire.
—from *Mauprat*, George Sand

Everyone talks about fighting to the last man, but only the Japanese actually do it.
—Field Marshal William Slim, Commander, Southeast India in World War II.

Date	Type of Machine	Number of Machine	Duration of Flight	Character of Flight	Pilot	PASSEN
1	F6F-5	72901	3.4	STRIKE	Self. Okinawa	
2	..	71742	3.3	T-CAP	Okinawa	
2	..	72901	4.1	CAP		
3	..	58072	3.7	SWEEP	Iriomote Shima	
5	..	71781	4.5	STRIKE	Kikai Shima	
6	..	70546	4.1	T-CAP	Okinawa	
6	..	71603	4.0	CAP		
7	..	77683	4.3	STRIKE	Okinawa	
9	..	72846	3.5	CAP		
10	..	77680	4.1	SWEEP	Kikai - Ammamio Shima	
12	..	72279	4.0	T-CAP	Kikai	
13	..	70082	3.3	CAP		
14	..	70546	3.3	CAP		
14	..	72257	4.0	CAP		
15	..	70546	5.0	CAP		
16	..	71517	4.6	T-CAP	Okinawa	
16	..	71950	3.5	T-CAP	Kikai	
18	..	72545	3.6	T-CAP	Kikai	
18	..	71979	3.3	CAP		
20	..	77675	3.3	STRIKE	Kikai	

Total time to date, 76.9

REMARKS

S		REMARKS
02	a	
03	a	Squadron shot down
04	a	total of 46 Jap planes
05	a	on 6 april.
106	a	
107	a	
108	a	※ TOJO
109	a	LOST G.W. McADOO - later found in POW camp.
110	a	On 7 april all available planes attacked Jap task force and sunk the BB YAMATO
111	a	
112	a	※ Kate ※ George
113	a	Squadron shot down 33
114	a	Jap planes on 13 april.
115	a	19 Japs splashed on 13 april.
116	a	Japs dropped flares over
117	a	Task force about 0400
118	a	in the morning.
119	a	
120	a	
121	a	

Ensign Tommy Harris of VF-17, flying an F6F-5 Hellcat in March 1945, shot down four Japanese fighters in two days, ending the war credited with nine aerial victories. At left, a page from his flying logbook.

Ens. Tommy Ha

Helicopter operations on HMS *Illustrious* in the 1990s.

At NAS Miramar in southern California, an aviator suits up for a hop in an F-14 Tomcat in 2000.

THE AVERAGE AGE OF THOSE RESPONSIBLE for carrying out the many vital tasks which keep things running smoothly on the flight deck of a United States supercarrier—is nineteen.

The men and women who do the jobs that make flight operations possible on a U.S. Navy carrier are easily identifiable by the colors of the jerseys they wear. BLUE jerseys are worn by airplane handlers, tractor drivers, aircraft elevator operators, and messengers / phone talkers. Air Wing plane captains and Air Wing line leading petty officers wear BROWN. Those wearing GREEN are the catapult and arresting gear crews, Air Wing quality assurance personnel, cargo handling personnel, ground support equipment trouble-shooters, hook runners, photographers, and helicopter landing signal enlisted personnel. Aviation fuel personnel wear PURPLE. Ordnance men wear RED, as do crash and salvage crews, and explosive ordnance disposal personnel. WHITE jerseys are worn by squadron plane inspectors, landing signal officers, air transfer officers, liquid oxygen crews, safety observers, and medical personnel. YELLOW jerseys signify aircraft handling officers, catapult and arresting gear officers, and plane directors.

On the aircraft carriers of the Royal Navy, none of which are currently operational, flight deck personnel wear a colored vest called a surcoat, which, as with the American jerseys, identifies personnel by function. YELLOW means flight deck officer, Chief of the Flight Deck, and aircraft directors. BLUE surcoats are for naval airmen / flight deck, and photographers. Aircraft and engine full supervisory ratings wear BROWN. Air electrical full supervisory ratings wear GREEN. GREEN WITH A BLUE STRIPE indicates air radio full supervi-

sory ratings. Crash and salvage parties wear RED. RED WITH A BLACK STRIPE is worn by weapon supply / all ratings. Flight deck assault guides wear RED WITH A WHITE STRIPE. Medical attendants wear WHITE WITH A RED CROSS. Deck supervisors, duty aircrew, watch chiefs, and Air Engineering officers wear WHITE. WHITE WITH A BLACK STRIPE is worn by flight deck engineers. Aircraft engine mechanics wear GREY.

When a U.S. aircraft carrier is to conduct flight operations, preparations normally begin the day before. An Air Plan outlining the scheduled activity is prepared and distributed the night before and includes all the required information for those concerned, including launch and recovery times, and information on the mission itself: the number of sorties to be flown, fuel and ordnance load requirements, and the tactical communication frequencies to be used. Flight quarters are announced and manned. No crew members who are not directly involved in the flight operations are allowed to be on the flight deck or in the deck edge catwalks.

The pilots and aircrew are briefed on the specifics of the mission and on the sequence of events. They will go to their aircraft thirty to forty-five minutes before they are scheduled to launch, and will do a thorough preflight inspection of the aircraft prior to the order to start engines.

Meanwhile, the various flight deck personnel are preparing their equipment and personal gear for the upcoming ops. Before any aircraft engines are started, a ritual FOD (foreign object damage) walk-down is conducted, in which all off-duty personnel, mainly flight deck and Air Wing, are requested to participate. Often the walk-down is sponsored

by one of the Air Wing squadrons, with music provided for motivation. With the range of aircraft minor maintenance and repair activity occurring on the flight deck, it is inevitable that items such as small tools, rivets, and bits of safety wire hit the deck and are not noticed at the time. When aircraft engines are running, these objects can be blown about and cause significant injury to people and engines. When flight deck ops are not underway, ship's personnel are frequently allowed to exercise there, usually by running laps around the deck. They, too, can be a source for foreign objects finding their way to the flight deck. The potentially deadly objects are often hidden in the recessed "pad-eye" tie-down points spotted all over the flight deck. Personnel manning air hoses precede the main walk-down force to blow any collected debris or water from these pad-eyes. The deck-wide line of FOD walkers proceeds slowly down the whole length of the flight deck, picking up all objects that may pose even the slightest threat to man and machine. They are followed by scrubber vacuums which suck up anything that may have been overlooked by the walkers. FOD is a deadly menace to both men and machines and the walk-down procedure is taken seriously. Only after it has been completed is the order to start engines given.

The first craft to start up and launch are the plane guard helicopters who leave the deck to orbit in a D-shaped flight path, designed to let them quickly rescue an airman or crewman should that be necessary.

Just prior to the launch of the mission aircraft, the supercarrier is turned to a heading that will allow for sufficient wind, usually about thirty knots over the flight deck, to assist the planes in getting airborne. The

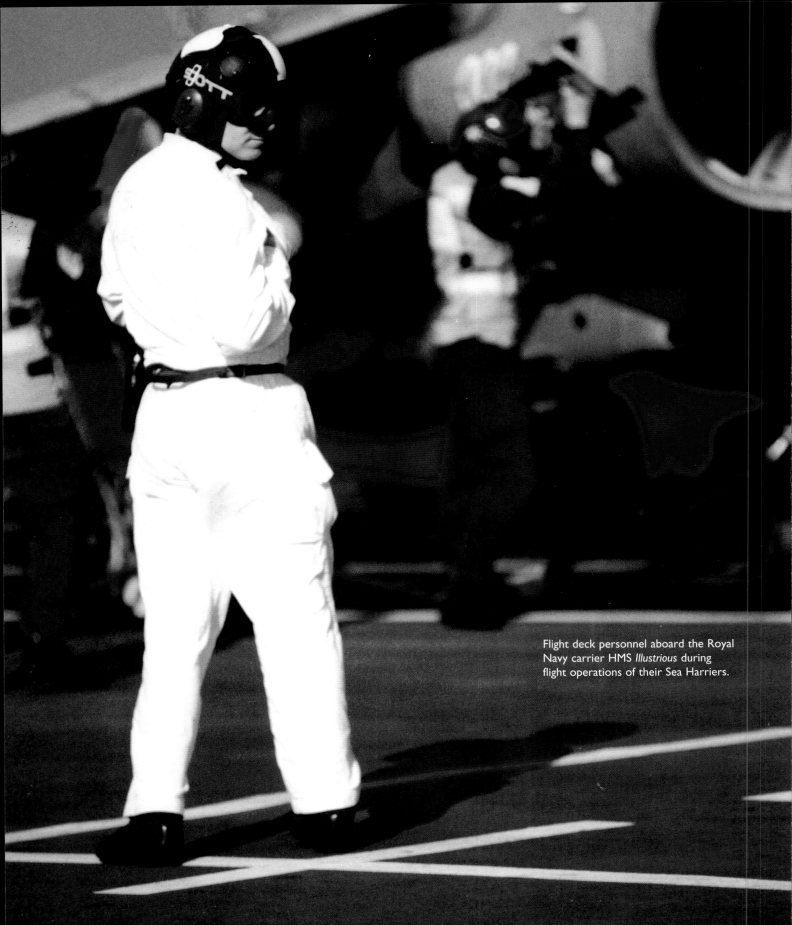

Flight deck personnel aboard the Royal Navy carrier HMS *Illustrious* during flight operations of their Sea Harriers.

yellow-shirted plane directors begin to guide the first aircraft to be launched to precise spots on the two forward steam catapults. When spotted there, large blast deflectors rise from the deck just behind the planes, to protect deck personnel aft of the catapults. Hook-up green shirts crouch at the nose wheel of each of the aircraft on cats one and two and attach the nose gear to the catapult shuttle with nose-tow and hold-back bars. A green shirt moves in to the right of one plane's canopy and holds up a black box with illuminated numerals which flash the predicted weight of the aircraft. The pilot must concur that the figure is correct. That done, the cat launch personnel calibrate the power of the cat to the requirement of the plane about to launch. Low clouds of steam billow down the length of the cats as a yellow shirt signals the pilot, who releases the brakes and applies full power. The cat officer signals with a rotating hand, two fingers extended, as the pilot does a quick final check that the aircraft and controls are functioning correctly. The pilot then salutes to indicate that he is ready to launch, and braces himself. If he is flying an F/A-18 Hornet, procedure requires him to place his right (stick) hand on the canopy frame grab handle and keep it there for the duration of the cat shot, in order not to disturb the computer-set trim during the shot.

At this point the catapult officer checks the final readiness of the cat and receives confirmation from other deck personnel that the aircraft is ready for flight. He then signals the shooter in the enclosed launch station bubble (by touching the deck), to press the cat firing button.

Launch . . . and the four-g force of the steam cat hurls the airplane from the flight deck. The plane achieves 150 knots air speed from a standing

start in two seconds, sending the flesh and facial muscles of the pilot racing toward the back of his skull.

The first two aircraft of the mission have departed and the catapult crews rush to position and attach the next planes in the queue for launch. These crews can ready and launch an aircraft every thirty seconds if necessary, and are frequently required to set up and launch more than 100 times in a day. For the flight deck operation to go smoothly, an endless regime of planning, discipline, expert engineering, skilled maintenance, training, motivation, and extraordinary attention to detail is employed. And safety is the prime concern of all.

Chris Hurst was a Leading Aircraftsman / Aircraft Handler with the Air Department aboard HMS *Illustrious*, and he describes a Sea Harrier launch sequence: "Ten minutes prior to launch, we will get a verbal communication from the flight control position to start the aircraft. Permission will then be given to the aircraft mechanics to liaise with the pilots to start the engines and go through their various acceleration checks, making sure the wing flaps, etc. are at the right angles for launch, depending on the aircraft weights and weapon loads. The mechanics will also take off the outrigger ground locks and the lashings that are not required. Then they will be ready on deck.

"The aircraft directors will face toward the flying control position, watching for an amber light which means that the ship is on a designated flying course and we have permission to taxi the aircraft onto the runway. The pilot will be told to 'unbrakes'. The two remaining nose lashings and the chocks will be removed. Then a Leading Aircraftsman will guide the aircraft out of the range and pass it on

to the Petty Officer of the Deck who is standing on the runway at the designated launch distance. He will then marshal it onto that launch distance, stop it in the brakes and pass the control of the aircraft to either the Captain of the flight deck, or the Flight Deck Officer, whichever is on watch at the time.

"The duty squadron Air Engineering Officer will then look round the aircraft and make sure that everything is safe, all the relevant pins have been removed, etc. When he is satisfied, he will give a thumbs-up to the Flight Deck Officer, who will wait for a steady green light from Flyco, which means he has the Captain's permission to launch fixed-wing aircraft.

"Then, when he has checked up and down the runway that all is clear, he will raise a small green flag. The pilot will turn on a white nose wheel light and roar away up the deck and off the ski ramp. As the aircraft is launched, the next aircraft will be drawn out of the range and marshalled on in sequence until all the aircraft have gone. All the time this is going on, there is a spare aircraft handling team ready in the 'graveyard' at the front end of the deck, should anything go wrong. We call it the graveyard because it is for "dead" aircraft. They have a tractor ready to attach to the aircraft. Certain minor unserviceabilities could mean an aircraft not launching, but having to taxi all the way up to the graveyard to get it out of the way, to clear the deck and make everything ready for the next aircraft to launch. There is nothing worse than an aircraft having a minor radio problem, sitting there with all its intake blanks missing. It would be dangerous. Foreign object damage could occur with an aircraft zooming up the deck, so we prefer to get him straight to the graveyard and out of the way."

"The *Enterprise* flight deck was 109 feet abeam, including the island, and approximately 800 feet long. Usually less than half of that length was availible for Scouting Six, because the TBDs of Torpedo Six and SBDs of Bombing Six were always in the pack behind us.

"We frequently watched a bomb-laden SBD drop out of sight as it took off and passed the bow of the ship. It then reappeared, picking up speed, getting a boost from the 65-foot deck height and the 'ground effect' between wings and water.

"One day I was up on deck watching as a young pilot really almost touched the waves ahead of the ship. He later confided that he had taken off with his controls fully locked. Somehow he managed to remove the unlocking pin under the control stick, barely avoiding a crash into the sea. He must have been a contortionist."
—Jack 'Dusty' Kleiss, former U.S. Navy pilot

Airline pilot David Smith is a veteran of more than 1,000 hours flying the Grumman F-14 Tomcat, between 1982 and 1991. In that time, he made 342 carrier landings in the course of two Mediterranean cruises aboard the USS *John F. Kennedy* (CVA-67). He was then assigned as an instructor, training fleet F-14 and F/A-18 pilots in adversary flight tactics at Key West, Florida. All of the F/A-18 Hornet squadrons that took part in the Gulf War Operation Desert Storm attended the Key West course. "We F-14 pilots flew whenever the ship had air operations. In a normal schedule we flew during the day and every other night. Some of us flew every night to make up for some of the weak night pilots and the senior squadron officers who just didn't want to fly at night. Flying at night was not fun. Flying in

A BAE Sea Harrier undergoing servicing in the hangar deck of HMS *Illustrious* in 1999; right: FA-2 Sea Harrier pilot Pete Wilson of No 801 Squadron, Royal Navy, in the cockpit of his aircraft aboard *Illustrious* in 2000.

the day was, and everyone wanted to do that.

"Most flight ops lasted either one hour and thirty minutes, or one hour and forty-five minutes. In peacetime, the briefs started between one-and-a-half and two hours before lunch. The topics included such admin items as weather, aircraft, crews, join-up (rendezvous), lost communications, gas (in-flight refuelling amounts, altitudes, and locations), and the mission briefing itself, which took longer and varied from ship support, to air-to-air basic fighter maneuvering, to air intercept, to strafing, to section or division tac- tics. If operating near land, we might be supporting an overland operation or working with another country. The brief was where you transitioned from just being aboard the ship, to be reminded of why you were there. The actual brief was almost a formal- ity because you had heard it all many times before, but it always served to make me focus on what I was about to do.

"If the brief ran long, you would walk immediately to maintenance control to check out the logbook on your airplane. You then signed for the airplane and went to the paraloft where flight equipment was stored. On the *Kennedy* it was a small room, no bigger than an average bedroom. With all of the hanging equipment, it could barely accommodate four per- sons. This was where you became an aviator. You went about the task of suiting up and preparing to go topside to do something that no one else on the planet was going to do at that moment.

"On the flight deck it was usual- ly very quiet and rather peaceful at the beginning of a new ops cycle. Normally, it was a very dangerous place to be.

"The first task was to find your plane. There was never a clue as to where it would be spotted. You walked around the flight deck until you found the aircraft number you were looking for. People have been known to man the wrong airplane. Finding your airplane at night can be difficult and frustrating. When you found it, the plane captain, who might be just eighteen years old, would exchange a few words with you about the only thing you really had in common—that airplane. I knew all my plane captains and all the maintenance personnel very well.

"Pre-flighting an F-14 on board a carrier can be the most dangerous part of the mission. Some of them were parked with their tails hanging out over the edge of the ship. There could be twenty to thirty knots of wind over the deck, and trying to do a thorough pre-flight might put you in the safety nets, if not actually overboard. Walking around the plane you encountered chains that were trying to trip you, missile fins aiming to leave an impression on you, and many other little gotchas out to ruin your day.

"Climbing in and sitting in the seat of the Tomcat was a relief, a place of comfort. You knew your way around the cockpit with your eyes closed, and you felt safe. Because the F-14 burns gas fast, we always launched right after the E-2 Hawkeye (our eyes and ears) and the A-6 Intruder / tanker (our gas). A couple of F-14s would be spotted either on the catapults or just behind them. When the order was given, engines were started and we went through the various after-start checks.

"We had afterburners, but did not always need them for the cat shot. On deployment, when you are going to launch missiles and have a full load of fuel, you would always be using afterburners in the launch.

"You followed the plane director's instructions and he would steer you into alignment just behind the catapult. He would then point to another plane director who was straddling the cat track at a point about thirty feet ahead of your plane. He would slowly lead you forward until you were just behind the cat shuttle. Another director would guide you very precisely onto the shuttle and you would then be turned over to the CAT officer. When satisfied that your hook-up was correct, he would have the tension taken on your plane. Under tension, you would be required to go to full power. You did not come out of full power under any circumstances unless the CAT officer stepped in front of your plane and gave you the 'throttle back' signal. This was a trust that had been violated in the past, costing lives. Once under tension and in full power, you were going flying.

"During the day you can see all of the actors on the stage. At night you see nothing but the yellow wands. Two totally different worlds. The difference is almost indescribable.

"The plane is under tension and at full power and, when the CAT officer is content that all of the check-list items have been checked, he will give the signal to launch by touching the deck. Now the fun begins.

"Our initial indication of the launch is when the launch bar releases. F-14 pilots have long been accused of trying to be 'cool' by holding the head forward during a launch, instead of keeping it back against the headrest as most aviators do. Actually, when that launch bar releases, the airplane abruptly squats; it's almost like hitting a pothole in the road. Your head is forced down and forward for a split second. This is quickly followed by an immediate and, hopefully, incredible acceleration forward. The neo-

phyte who puts his or her head back against the headrest at the start of this sequence, will have it jolted forward, and then back, with amazing sharpness that will literally make him or her see stars.

"The intensity of the acceleration can vary, depending on the initial gross weight of the plane and the natural wind over the deck. You need a given end / air speed to go flying, and the heavier your plane is, the greater that air speed has to be. Less wind over the deck requires a harder, more powerful cat shot. At a maximum gross weight of 72,000 pounds, an F-14A, with little or no wind over the deck, requires a cat shot that will take the breath out of you. The acceleration is so rapid, it hurts. Such cat shots are not only hard on the pilot and RIO (Radar Intercept Officer in the back seat); they are hard on the plane as well. Generators, inertial navigation system alignments, radars . . . all are in jeopardy in such launches. Stories of instruments coming out and striking air crew in the face and chest are not uncommon.

"On an extremely windy day, when the ship is barely moving, you may become concerned that your launch will not be hard enough to send you flying. That concern is directed toward the CAT officer, who may be about to shoot you into water breaking over the deck. He will try to time the launch with the ship's pitches, but a cat shot into a severe down cycle will give you a windscreen full of ocean that you won't soon forget. Still, when things work, and they almost always do, the cat shot is the most enjoyable part of the cycle. Getting back on board is something else."

"Cat shots never bothered me. You are as much passenger as pilot. Even if you shut down the engines and set the park-

Catapult and arresting gear crewmen on the carriers of the U.S. Navy wear green jerseys.

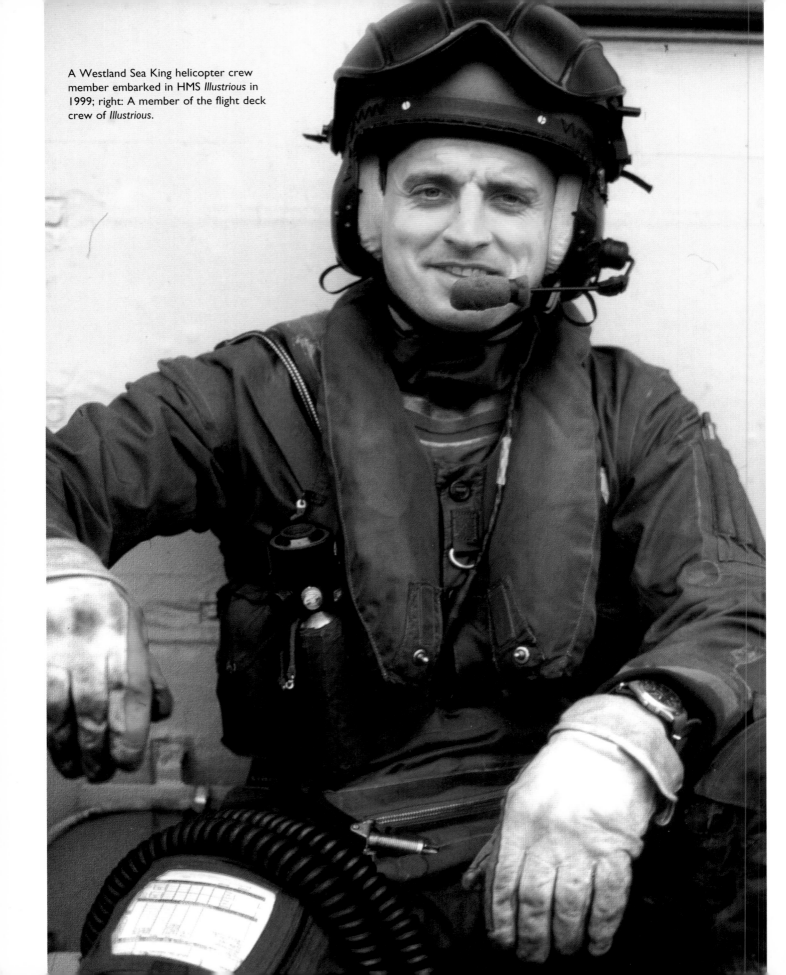

A Westland Sea King helicopter crew member embarked in HMS *Illustrious* in 1999; right: A member of the flight deck crew of *Illustrious*.

ing brake, you were going off the cat. Just five knots slower. The first one is the first one. It was memorable and very exhilarating. My subsequent shots were in unison with hooting and hollering, maybe another reason why instructors don't ride along. Once you've finished your required number of traps (arrested landings on a carrier deck), you sit on the deck, refuelling and anxiously waiting for the radio call from the LSO and the magic words: 'You're a qual.' Back on land, we were all very excited and animated. I had been in the Navy for only a year, and flying for only eight months. That night I slept like a baby. The next step was advanced jet training."
—Frank Furbish, former U.S. Navy fighter pilot

"One day when I was flying wing out over the ocean west of NAS Miramar near San Diego, my engine began making grinding sounds. I asked my section leader to take us home. When we arrived, I wrote up the bad engine. The crew chief refused to believe my write-up because I was the new kid, the most junior officer. I tried to convince him about what I had experienced, and left the ops shack to return to the squadron area. Soon after I got there, the chief phoned me to chew me out, saying I was wrong, that it had only been carburetor icing. Obviously, he didn't want to go to work checking the oil filter on the opinion of a snot-nosed ensign. I was just a kid and he an old chief. My mistake was in not contesting his judgement or challenging his lack of respect. He released the plane for ops without checking the oil filter. The next day a squadron buddy of mine flew that same Skyraider and suffered engine failure on take-off, but managed to get it back on the runway. The filter had metal particles in it. The chief did not apologize for his stupidity."

—Paul Ludwig, former U.S. Navy attack pilot

"One afternoon while Ensign Willie P. West and I were walking and talking to each other on the flight deck, neither of us heard the centerline elevator warning signal—if it was sounded. Suddenly, Willie took a step into space, and I was right on the edge of the gaping hole. I expected to find him in a crumpled heap at the end of a thirty-foot drop. Instead, he walked away unhurt. He said that the elevator was moving downward almost as fast as he was falling, and that jumping on it was like landing on a feather bed."
—Jack Kleiss, former U.S. Navy fighter pilot.

"We had just left Majuro anchorage on our way to Hollandia. We were getting close to Hollandia, in an area where strict security required a darkened ship. AOM2/c Petty had left Fighter Armory with AOM1/c F.S. Rice, heading toward the port bow. It was one of those nights when you literally could not see your hand in front of your face. Both men were cautious and felt somewhat safe because they thought the 'safety chain' was up across the bow. Neither realized that we had spotted two F4U night fighters at 'ready' on the catapults, with the pilots in them prepared for instant take-off. The safety chain was down.

"Petty was a step or two in front of Rice when suddenly Rice heard a muffled grunt. It didn't take him long to realize that Petty had walked off the bow. Rice immediately ran aft to the LSO (Landing Signal Officer) platform where he grabbed some float lights and, without thinking of the consequences, threw some of them overboard. What a sight to suddenly see lights behind the ship in that total darkness. Alert men on watch were quick to report. GQ (general quarters) was sounded and this particular GQ caught everyone at a time when 'tense' didn't begin to describe how jumpy we were.

"The Officer of the Deck sounded 'Man Overboard' and every division met for immediate muster and roll call. Destroyers guarding the rear of the task force were given the OK to search for Petty. They directed their efforts to the float lights, but there was only one thing wrong with that. The length of flight deck that Rice had to travel to get to the LSO platform would take a fast runner forty to sixty seconds and the ship was moving at a fair rate of speed. In the time he took to run that distance, the closest light to Petty was judged to be a half mile

away. Seas were also running choppy at four feet. The odds of finding Petty were in the needle-in-a-haystack category. We were thinking we would never see him again.

"However, there are survivors, some of which are extremely lucky and some personally self-sufficient. Petty was both. The whale boats which the destroyers sent to look for him did an ever-expanding circle search out from the float lights. They had just decided to halt the search when they heard Petty whistle. He could not see them, but he heard their voices, so he managed to whistle with his fingers to his teeth. That is what saved him. He also helped himself by tying knots in his dungarees and filling them full of air as a float.

"We were back at Pearl in January 1944. Petty had gone on liberty and come back with tattoos of a rooster on one foot and a pig on the other. Old seamen's lore has it that a sailor who does that will never drown. When we next returned to Pearl in July, we had sailors by the dozen getting tattooed with pigs and roosters on their insteps."
—M.S. Cochran, formerly assigned to the USS *Enterprise*

"I was wired to the port catapult of the *San Jacinto* when the boing, boing, boing went off, followed by 'This is no drill!' I saw a Japanese Jill aircraft coming across the front of our ship, starboard to port. He was low, about 100 feet, and every ship in the fleet was shooting at him. I started yelling at the catapult officer to launch my plane. It seemed to take forever. I charged my guns while waiting. The Japanese plane had bore-sighted another carrier to our port side. Finally, the cat fired. The Jill, with bomb or torpedo in plain view, was crossing my launch path. I squeezed the trigger. Nothing. The

gear was still down. The guns are not supposed to fire with the gear down. I hit the gear-up lever. The Jill was closing at full deflection. I was squeezing the trigger. At last all six .50s were firing just as the Jill crossed in front of me. It exploded as it flew into my line of fire. I had been in the air less than thirty seconds. My aircraft was hit several times by shrapnel, but I continued my combat air patrol and landed just under four hours later."
—James B. Cain, former U.S. Navy fighter pilot

"After reinstallation, every jet engine was thoroughly checked out, and the more 'Walter Mitty-like' mechanics, including me, eagerly looked forward to this task. One did feel slightly elated, clambering into the cockpit, starting the engine and testing it. While stationed at land bases we sometimes needed to taxi the aircraft short distances, and one couldn't help wondering how it would feel to actually take off."
—Bill Hannan, former U.S. Navy jet engine mechanic

right: A survivor of the Argentine attack on the Royal Navy destroyer HMS *Sheffield* being rushed from a rescuing helicopter to the sick bay of the aircraft carrier *Hermes* during the Falklands War in 1982.

KOREAN AIR WAR

U.S. Navy Chance Vought F4U Corsair fighters over the carrier USS *Boxer* during the Korean conflict in the early 1950s.

The main British front-line fighter in Korea was the Hawker Sea Fury, which was operated from Royal Navy carriers including HMS *Glory*.

FROM JUNE 1950 UNTIL JUNE 1953, a war called "a police action" raged on the Korean peninsula, during which attack missions flown by U.S. and British naval aviators took a huge toll on the military assets and infrastructure of their North Korean enemy. The pilots destroyed eighty-three enemy aircraft, 313 bridges, 12,789 military buildings, 262 junks and river craft, 220 locomotives, 1,421 rail cars, 163 tanks, and nearly 3,000 support vehicles. The Korean conflict was one of only two events in which United Nations forces had gone to war against an aggressor nation. It was only the absence of the Soviet Union from the UN Security Council (which it was boycotting when war broke out in Korea) that enabled the UN to approve military action there under its auspices, as the Russians would certainly have exercised their veto had they been present.

John Franklin Bolt flew U.S. Marine Corps F4U Corsairs in the Pacific during World War II. He came home with six Japanese Zeke fighters to his credit, and a few years later was to become the only Navy Department jet ace of the Korean war, having disposed of six MiG-15s in air action there.

Jack Bolt wanted a piece of the Korean action. "I chose an Air Force exchange tour of duty because at that point the only thing standing up to the MiGs were the F-86s. I knew that none were coming to the Marine Corps, and I was anxious to get back to the air-to-air fight. The only possibility of doing that was by getting in an F-86 squadron. The MiGs were beating the hell out of everything else, and the F-86s were our sole air superiority plane in Korea from early on. So I managed to get a year's tour with the Air Force, and toward the end of it I managed to get into an F-86 squadron of the Oregon Air National Guard.

"I would grind out the hours in that thing, standing air defense alerts. Those were the days when the threat of nuclear war with Russia hung heavily over our heads. We really thought we were going to get into it. It was late in 1951 or early 1952 and the squadron was part of the Northwest Air Defense Command. Our guys were on stand-by and would be down in the ready room in flight gear, not sitting in the planes the way they did later. They would be playing bridge and so forth, but I would be up flying, getting hours in that F-86. When my guard tour was over, I was able to get out to Korea in about May of '52 and flew ninety-four missions in F9F-4 Panthers, interdictions, air-to-ground, and close air support. We were down at K3, an airfield near Po Hang Do, with VMF-115.

"We were using napalm to attack rice-straw thatched-roof targets. They were all supposed to contain enemy troops, but I'm sure most of them were probably innocent civilians. We were attacking the villages with napalm. Then, of course, the proper military targets used thatching for waterproofing too, a supply depot for food or materiel, fuel or ammo. We used lots of napalm against all of those targets.

"My tour in Panthers came to an end and I took some R and R. I looked up an Air Force squadron commander named George Ruddell. I had met him at El Toro in 1947 when he flew an F-80 over to lecture our squadron about it and gave us a little demonstration of what that airplane could do. I found George at K13 where he was commanding the 39th Fighter-Interceptor Squadron. I told him about my 100 hours in the F-86F, the same type of Sabre his squadron was flying. I had the experience he needed, and he was friendly towards

The cockpit and instrument panel of a MiG-15, the primary Soviet fighter of the Korean War era.

me and let me take a few fam flights with some of his boys.

"On a second R and R trip around Christmas of '52, it happened that Joe McConnell, who was to become the top-scoring U.S. fighter ace of the Korean war with sixteen kills, had just been grounded from operations, and Ruddell very generously sent him over to teach me some tactics. I flew a few fam hops with McConnell and he was good. We became friends and he taught me a lot about his tactics in the F-86. He was very deserving of the fame that he had earned as the leading ace of that war. Tragically, he was killed soon after the war on a test flight at Edwards Air Force base in California.

"After that second R and R, I put in for another Air Force exchange tour. The Group Personnel Officer said, 'Bolt, I know you've been trying to worm your way into this, going up there on R and R. I'll tell you, you've had a year with the Air Force and you ain't goin' up there. You think you are. I'm telling you now, it ain't gonna happen.' They felt that I'd had more than my share of gravy assignments, so I got in touch with Ruddell and he got the general up there to send a wire down to the Marine Corps general. They only had two F-86 groups, the 4th and the 51st, and they had two Marines in each. One of them, a guy named Roy Reed, was leaving shortly. This was the opening I needed. The Air Force general's wire read: 'We're willing to have your pilots, but they come up here having never flown the plane, and they present a training burden on our people. But now we have a rare instance of having a pilot who's shown enough initiative to come up here and get checked out, and he's ready to go. Would you mind appointing John Bolt?'

"There was nothing else the Group could do. I was put in Ruddell's squadron and I was flying on McConnell's wing for my first half dozen flights. I was in Dog Flight. Ruddell was a very tough guy, but he was as nice as he could be. He had four or five kills, but the MiGs had stopped coming south of the Yalu River and we weren't allowed to go north of it. The Chinese were yelling about 'the pirates' that were coming over there, but that's where the action was.

"When McConnell left, I took over the command of Dog Flight, a quarter of the squadron with about twelve pilots. We lived together in one big Quonset hut.

"Ruddell wasn't getting any MiGs because they weren't coming south of the river. He'd been threatening everybody that he'd kill 'em, cut their heads off if they went north of the river after MiGs. But one night he weakened. He'd had a few drinks and he called me into this little cubbyhole where he had his quarters. During the discussion tears came into his eyes— running down his cheeks—as he was saying how he wanted to be a good Air Force officer, and he loved the Air Force, and if they told him to do something, he'd do it, and if they told him not to do something, he'd not do it. But getting those MiGs meant more to him than his career and life itself. And, since he had been beating up on his own flight about not going across the river, he'd be embarrassed to ask any of them to go across with him. He didn't know whether they would want to anyway—two or three members of Dog Flight didn't like to do it. (They would have been in big trouble if they'd been identified as going up there. I don't know if the ones they picked up later on, who were shot down north of the river, were ever disciplined when the war was over. But at the time, the threat

Practicing water survival exercises at NAS Pensacola.

was believed and hanging very heavily over us.) Ruddell said, 'Would you give me some of your flight? I want to go across the river. I've gotta have some action.' Ruddell's boys had been several days with no action. I said, 'Sure, I'd be delighted,' so we planned one for the next day.

"I was to fly his second section. On a river crossing flight, we would take off and go full bore. We'd fly those planes at 100 percent power setting until we got out of combat. Engine life was planned for 800 hours and we were getting about 550 or so. Turbine blade cracks were developing. We were running the engines at maximum temperature. You could put these little constrictors in the tailpipe—we called them 'rats'—and you could 'rat 'em up' until they ran at maximum temperature. They were real hot rods. You'd run your drop tanks dry just about the time you got up to the river, and if you didn't have a contact, you weren't supposed to drop your tanks. We skinned 'em every time anyway. On at least four occasions, by the end of the flight I had been to over 50,000 feet. When it was empty and I still hadn't pulled the power back from 100 percent, the airplane would really get up there. The MiG-15 could get right up there too.

"On the flight with Ruddell, we got up there and dropped our tanks. At least the pilots going across the river dropped them. There were big clouds up as we crossed the river. It was early morning and we heard on the radio that there was a fight going on. There were some MiGs flying this day. We came from the sunny side of the clouds to the back side of a big cumulous; there were some black puffs of flak and there were some planes down there. We were half blind from the diminished illumination on the back side of the cloud. It was a confusing

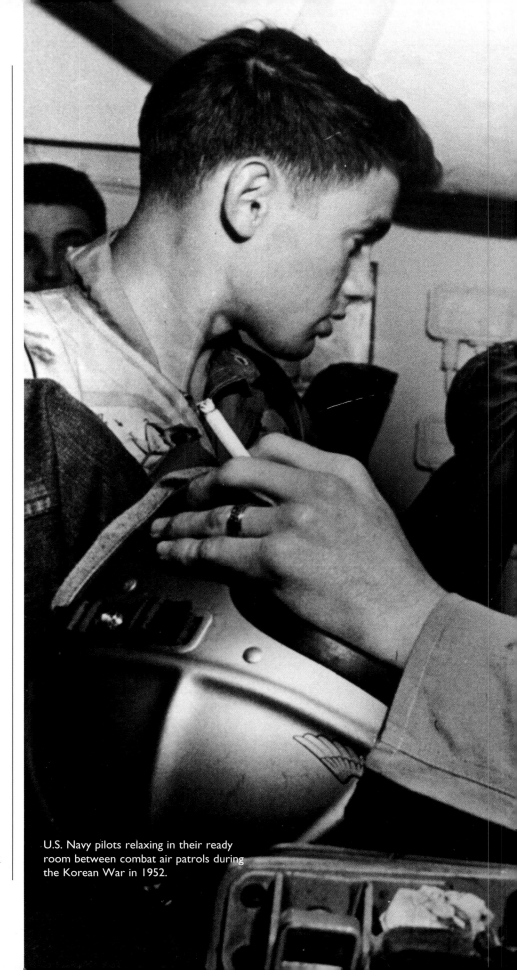

U.S. Navy pilots relaxing in their ready room between combat air patrols during the Korean War in 1952.

Bill Hannan served as a jet engine mechanic on board the USS *Kearsarge* off the coast of Korea in 1951. He is seen here atop a Grumman F9F Panther.

situation. We dove down and there was a MiG. Ruddell got it in sight and we dropped from 43,000 feet down to about 15,000, just dropped straight down. He got into shooting position behind the MiG but didn't shoot . . . didn't shoot . . . didn't shoot. I had experience at jumping planes and one of the things you did when you came down from extreme altitude (MiGs were frequently found down low when north of the river) was put your armor-glass defrost on full bore. It would get so hot it was almost painful, but it kept the front windscreen clear. You also tested your guns and your g-suit. Ruddell's windscreen had fogged over. He was sitting there in a kill position and couldn't see properly to shoot. So I went by him and got the MiG. Of course, the squadron was abuzz that the colonel had started crossing the river and gotten aced out of his first kill up there. I was a 'MiG killer.' I'd gotten three or four. When I got back, they had all these signs pasted up all over the Dog Flight Quonset hut. One read: MARINE WETBACK STEALS COLONEL'S MIG!

"The 'kill rules' were, if you got seven hits on an enemy aircraft, you would be given a kill. The MiGs didn't torch off at high altitude; they simply would not burn because of the air density. So, incendiary hits would be counted (we had good gun cameras) and if you got seven hits in the enemy's fuselage, the odds were it was dead, and they'd give you a kill. We knew that every third round was an incendiary so, in effect, if you got three incendiary hits showing on the gun camera, it was considered a dead MiG.

"My first kill was at about 43,000 feet. I had missed a couple of kills before it by not being aggressive or determined enough. I was almost desperate for a MiG kill. I was leader of my flight and I'd screwed up a couple

of bounces. My self-esteem and my esteem in the Flight were low, and I decided that the next MiG I saw was a dead man and I didn't care where he was.

"The next MiG was part of a gaggle; MiGs as far as you could see. I made a good run on one of them and pulled into firing position, but other MiGs were shooting at me and my wingman, and they were very close. I got some hits on my MiG and he went into a scissor, which was a good tactic. I think the F-86 may have had a better roll rate. I was trying to shoot as he passed through my firing angle. Each time I fired I delayed my turn, so he was gaining on me and drifting back. He almost got behind me and was so close that his plane blanked out the camera frame. I think he realized that I would have crashed into him rather than let him get behind me, and he rolled out and dove. Then I got several more hits on him and he pulled up (he was probably dead at this point). That scissor was the right thing to do; he just shouldn't have broken off. He was getting back to a position where he could have taken the advantage.

"The salvation of the F-86 was that it had good transonic controls; the MiG's controls were subsonic. In the Sabre, you could readily cruise at about .84 Mach. The MiG had to go into its uncontrollable range to attack you, and its stick forces were unmanageable. As I recall, the kill ratio between the F-86 and the MiG was eight to one. This was due almost entirely to the flying tail of the Sabre, although it had other superior features. The gun package of the MiG was intended for shooting down bombers like the B-29 and B-50. It carried a 37mm and two 23mm cannon, which was overkill against fighters. Although the F-86 used essentially the same machine-guns as a World

The Chance Vought F4U Corsair fought its last major action in the Korean War.

far left: The cockpit of a North American F-86 Sabre jet fighter of the Korean War era; below: Right side gun ports of the Sabre; above: The famous North American-built trainer known as the Harvard, Texan, and the SNJ, which was the naval version.

War Two fighter, the rate of fire had been doubled, and it was a very good package against other fighters.

"Down low, where we were out of the transsonic superiority range, we wore a g-suit and they didn't. You can fight defensively when you are blacked out, but you can't fight offensively. If you had enough speed to pull a good 6g turn, you would 'go black' in twenty to thirty degrees of the turn. The MiG pilot couldn't follow you because he was blacked out too. You are still conscious, though you have three to five seconds of vision loss. When you had gone about as far in the turn as you thought you could carry it, you could pop the stick forward and your vision would return immediately. You had already started your roll, and the MiG was right there in front of you, every time, because, not having a g-suit, he had eased off in the turn. His g-tolerance was only half of yours. So he was right there and most probably would overshoot you."

"With little more than a hundred hours in the AD Skyraider, I got orders to an AD squadron on the west coast. After I got there I wanted some additional cross-country time so a friend and I flew our Skyraiders up the coast to NAS Alameda near Oakland. While over Los Angeles that night I felt very uneasy because everywhere I looked all I could see was a sea of lights. Over Los Angeles is not the place to lose an engine in a single-engine airplane. There was no place to set down if the engine quit. For several long minutes we flew along over that huge city with me thinking that if the engine quit I would have to ride that free-falling anvil into any unlighted patch I could find. I didn't want to drop an AD into a house. There were no black holes to be seen."
—Paul Ludwig, former U.S. Navy attack pilot

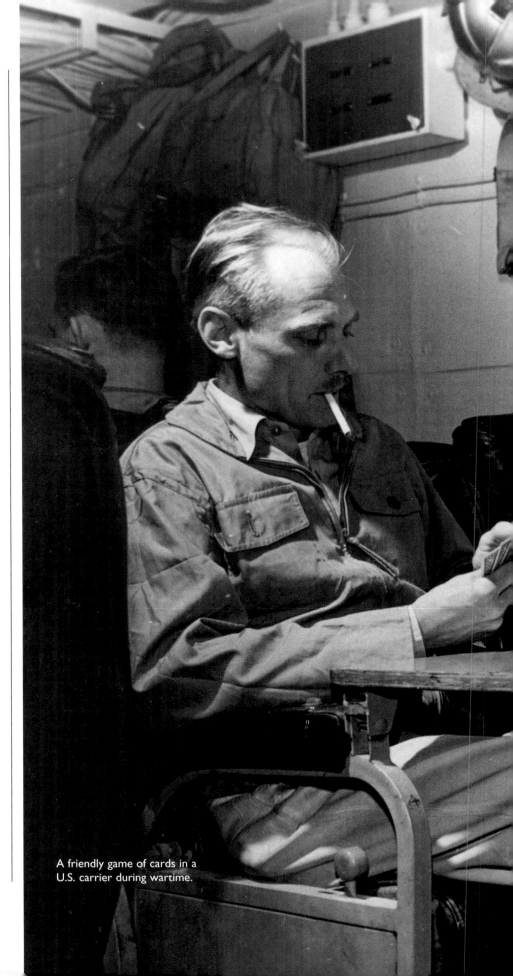

A friendly game of cards in a U.S. carrier during wartime.

LEARNING CURVE

A vital part of the fundamental training at
NAS Pensacola is survival in the sea. Coming
down on water is an experience relished
by few naval aviators, but one that must be
anticipated and prepared for by all.

THEIR TRAINING STANDARDS ARE AMONG the highest in the world. They have to be. Naval aviators must be capable of operating safely and efficiently in the most adverse circumstances. When the pilots of a carrier air wing come out to the boat for a refresher carrier qualification (part of the ship's work-up prior to a six-month deployment) they normally practice their landing approaches when the ship is within a reasonably short distance of the beach. They know that if they have to, chances are that they will be able to divert and land safely on a nearby airfield. The practice is good for perfecting their skills and helps build their confidence for doing what is probably the most important and demanding part of the job: bringing their multi-million dollar airplanes, and themselves, safely back aboard the carrier. Once deployed, however, they can no longer rely on that safe proximity to a friendly airfield ashore should they need it.

For them it's the boat or nothing. They need to have worked out any kinks in their approach and landing technique before they can perform safely and confidently in the blue water environment, out of reach of the beach. A pilot who gets too many bolters, or has a tendency to be a bit low in the approach, for example, must cure himself of such habits and achieve consistency in his traps, both day and night, to become truly blue water-competent. Key in the final weeks of the pre-deployment work-up is the identification of any such flaws. If these habits cannot be overcome, both mechanically and psychologically, the pilot will be deemed not up to scratch and unsuitable for operational deployment.

Who are these men and women who fly the warplanes of the Navy? Where do they come from, these

pilots and aircrew who carefully don flight suits, g-suits, survival gear, helmets, oxygen masks, and more, and shoehorn themselves into tight-fitting cockpits so they can sling-shot from the relative security of their carrier to whatever may await them on their assigned mission? How did they get to the fleet, these people who, in all weathers and the blackest of nights, must return from their missions and somehow locate their ship, often with no visual cues, and come aboard, no matter what, because there is no other place to land? They are the best of the best, drawn, like moths to light, to the greatest challenge in aviation.

Jeff Mulkey flew with Helicopter Anti-Submarine Squadron 8 aboard the USS *John C. Stennis*. A 1993 graduate of the United States Naval Academy, Annapolis, he describes the path taken by those who want to fly with the U.S. Navy. "A typical American naval aviator comes to NAS Pensacola, Florida, the cradle of naval aviation, from either the Naval Academy or a college ROTC program, or from Officer Candidate School. It all starts in Pensacola with Aviation Preflight Indoctrination, API, which lasts for about six weeks. Then you go on to a Primary Flight Training squadron, known as a VT, at either Pensacola or Corpus Christi, Texas. All naval aviators, regardless of whether they become jet pilots, fixed-wing propeller pilots, helicopter pilots, or Naval Flight Officers—start Primary training in fixed-wing, flying the T-34 Charlie, a single-engine, turboprop sporty model. Everybody learns to fly fixed-wing and the basic training is all the same no matter what type of aviator you are in the Navy.

"From Primary training it branches out, based on the needs of the Navy in the week that you are graduated.

The grades that you receive during that training also affect the Navy's decision about which aircraft community you will be sent to. It will send you to one of several pipelines, the biggest ones being Propeller, in which you would end up flying P3s, C-130s, or some other prop type; Helicopter, which can branch out to any of the types of helicopters we fly; and Jets, which could be F/A-18 Hornets, E/A-18 Growlers, F/A-18E/F Super Hornets, and F-35 Lightning IIs. If you go into the helicopter pipeline, you stay there at Pensacola and train in the TH-57 up at Whiting Field. The pipelines then branch out to Advanced Training. For Advanced in jets, you go on to either Meridian, Mississippi, or Kingsville, Texas; for Advanced propeller, it's Corpus Christi, Texas. At the completion of Advanced training, pilots are 'winged' and officially become naval aviators at that point. Then you go to the Fleet Replacement Squadron (FRS), also known as the RAG or Replacement Air Group. At the FRS or RAG, you learn to fly the particular type of aircraft that you will fly permanently in the fleet. That is where a jet pilot may become an F-18 pilot, or a helicopter pilot may become an HH-60 pilot. There you are sent to your community within the communities at the FRS.

"In terms of elapsed time before you get to the fleet, it depends on the particular pipeline and how smoothly things are running for you, but if all goes well, you can get to the FRS in a year and a half to two years. At completion of the FRS, you head to your first sea tour or fleet squadron. The flow of the pipelines works pretty much the same for all naval aviators, whether helicopter, jet, or prop. On average, the total process these days takes you about three years to get to your first fleet

Shannon Callahan trained to become a Naval Flight Officer at NAS Pensacola. A Naval Academy graduate and the granddaughter of a U.S. Navy enlisted man who served on the USS *Gambier Bay*, an escort carrier that was sunk in the Battle of Leyte Gulf in the Second World War, she completed the NFO course in March 2000 and was selected for the EA-6B Prowler community.

Seen here finishing her water survival instruction, Naval Flight Officer candidate Shannon Callahan moves efficiently through the requirements and demands of the Navy's thorough training regimen.

squadron—a pretty long time. But they are making an effort to weed out some of the 'pools' that have built up in the past, and the demand at the turn of the century was certainly high for pilots in the Navy, so they began to move more quickly through the pipelines. The primary reason for the increased demand was the number of mid-grade pilots that were electing to leave . . . that were not staying in the service. The Navy was losing a lot more of the senior folks; the mid-career officers who had finished their initial commitments and opted to get out and pursue other interests, whether those were commercial aviation or some other type of job. The senior leadership was still there The new guys were still coming in, but the middle was eroding a bit. It was the same across the board . . . fixed-wing, rotary, and jets.

"Everyone in naval aviation is aware of their obligation. No one enters into it without realizing how much time they're gonna owe. But life changes. Most people are not married and do not have children when they start flight training. If you do get married and have children, suddenly you are five years into it and your outlook may be quite a bit different from what it was when your were single. It's talked about—separation—but until you have actually done it, until you have gone through a carrier work-up cycle, until you have been away from home for six months or more and gone through a cruise and experienced what it's like, only then can you know. Everyone thinks at the outset that they are ready to accept the life and the obligation, but they don't really know until they've been there. The Navy sets the commitment that both it and the individual agree to and accept. It's a contract and all sides understand that. You know what

the Navy expects and everyone honors that. Certain people deal with it better than others, but the contract is always honored, whether for personal reasons, or because the Navy says you will, or out of a sense of honor and obligation, or because of monetary reasons. A whole lot of money is spent training a person to do what we do and the Navy has every right to expect to get our services for a number of years, for training us to do this."

Early in the twenty-first century Dale Dean was director of the Aviation Training School at NAS Pensacola: "We give you a test to see how smart you are and how good you are at problem-solving. If I were to define the perfect person for us, it would be someone who scored well on the test and is about five feet eight inches tall. That's important because we have anthropometric concerns. When you are sitting in the aircraft, you have to be able to see over the glare shield, to reach all the switches, to fully throw the controls in out-of-control flight, maybe negative g, and you have to be able to reach the rudder pedals, and, if you have to eject, not tear your legs off. If you are five feet two inches tall and have little T-Rex arms, you're probably not going to qualify. If you are six feet seven inches tall and your legs go under the glare shield, you are probably not going to qualify, at least not for jets. We want that academic profile and we're looking for a fairly athletic, medium-build person. And then there is the part that is hard to define . . . motivation. You have to really want to be here. You're not just coming to get your ticket punched, spend a couple of years flying here and then go on to the airlines. How badly do you want to be here? Are you willing to gut it out and put up with the inconveniences to get to fly?

"So, it's a three-part requirement. You have to be able to do the job, fit in the plane, and really want to be here. The people who do best as Naval Flight Officers are not necessarily the ones who have engineering degrees; it's the ones who really want to fly, they just want to fly. They are really smart, have good eyesight, good hand-eye coordination, a quick mind, able to grasp detail. In general, most successful naval pilots or NFOs are successful naval officers as well. They do pretty well with their ground jobs, are multi-faceted and able to handle more than one detail at a time. A lot of it is attitude. You have to want to be here. You have to enjoy it. You have to want to be in charge, to take control of the situation. That's where success comes from."

What sort of person flies the F/A-18 Hornet front-line fighter in the U.S. Navy? One example is David Tarry who spoke with the author in 2000 aboard the USS *John C. Stennis*: "I've been flying the F-18 for about fourteen months—ten months getting through the initial training and four months with the squadron. The primary purpose of the airplane is to cover both the fighter and attack roles. We have different master modes for our computer that let us fight our way in, drop our ordnance and then fight our way out, without dedicated fighter support. The Navy is moving toward a multi-role airplane and away from the dedicated fighter and the dedicated attack plane. The F-14 will be phased out, and the Super Hornet wil be our next line, followed eventually by the Joint Strike Fighter (JSF). The Super Hornet will also take over tanking, which the A-6 used to do, and will be the future of naval aviation until we can get the JSF on line. We're supposed to start training pilots for the Super Hornet in 2001. It will have a dual-seat configuration. Right now, the Marines fly a dual-seat variant of the F-18—land-based—for doing forward air control and high-task-loading issues.

"When we launch from the cat, the F-18 pilot grabs the 'towel rack,' a grab handle on the canopy frame, prior to and during the launch. The aircraft rotates on its own with the trim that we set, but right after you come off the front end, you grab the stick immediately. They just don't want you to put in any stick control because it would disturb the trim. You can do the same taking off at the field. It's pretty much hands off. As you get the air speed and wind over the wing, it just naturally rotates and takes off. It's a very user-friendly plane. The computer systems we have allow us to go from a two-seat cockpit, like the F-14 or the A-6, dedicated fighter or dedicated attack, to where we can do all of that with a single-seat plane because it is so user-friendly, with the hands-on throttle and stick system (HOTAS). You can run your computer and all your displays, and almost never take your hands off the stick and throttle. It takes most of the work out of flying and actually lets you concentrate on working the weapons systems and flying the plane as a weapon. Higher level guys who have at least a few hundred hours in the plane are very comfortable working their way in and working their way out, and not having a backseater to help them. The computer is really your backseater, taking care of a lot of the administrative tasks.

"To land an F-18 on a carrier, you are coming in at somewhere between 130 and 140 knots and trying to hit that little piece of ground and stop that quick. Lots of my friends can't

believe I do it. They can't see how you can do something that precise. But really, with the training you have, you just start off and everything is baby steps. They never have you take a big step. You start out in a small turboprop, just learning basic flying and how to land at the field. You go to an intermediate jet trainer where you start working with higher speed maneuvers, but still just working at the field. You get into Advanced training and start learning more tactical things. You start doing some bombing, some air-to-air fighting. Then you do a long period of field carrier qualifications, using the lens to land at the field. They work you up and work you up, and then you go to the boat in Advanced training during the day. Then you go to the FRS, the RAG, where you learn how to fly the F-18, or whatever you happen to be flying. You learn how to do the bombing, the air-to-air fighting, and then you do day and night field carrier work and, eventually, carrier qualification. But everything is done in baby steps. By the time you get to the fleet, it's not an unfamiliar environment. That's a big step. Seeing the sight picture; looking down from 16,000 feet while holding overhead and thinking, 'I'm gonna land on that postage stamp down there,' sure gets your heart rate going. But they baby-step you along so much that it's really not a huge leap of faith to be able to do it.

"When you learn to land at night on a carrier, it's basically the same pattern that you fly during the day. So when you make the transition to night, you're basically doing the same thing you do in the day. You just don't have the visual reference, but if you do everything at night the way you are supposed to do it during the day, you should roll out in exactly the

same spot. Again, it's a little step. Take away the visual reference. But you do it enough at the field, and you start flying extended patterns, or holding in a marshal stack and then flying straight in to pick up the Instrument Landing System (ILS) or the Automatic Carrier Landing System. I find that night landing is actually a little easier, because you are doing a straight-in. You aren't doing the approach, hitting specific numbers and having to roll out. Rolling out, making the transition from the turn to wings level, is a pretty big power correction. With the small, stubby wing that we have, you're pretty high up on the power in that approach turn, so when you roll out you get all that lift back under your wings. You've got to come quite a bit off the power, keep the rate of descent, and then get back on the power so you can find the middle ground again. You're really fighting to find the middle happy place. But if you are coming in on a straight-in approach, you are three miles out and making the transition from straight and level flight to about three degrees glide slope down, a little power off, a little power back on, establish yourself on glide slope and then, for three miles you're just fine-tuning. By the time you are flying the ball, it's just little corrections and maybe a little power on as you fly through the burble, depending on how the winds are across the deck.

"Once you get used to flying at night, and get over the mental aspect, which is really what the problem with night . . . it's more of a mental thing . . . that you don't have the horizon and the visual reference, but once you get over that it's really not bad at all. You use the same rules that the Landing Signal Officers (LSO) teach us all the time. If you're a little high, lead it and step it down. If you're low, get it back

U.S. Marine Corps nightfighter pilot Bruce Porter became one of naval aviation's greatest fighter aces of the Second World War.

Naval Air Service ladies at Pensacola in 1918.

up where it's supposed to be. There is no life below the datums. You don't want to be down there, so get it back up. Ball flying is ball flying, whether it's dark or light out. You do so much of it at the field that it becomes more muscle-memory than anything. 'OK, the ball is down. I've got to get it back up.' It becomes subconscious. They talk about the zen of ball flying. It's an art, it's a religion to have that touch, that feel. I don't know that I have it yet. I'm still working on it.

"The F-18 is fun to fly. It's the greatest job in the world. Every day I fly, I can't believe that I'm doing it. I can't believe that anybody would let somebody do it. We're no different from anybody else; there's nothing that sets us apart from everybody else except, maybe, that we have the eyesight to get in. That's the big thing with carrier aviation. It keeps out a huge percentage of people who would love to do this and are more than smart enough to be able to go through the training and do it. But the Navy has such rigorous eyesight standards, mostly because of night landing. You have to have really good eyesight. The Hornet is a great airplane; a great ball-flying airplane. It's easy to put the ball where you want it, easier than the F-14 or the Prowler whose systems are more manual and take a lot more work to fly. The F-18 has a great system that helps us to be safe and get aboard safely. The LSOs are always pushing: 'Just be safe.' You don't want to be low on approach because it's not safe. If you are high you can always go around and try again. If you do that four times and you have to tank, we have tankers. Go get some more gas, but always be safe. Never drag the ball in low just to get aboard, taking the risk of settling right at the back end of the boat. Our bosses tell us that our job

is to go downtown and drop bombs, or fight our way, or defend the strike package that's going in. Getting back on the boat is just admin, but it's one of the prime spots where you can get in trouble."

"Usually a student is kept free of trouble by instructors, and the student tries to keep himself out of trouble because he wants to succeed alongside his peers. But stupidity appears to many of us at the very time we are happiest. In 1954, during Primary training at Pensacola after I had soloed, I thought I had mastered the SNJ trainer, and one day over Perdido Bay I was practicing aerobatics for my next check ride. I did a slow roll and hadn't got the nose high enough on the entry. When I was upside down I let the nose fall through and, rather than roll out, I split-essed. I blacked out from g during the pullout and awakened to see the indicated air speed needle exceeding the red line and expected to see the wings tear off, but the airplane held together. It shook me up but I got over it."
—Paul Ludwig, former U.S. Navy attack pilot

Royal Navy pilot Danny Stembridge flew AF-2 Sea Harriers with 801 Squadron from HMS *Illustrious*: "I went through flying training to fly the Lynx maritime attack helicopter. I had a fantastic time doing it and part of me actually still misses it. It wasn't as satisfying as flying a fast jet, but I think it was more enjoyable. When you are flying a fighter, there is very little time to think, 'Wow, this is fun.' That's more in retrospect. I think that the satisfaction I got from flying Sea Harriers outweighed the fun I had flying helicopters. The Sea Harrier is very demanding. It's not hugely ergonomic inside, and you are working

hard because of that. The air defense environment is a busy one, and you're on your own. Then you have to come back and land on a ship in a VSTOL fighter. Bringing the Sea Harrier alongside, with its lack of systems to help you and its inherent lack of thrust, and therefore the amount of fuel that you require to come aboard . . . it takes a lot of brain power and piloting ability. You're working from the minute you start preparing for a sortie 'til the minute you finish debriefing it, and afterwards, if it has gone right, it's immensely satisfying. It's a job that has to be done, when you're airborne, whether you are training or not, and the satisfaction comes afterwards.

"If you mishandle the Sea Harrier in any way, particularly in the VSTOL regime, it will bite you hard. It will really punish you if you make a basic error in VSTOL regime. But the training is pretty intense and pretty long as well. Because of my rotary flying background, I had a slightly different pipeline, but the Sea Harrier training is a very long course and a lot of it is spent in learning to tame the plane in the VSTOL regime, just flying it. With other fighters, once you've learned, they are similar to other types, but with the Harrier, you are always learning how to fly it and how to operate it in the role for which it was designed.

"Coming from flying helicopters, I have found it easier and a lot more comfortable around the ship than other people do, because of my experience of about 1,200 deck landings on very small ships in a helicopter, many of them at night. Shipborne operations are unique, and to have that to fall back on when everything else is looking horrible . . . you're coming down the glide slope, you're in cloud and wondering if the ship is actually gonna be there at the end . . . I'm used to

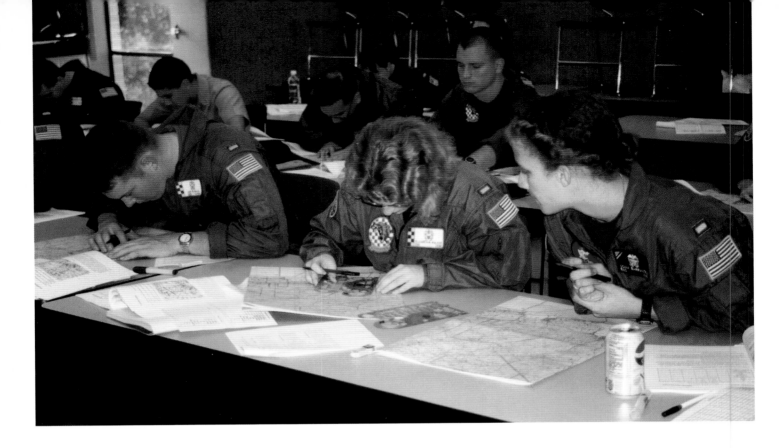

seeing the ship pop out of the gloop at the bottom. Other people may not be. I also think that hovering experience has helped me immensely.

"I'm looking forward to my first deployment in the Gulf flying Sea Harriers. I've been to the Gulf twice, for six months, so the area is not new to me, but the mission I will be carrying out will be totally different, and professionally, I'm looking forward to it. As for the danger involved in the flying, it doesn't keep me awake at night, nor does going to the Gulf. In the past I've done what could be construed as scary things, and that hasn't kept me awake. Maybe in six months my view will have changed, but I think if you're the kind of person to do this, then it's very unlikely to worry you. Otherwise you wouldn't be doing it."

Shannon Callahan is the granddaughter of a U.S. Navy enlisted man who served on the *Gambier Bay*, a small

carrier that was sunk in the Battle of Leyte Gulf during the Second World War. In March 2000 she completed the Naval Flight Officer course at NAS Pensacola and was selected for the EA-6B Prowler community. "When I was in high school I took a trip to the Air Force Academy and fell in love with the place. I definitely wanted to go there. But the Air Force officers I talked to convinced me that, to be in the Air Force one should really be a pilot, and I didn't think I could be a pilot because I didn't have 20/20 vision. I looked at the other service academies and decided on the Naval Academy, where I learned that even without 20/20 (I have 20/40) I could qualify to be a Naval Flight Officer. It is ironic that I actually could have been a pilot in the Air Force, because their eyesight requirements are lower than those of the Navy, but I didn't know that at the time. Fortunately, I found my calling because

I really love carrier aviation. I went out on a carrier on a midshipman cruise one summer while at the Academy, and was enamored with the whole thing. I got five cat shots in a Prowler and after that there was no going back. I graduated from the Academy in '98, got my Masters degree in National Security, and showed up at flight school at Pensacola in '99.

"My first choice would be Radar Intercept Officer on an F-14; second choice would be Electronic Countermeasures Officer on an EA-6B Prowler. The Prowlers will probably be replaced by the F/A-18G; they call it the Growler. So it seems like I will end up in the Super Hornet if I stay in, which I really want to do. I'll be happy with whatever I get. Every aviator loves their platform. Nobody ever regrets the direction they went or their choice. Everyone is positive and always trying to sell you on their platform.

left: Naval Flight Officer students moving through their navigation training; above: NFO candidates take their turns in the famous Dilbert Dunker where they learn escape techniques from an aircraft downed in the sea.

"Every event, every training flight is graded. They keep track of how each student is doing with what they call the Navy Standard Scores (NSS). The scoring system for flights is: Above Average, Average, Below Average, and Unsatisfactory, which is a 'Down.' Two Belows equals one Down. Your NSS reflects how many Aboves and Belows you have, compared to the 200 to 300 students who went just before you, so its all comparative. This is because the instructors come and go, and thus the grading changes a little bit; it's kind of fluid. To keep track of where I am in relation to my class mates, it's just a matter of counting up those NSS grades, and some people do that. That's not something I obsess about. You'll drive yourself nuts if you keep comparing yourself to your buddies. The thing to do is just to go into every flight and give it your best, 100 percent. I have faith in my instructors. I think they

are pretty good and pretty fair, and I know it's all gonna work out the way it should because these people have been in aviation for years. I trust them with the grades.

"I'm sure people on the outside probably think it's pretty cut-throat, but it's not. I've never known anyone who screwed a buddy to get ahead in this program. Everybody always helps everybody else. You have to cooperate to get winged. That's hard enough, and there is a huge attrition rate, even in Pre-flight, so you really can't make it without your buddies. The workload is so intense that you have to split up the work. I haven't met any lone rangers. You just can't do it. I've worked in groups from the beginning. The instructors encourage it. I think it's a necessity. You have to, to get it all done. And you rely on your buddies to cheer you up, to keep you stable and centered. It can be pretty stressful.

"There are no particular problems in being female in the program. There are still not that many of us, so, naturally most of my friends are guys. There hasn't been anything that has really got in my way. I think that if anybody does have prejudices and stereotypes, they brought them with them from the civilian world into the Navy, the way they were raised or the area of the country they come from. I don't think the Navy breeds that at all. Most people just want to know, can you do your job? Are you safe to fly with? The percentage of women in the program is small, especially when you get to this stage. Right now I think there are six or seven female students in the squadron, out of over a hundred students. There are few of us, markedly fewer of us, but at the same time we are not such an oddity anymore. There are not many female instructors. I've flown with one since I started, and that's from Primary on. I work in a pretty

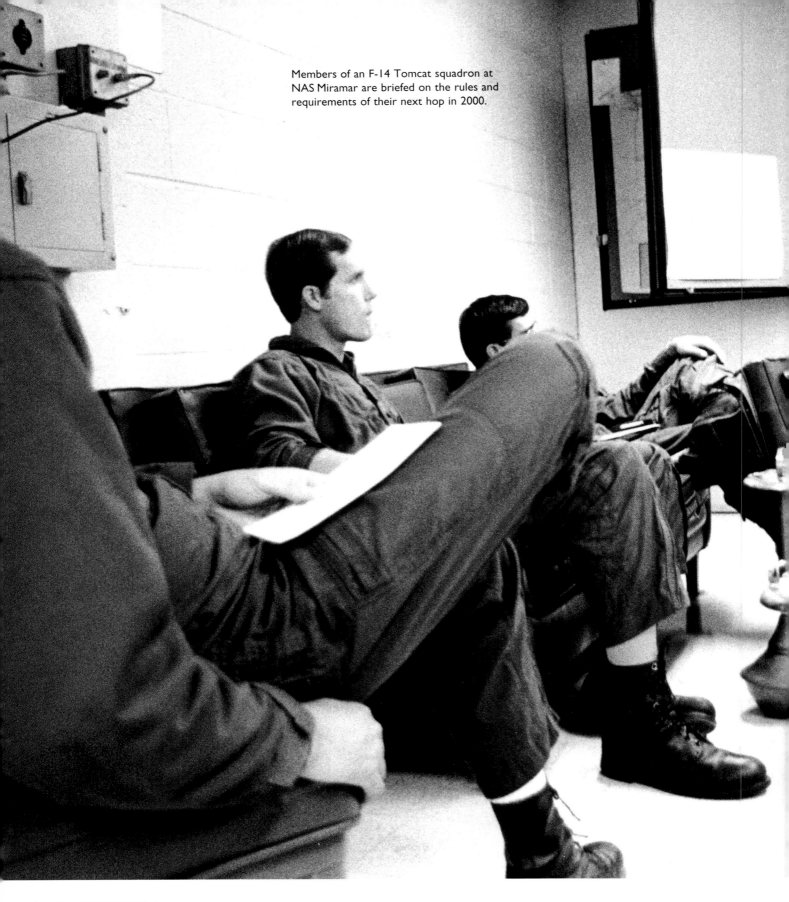

Members of an F-14 Tomcat squadron at NAS Miramar are briefed on the rules and requirements of their next hop in 2000.

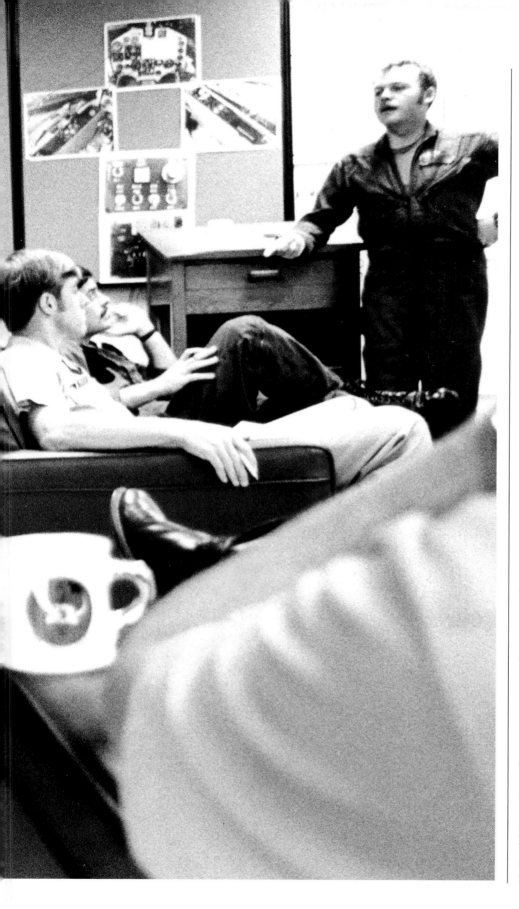

much all-male environment but I'm used to it. The Academy trained me for that. It would have been a bigger adjustment had I come from a civilian school where the ratio was 50/50, so I was kind of lucky in that respect. The military is kind of inherently masculine. That's not necessary anymore. I think the situation has changed. You can just be yourself. Everything feminine isn't bad anymore, and it doesn't necessarily mean you are weak to be feminine. Again, people are interested in the bottom line. Can you fly? Can you navigate to the target? Can you get to the target on time? Are you safe? Do you know your emergency procedures? Can you make good judgement calls? Do you do thorough pre-flight planning? All that stuff is pretty much gender neutral.

"To get through this program you really have to love it. That's what I tell people who are just starting. If you don't love it, don't bother, 'cause it only gets harder and more demanding. Your attitude has to be: 'I get to do this.' Not, 'I have to do this.' I'm really lucky to be doing this. I saw a lot of my buddies get attrited for medical problems or because they didn't have the grades for aviation. I've been really fortunate to be in this program and I'm not gonna make myself miserable just because it's hard. You have to earn something to appreciate it. I knew a long time ago that I wanted to be in the Navy for a long-term career. If you love your job, it's the biggest blessing in life. I would do this if they paid me in sand. I'd like to command a carrier one of these days. Right now, I'm just trying to get winged and fly as much as I possibly can.

"The Naval Academy is a great place. It had a big part in making me who I am today. I'll always be grateful and proud that I went there."
Recent Pensacola graduate Scott

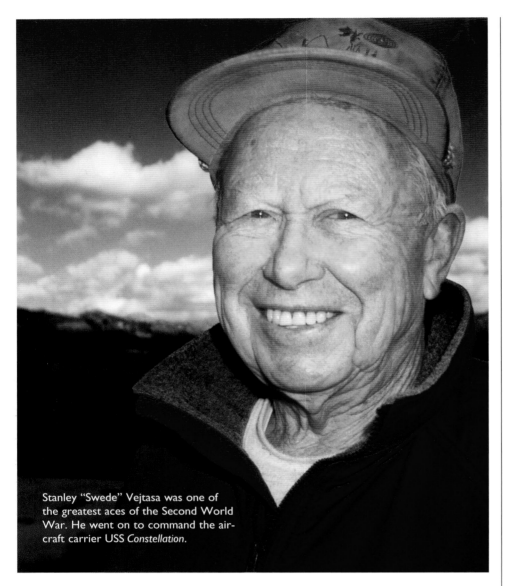

Stanley "Swede" Vejtasa was one of the greatest aces of the Second World War. He went on to command the aircraft carrier USS *Constellation*.

Whelpley is also headed for the Prowler community. Scott made it to the NFO program by an unusual route: "For nearly six years I was an enlisted Aviation Electronics Technician in the Navy. I applied for Officer Candidate School for Aviation and was turned down. I applied again and was accepted, but for the supply corps. I was told that I was too old for naval aviation. After the tenth week at OCS I asked if I could switch to aviation. 'You're too old and there is nothing we can do about it.' I was thirty-one at the time. So I was commissioned a supply corps officer. Then I met a lieutenant commander who thought that what I had been told might not be true. He himself had been thirty-one when he went through the NFO program. He made some calls for me, and, after about four months and more rejections due to my age, I was finally accepted.

"I got a month's advance pay, threw all my stuff in a U-Haul and was on the road to Pensacola. I'm older than most. A lot of these guys out of the Academy are twenty-three. I really admire them. They are so smart and grasp the stuff so quickly. I'm a little more stressed and concerned because I feel like this is my last hurrah, so I really need to get through the program. I'm having a good time but I've put a lot of pressure on myself because this will be the greatest thing that I've ever accomplished. I study all the time. I have to. I know the

Instructors at NAS Pensacola between training sessions in 2000.

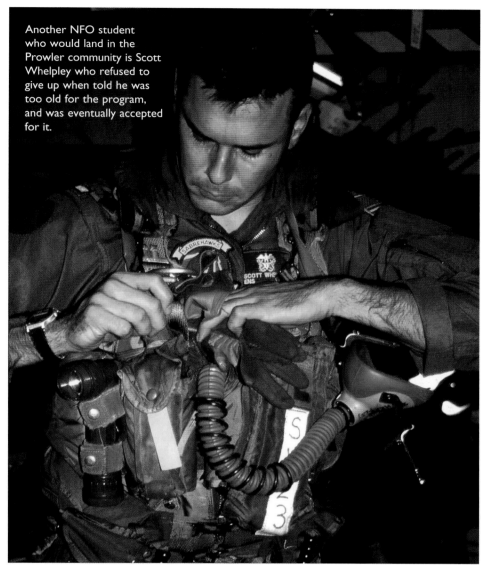

Another NFO student who would land in the Prowler community is Scott Whelpley who refused to give up when told he was too old for the program, and was eventually accepted for it.

physiology guys would throw a fit if they knew, but there are times when I'm up 'til one and then get up at five, because I have to. It's the only way I'll get through it. It's been ten years since I was in college.

"Everybody here wants to be the number one flight officer in the program. I know I'm somewhere in the middle of the pack but that never stops any of us from competing and trying to be better and better. We are tested and graded every single day. We have to know all the systems of the aircraft, all the procedures, all the checklists, all the emergency procedures . . . every single day something is added on top of what we just learned. But I'm so happy to be here. I'm very lucky. Back home, everybody is like, 'Wow, Scott, you're gonna be flyin' a jet.' If only they knew. It's just me, me, the same guy you used to run around with and get in trouble with. If I can do this, anybody can do this.

Obviously, you have to want it badly enough. It's a Big Boy program here. You are responsible for knowing your stuff. Go ahead. Go home and do whatever you want to do, but you'd better know your stuff when you come back. It's taught me discipline. Being 'enlisted' really humbled me and I think I needed that. It was what I needed prior to doing this. I think it has made me a better officer.

"Yesterday was my fourth hop. Today will be my fifth and after that

NAS Pensacola flight instructors on the flight line.

I have seven left. I'm not a pessimist or an optimist; I'm a realist. Anything can happen, so I'm just hoping. Hold on to your hat and don't let go. Eight more events and that's it, I get my wings. As soon as you are done with your last flight they come out and wet you down with champagne. They rip off your name tag and put on your 'soft wings,' and you get a punch in the chest, which is politically incorrect. After that we have a giant ceremony at the Naval Aviation Museum with the families invited. After we get winged, we are selected. I'm probably going to get S-3s or Prowlers. My first choice is Prowlers. I've been in the Navy for six years and I'll owe them six after this. I really enjoy the Navy. It's funny, I miss going out to sea. That might seem crazy but I really do. It's one of the few things in this world that is still an adventure. You never know what's gonna happen. I was on a small aircraft carrier, the USS *New Orleans*, in 1997 when we took a 45° roll during Typhoon Justin off the coast of New Guinea. That was pretty scary. We almost lost it. I've never been so frightened in my life. Everybody was surprised that the island didn't break off. The ship had some really heavy damage. That is real adventure, it's dangerous, but there is nothing in the world that I would rather be doing. No matter all the grey hair, I plan to stay in as long as they will keep me. I'll get to the highest rank I possibly can. It's all about being proficient. I'll do whatever it takes. I'm willing to learn, and wherever the Navy takes me, I'm ready to go.

"Grades. Sometimes you get bad grades. Sometimes you have a bad flight. It's humbling and sometimes you feel you're not worthy. I had a great hop on Friday, Above Average, and I felt like I was the best flight officer. Yesterday I had an average hop and got an Average grade. Driving home, I was kicking myself—what did I do wrong? I suck. I'm horrible. It can go from one extreme to the other. You just push it all away and go back the next day.

The days and weeks have flown. I'm almost afraid to look up and see how much more of the hill I have to conquer. I like looking back down behind me and thinking, 'Hey, I've come this far. I'll just keep my head down and take one day at a time, and just keep chuggin' away.' "

Another who came late to flying is Nick Wallace, who flew Sea Harriers with 801 Squadron, RN. Nick was a ship driver until July 1994, when he entered flying training. "I hit the front line in Sea Harriers in July 1999. Our orientation for going to the Gulf in January 2000 has really been going on all through our flying training. The Sea Harrier training squadron is given a weekly brief by an intelligence officer who often covers the Gulf or Bosnia. Before deploying to the Gulf, we go through a series of formal briefings and the rest of the squadron gets

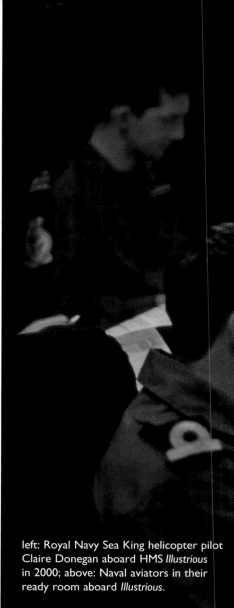

left: Royal Navy Sea King helicopter pilot Claire Donegan aboard HMS *Illustrious* in 2000; above: Naval aviators in their ready room aboard *Illustrious*.

involved in station-level briefings by intelligence officers. The week before we sail we'll get a threat update and an analysis update. Once we are on board, the briefs will continue. We'll be well prepared for the threat we are possibly facing out there.

"It seems strange to say, but I hope I never have to go and do my job for real, because if you do go and do the job that we train for for real, it means that we are at war and diplomacy has failed. We will be patrolling the no-fly zones set up over Iraq and it's quite possible that we'll have contact with Iraqi aircraft. We'll be flying in conjunction with American aircraft which provide the bulk of the numbers on the combat air patrols there, with help from the Sea Harriers and from various other countries as well. We'll be working very closely with the Americans.

"The Sea Harrier is unique. It's not the fastest or the most modern airplane. It's got a great radar, a great weapon, which makes it very formidable as an air defense fighter. And it's got these nozzles which make it unique. Learning to fly it was . . . very different. You get used to learning how to fly aircraft faster and faster and lower and lower, and then you get to the Sea Harrier and they teach you how to stop in flight. From about 100 knots downward, its wing is not very efficient and produces very little lift, so once through 100 knots in a decelerating phase, you have to pro-

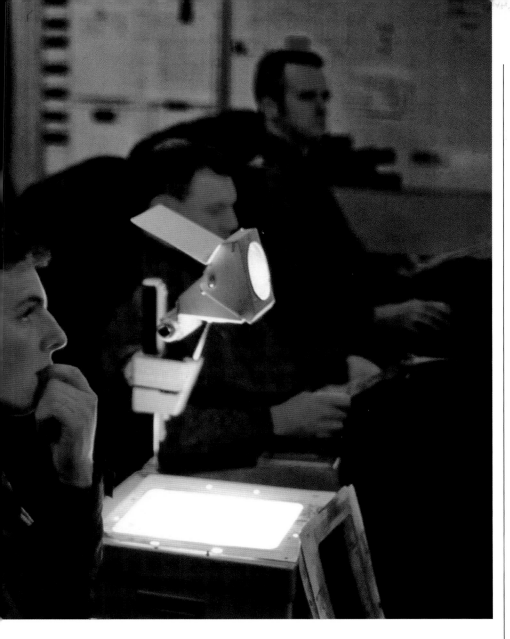

careful about how you manage your fuel. If you are going to start dumping it, which you have to do on most sorties to make your weight back at the boat, you need to dump down at the correct time, generally about fifteen minutes before your recovery so you can properly slot into the boat.

"Assuming it's a nice day, it's then up to us to come back to the boat on our own. We might get some assistance from the air directors in the ops room who can pick us up on radar and give us steers back to the overhead. We then set up a holding pattern 1,000 feet over the ship. The pattern is about two and a half minutes long. You go round in a circle above the ship and, two and a half minutes prior to your landing, or Charlie time, you fly past the ship at 600 feet and slightly on the starboard side of it. That's called the slot, and once you have slotted, you then turn in front of the boat so that you are effectively on a cross-wind leg and you roll out going down-wind . . . the opposite way to the boat. As you approach the back of the boat, with all your checks complete and your landing gear down, you tip into the finals turn and it's around that turn that you start to wash off your speed by using some of the nozzles. You take about 40° of nozzle around the finals turn, maintaining it flat initially and then using about 90 percent power, monitoring the engine temperature so you don't trip off the water injection system. You use the nozzles around the final turn. You are playing the nozzles to keep your speed and your angle of attack under control around the turn. As you approach, you roll out behind the boat and start in towards it. You then judge when to take the hover stop, to move the nozzles all the way downward to allow the aircraft to hover. Obviously, this means

gressively put more and more power on to keep the aircraft in the air. Coordination. It certainly concentrates the mind, recovering to the ship. Going into a big airfield is fine. Half the time we land conventionally, going forward at speed. But on the boat it's vertical landings every time; recovering to a moving airfield that is going up and down as well as forward, is a real challenge.

"Coming back to the ship is very well controlled. We have a certain time to be landing on deck. In the initial brief we will know what time we are landing on board; it's called a charlie time and it is given to us by the ship to fit in with the rest of the ship's programs. Once airborne we are managing our fuel, both to achieve the mission aims, do our training or whatever, and also so that we can arrive back in the vicinity of the ship with the correct amount of fuel, so we are not too heavy for the vertical landing. You have to be quite critical and that there is no thrust going out the back of the aircraft, so it starts to slow down a bit more rapidly. The idea is to arrive alongside the boat in a steady hover next to the landing area you have been allocated for that particular landing, at about eighty feet or so above the sea level and just off to the left side of the boat so you are not quite over the deck but fairly close to it.

"Once you have steadied yourself into a nice position and you're happy with your references next to the boat, you do a transition across by moving sideways about thirty feet to line up just over the mark that you have picked. You reduce power just a bit and the aircraft starts to sink. It's quite a firm landing because on a wet or pitching deck, if the wheels don't make a good contact, it would be easy to slide about.

"You think about the danger, although not all the time. You're very aware that the Sea Harrier is a difficult machine to fly; that if you don't keep on top of it, if you don't concentrate during decelerations and accelerations into and out of the hover, it can go wrong very quickly. There is a higher chance in this airplane that you may have an accident or crash or have to eject, or even be killed. It's something that you do think about periodically. I don't think about it when I strap into an airplane, when I go flying. The training you get is very good, and there is no way they are going to send someone out to fly the airplane if they don't think they can do it. You think about the danger when you have the aircraft systems failures or when you have a problem with the aircraft . . . when you are just that little step closer to maybe having to eject. Fortunately, they are rare. When something happens to someone you know, that brings it home to you. Yes,

it is a dangerous occupation, and yes, you do have to stay on top of the airplane at all times, but I don't think it would ever make me so scared that I wouldn't want to do it."

Jason Phillips, an Observer Instructor and Warfare Instructor in Sea King helicopters with 820 Squadron, Royal Navy aboard HMS *Illustrious* recalled: "Our primary role on the squadron was to hunt submarines. We used sonar and had two sonars on board. The active sonar is like a big microphone, a long bit of electric string that we'd lower into the water. We'd press a button and it sent out a pulse of noise. If anything was out there, the pulse bounced off it, came back, and was displayed on the computer's green waterfall display. Because we put out a 'ping' when using active sonar, that let the submariner know that we were there. Ideally, we'd like to sneak up on him to give our weapon the best chance. We also used a passive sonar: a smaller microphone on a thinner bit of electric string. It went down in the water to just listen. It floated to the surface and had a little radio antenna. Everything it heard uplinked to the aircraft and displayed on the same screens. No noise, no pings. It just listened. A trained aircrewman with supersensitive hearing would pick out the contact and pass the information across to the observer, who is the tactical coordinator. We would be the tactical nerve center when we got a contact with a submarine. I would then take over as the scene-of-action commander. No matter the seniority of the ships in the area, we could tell them to move out of the way while we dealt with the submarine. We controlled the weapons and carried up to four torpedos on board. The weapon we used was the Stingray, a highly intelligent

Pre-flight instruction in the Beechcraft T-34 Mentor, the primary piston-engined training aircraft of the U.S. Navy in 2000.

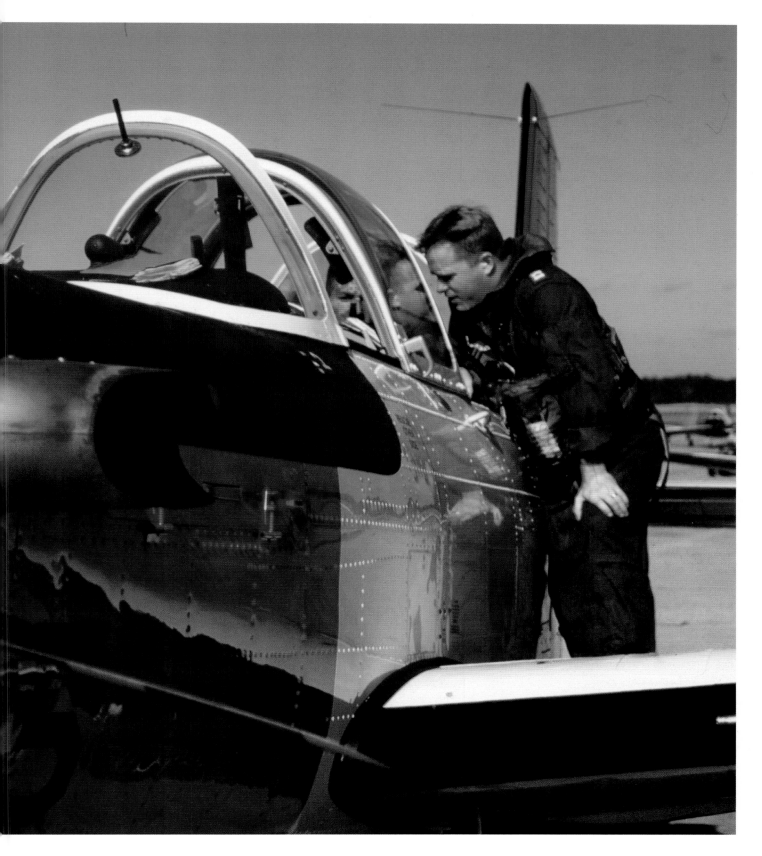

weapon. Another bit of equipment we had, the MAD or magnetic anomoly detector, detected magnetic disruptions in the earth's field. It's a big bar magnet and if we flew over something like a submarine—a big lump of metal—it caused a disturbance. We had a sensor which a crewman operated and the contact was also then painted on an old-fashioned chart recorder. If we believed there was a target down there, we would fly over it to corroborate our information."

Ed Copeland, former U.S. Navy fighter pilot: "In the Navy Pre-flight school that I went through, half of the time was spent on such relevant subjects as aircraft recognition, navigation, and naval traditions and customs. The other half was devoted to body contact athletics. Football was rough enough. We played basketball with ten men on a side, and the referee was there solely to break up the fist fights. We played water polo in the deep end of the pool and the instructor cracked the knuckles of anyone caught hanging onto the side. Pushball was another form of mayhem designed to inflict bodily harm on the other guy. In hand-to-hand combat we learned how to knife-fight and how to break a man's neck, go for the jugular, dislocate a shoulder, apply a knee to the groin, and so on.

"Physical fitness training, where competitiveness was stretched one step further to combativeness, was re-emphasized each step of the way in the flight training program, which lasted about ten months in 1942. I think it is fair to say that we came out of the cadet program with a certain killer instinct and an aggressive approach to survival. When it came time for me to go into combat against the Japanese, the issue was uncomplicated. They were out to kill me and

I was determined to do unto them before they did unto me."

Once told by his Navy flying instructor, "You will never solo. You are the dumbest cadet I have ever laid eyes on," U.S. Marine night-fighter ace Bruce Porter became one of the great fighter pilots of the Second World War. "As I stood watching my first night carrier ops, the feeling that crept over me was as eerie as any I had ever had. All I could hear was two high-performance engines. All I could see was two sets of landing lights. There was absolutely no moon to light the wake or give a hint of the ship's whereabouts. There was a slight breeze over the bow.

"Suddenly one set of lights was over the wake. The approach was textbook perfect, right up the wake at precisely the correct speed, attitude, and altitude. I heard the engine drone lower as the pilot took the cut and I watched the outline of the night-fighter arrest on the first or second wire. As the first Hellcat taxied forward to just beneath my perch, the second one set down in a textbook landing.

"For all the hours of training and instruction I had received, I had not really believed it possible before seeing it with my own eyes. We gathered around the two Navy veterans and asked a set of rapid-fire questions. Then someone with a bullhorn blared: 'Fly One, Marines, man your airplanes.'

"It had been decided that only one of us would launch and recover at a time, until everyone had completed one landing. I was the senior one in the group, so I would launch first. I did my best to hide my terror, and I think the only reason I was not found out was that everyone else was too deeply involved in masking their own fright to notice mine. My flight gear was still in the cockpit of my Grumman, so I climbed aboard

The learning experience in the U.S. Navy's North American T-2 Buckeye jet trainer.

RESCU

EMERGENCY ENTRA

CONTROL ON OTHER

and quickly snapped snaps and pulled straps. I recalled my first real moment of truth in an airplane, my qualifying solo at the elimination base at Long Beach, California, in 1940. Wow! I had come so far. I had been eager to fly then and had remained eager as I passed every milestone to this moment, when I found myself unforgivably apprehensive for the first time in my flying career. The prospect of first combat had not come as close to terrorizing me as this flight. I turned up the engine and allowed myself to be guided to the catapult.

"Before giving the catapult officer the 'ready signal,' I nervously checked and rechecked my harness, pulling the straps again for good measure. Then I ran through my pre-flight checklist; screw the men in the island who were moaning about how long I was taking: canopy back and locked, engine at full rpm, prop at full low pitch, flaps all the way down for maximum lift, right foot hovering above the right rudder pedal ready to overcome the left torque of the spinning prop, stick held loosely in my right hand, throttle grasped loosely in my left hand, head resting against the headrest to take up the shock of the catapult.

"I looked to my left and saluted. Ready! In response a dimly-perceived deckhand standing over the catapult crew's catwalk whirled a flashlight. Go! I turned my eyes front, loosened my grip on the stick, set my jaw and leaned back into my seat.

"WHACK. My conscious mind was aeons behind my senses, as it had been on all previous catapult launches. I had a very busy couple of seconds as I kicked the right rudder pedal and yanked the stick into the pit of my stomach. I had no time to dwell on how dark it was out there.

"My equilibrium returned. The Hellcat was climbing away to the left.

I got the wheels and flaps up in one motion. I had that familiar short sinking sensation as the flaps went up and the Hellcat dropped slightly. Then my mind kicked in: 'Needle—ball—airspeed, you dumb cluck.'

"A destroyer passed beneath my low left wing. I had just enough time to notice two blinking navigation lights before the inky black of the perfectly dark night enfolded me.

"All my training and experience saw me through a climb to 3,000 feet. While my mind reeled off a thousand facts about my flying, my voice talked to the ship in calm tones, reporting on routine matters the air officer would want to hear about. I was neither here nor there.

"I was cleared to land, which was of both relief and concern. I wanted to get down but first I had to find the carrier.

"I coaxed the Hellcat into one full circuit of the area in which I was pretty sure I had left the *Tripoli* and her escorts. I saw the two navigation lights on the forward destroyer I had overflown after launch. Then I saw two more which had to be the plane guard destroyer deployed a few thousand yards directly astern of the carrier, to pick up downed 'zoomies,' as we carrier pilots were known.

"Now I knew exactly where the flight deck lay. I also knew that, in the event of extreme danger, the carrier flight deck lights would be flicked on to help me find a safe roost. But that would mean failure, and there were too many people watching to let that happen.

"After reassuring myself that I was flying on a heading opposite that of the ship, I flew down the carrier's port side and approached the plane guard from ahead, keeping it just off my port wing. I could not help ruminating about how useless a night search for a bilged aviator must be.

"I flicked on my radio altimeter, a brand new instrument that had been installed in my cockpit just before we left San Diego. I had set it for 150 feet. If I flew above that altitude, I'd get a white signal light. If I flew below 150 feet, I'd get a red danger light, and if I was flying right at 150 feet, I'd get a comforting green light. The light was green when I turned on the altimeter.

"I flew upwind the length of the tiny destroyer and sighted her deck lights, which could only be seen from the air. This was the only concession to a pilot's natural tendency to become disoriented across even the briefest interval of night space.

"I had been timing my flight ever since passing the carrier and spotting the plane guard's lights. At what I judged to be the best moment, I turned 90° port, dropped my wheels and flaps, enriched the fuel mixture, partly opened the cowl flaps, put the prop in low pitch, and turned another 90° to arrive at a downwind position dead astern of the carrier.

"My night vision was, by then, as good as it would become. I had been training myself to find dim objects with my peripheral vision, which was the preferred method. Thus, I was able to pick out the dim shape of the totally darkened carrier as I floated up the wake.

"I was committed to the approach. All my attention was focused on sighting the LSO's luminous paddles. I momentarily panicked and said, or thought I might have said, 'Where the hell are you?'

"First I sensed the colored paddles; then I knew I saw them. The LSO's arms were both out straight. Roger! My ragged confidence was restored, though I was a good deal less cocky. I checked my airspeed, which was down to the required 90 knots. Before I knew it, I saw the cut.

The tailhook caught a wire and I was stopped.

"I taxied past the barrier, came to a rest beside the island and cut my engine. As had been the case after my first combat mission, my flight suit was reeking with sweat.

"During the rest of the night, my eight fellow fledglings each made one night landing. My subordinates accounted for more than a few wave-offs, but that was partly my doing. I had asked the LSO to be particularly unforgiving of minor gaffes. We all knew how important it was to get this exercise 100 percent perfect."

Paul Ludwig, former U.S. Navy attack pilot: "It has been said that those who stand and wait also serve. I didn't fly combat because there was no war. Like countless others, I was there if they needed me. I had to be content with peacetime operations, and I was. It excited me to fly the meatball or make paddles passes, to launch from a deck run over the bow or, once in a while, get a cat shot, and fly the downwind leg, judge the 180° turn in a stiff tailwind and come aboard smartly in a prop-tailwheel type air-craft, like my heroes in F6Fs and F4Us did in World War Two. I was a kid hoping to follow in their footsteps if there had been a war. Few are eager for a war, yet every kid joining the fleet thinks he is bullet-proof and that, if war comes, he'll just follow his lead-er and do whatever he does.

"Everyone remembers his solo flight, his first emergency, his first girl, first car, and so on. I ate up six months of peacetime carrier flying as though nothing else in the world mat-tered. In some ways, nothing has ever topped that, other than the love of a wife and the births of healthy chil-dren. Thank God there wasn't a war on when I served, but when you're in uniform, you serve. I am damned proud of what I did."

Jack Kleiss, former U.S. Navy pilot: "I first met AMM3/c Peter Gaido as I was preparing to make my first carrier landing. He asked, 'Can I go with you?' I replied, 'This is my first carrier land-ing and I am supposed to have only sandbags.' He said, 'You got wings, ain'tcha?' and replaced the sand-bags with his stout frame. With that supreme vote of confidence, I made half a dozen perfect landings.

"Peter later displayed his character as he observed a Japanese bombing plane attempting to crash into the *Enterprise*. He jumped into an empty SBD, fired the machine-gun at the approaching plane and continued firing at it as it sheared off the tail of his SBD. He continued firing as the Japanese plane moved in the opposite direction until it hit the ocean. He tried to remain anonymous in this action, but Vice Admiral Halsey finally found him and promoted him on the spot to AMM1/c.

"He flew with Ensign O'Flaherty during the Battle of Midway. They dropped their bombs on the Japanese carriers but later had to make a crash-landing. They were picked up from their rubber boat, rescued by the Japanese, interrogated, murdered, their bodies thrown into the sea. Peter Gaido was the bravest man I ever met."

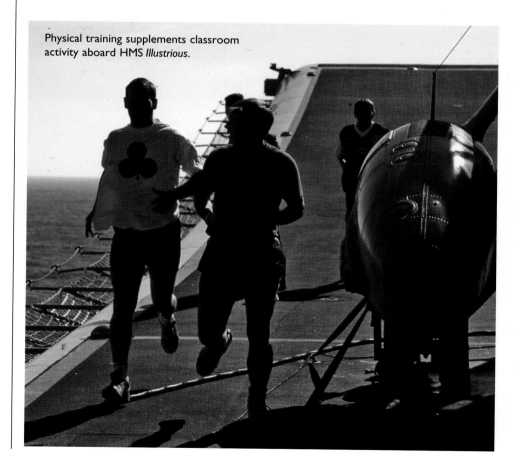
Physical training supplements classroom activity aboard HMS *Illustrious*.

BRING ME IN

A U.S. Navy Landing Signal
Officer on the job during
Operation Desert Storm in the
Persian Gulf, early 1991.

For all that has been said of the love
that certain natures (on shore) have
professed to feel for it, for all the
celebrations it has been the object of
in prose and song, the sea has never
been friendly to man. At most it has
been the accomplice of human rest-
lessness.
—from *The Mirror of the Sea* by
Joseph Conrad

THE LANDING SIGNAL OFFICER (LSO), OR
Batsman in the Royal Navy, is the
person who, for much of the time
that aircraft carriers have been in use,
has been responsible for guiding pilots
onto the flight deck to a safe landing or
"trap." Each squadron on today's U.S.
Navy carriers has its own landing signal
officer who assists his fellow aviators
down the approach, confining his communications to a minimum if the pilot
is doing it right. If he isn't, the LSO will
signal corrections to the pilot, and / or
talk him down with "candy calls" until
he makes the necessary adjustments.
If he fails to properly correct, the LSO
will give him a wave-off, a signal which
must be obeyed, sending him around to
rejoin the pattern and try again.

In the U.S. fleet today, the Carrier
Air Traffic Control Center (CATCC)
guides returning aircraft to the carrier
control area around the ship. When
planes return from missions and
adverse weather obviates a safe visual
approach to the ship, the CATCC
controls their arrival. It clears each
aircraft for approach at one-minute
intervals. The landing signal officer
then comes into play, helping the
pilot in his or her final approach to
a landing. A seasoned naval aviator
and carrier pilot, the LSO has been
thoroughly evaluated and well trained
at Landing Signal Officer school and
on board ship. The LSO is an expert
naval aviator who must bring sen-
sitivity, the wisdom of experience,

and exceptionally good judgement
to the job. He or she performs this
vital function using state-of-the-art
equipment from a platform area adjacent to the landing area, on the aft
port side of the carrier. In this prime
viewing spot the LSO, assistants, and
LSOs in training, monitor wind and
weather conditions, characteristics of
the operating aircraft, and the motion
of the deck. They must also take into
account the experience level of each
approaching pilot in turn.

In ordinary visual flying conditions,
carrier aircraft return from their missions and may be positioned in a
"marshal stack." When this happens,
flight leaders take their interval on
flights at lower altitude levels in the
stack. The actual landing procedure
begins as either two- or four-plane
formations enter the break for landing, astern of the carrier, on the same
heading and to the starboard side
at an 800-foot altitude. As the flight
leader reaches a projected point
ahead of the ship, he will break left
and align his airplane on a downwind
leg while descending to 600 feet and
completing his landing checklist. On
the final approach leg he will rely on
the carrier's automatic gyrostabilized
Fresnel lens optical landing system—
an arrangement of lenses and lights
positioned off the port edge of the
angled deck. If the carrier is rolling
and pitching beyond the limits of the
gyrostabilization capability, or if the
Fresnel lens system should fail, a manual optical-visual landing aid system
(MOVLAS) can be quickly set up for
use. When the weather cooperates
and conditions for aircraft recovery
are reasonably good, the LSO operates "zip-lip": without radio communication.

"On his final approach to the deck,
the pilot is flying at between 120 and
150 knots, depending on the type of

aircraft. To use the Fresnel system, he must first locate the array of lights and focus on the amber light or "meatball" in the center of the mirrored lenses. If he has properly aligned his aircraft on the glide slope, he will see the "ball" aligned with a horizontal line of green reference lights on either side of the center lens. If his aircraft is too high (above the glide slope), the ball will appear in one of the lenses above the center lens; if the aircraft is too low, the ball will show on one of the lower lenses. An optimal carrier landing requires that the pilot visually keep the ball centered all the way down the glide slope to touchdown on the deck, and then engage the "number three wire", the third of four heavy cables which are stretched across the aft area of the flight deck from just ahead of the ramp or rounded aft end of the deck. It is the pilot's responsibility to "fly the ball." The LSO can and does help him down with light signals and / or voice instructions.

When a pilot has flown his plane to a point roughly three quarters of a mile from the carrier in the final approach to the deck, the ship's air traffic control center delegates control of the aircraft to the LSO. The LSO and his half-dozen or so assistants, many with binoculars trained on the incoming plane, check first to be sure that its landing gear and flaps are in the proper down position, that the plane is lined up on the centerline of the flight deck, that its wings are level, and that it appears to be descending at the correct rate to catch one of the four arresting wires when it slams onto the deck.

Bringing a hot and heavy beast like an F/A-18 Hornet aboard a carrier is a precise and demanding task, with little margin for error. The pilot must establish his plane's position and attitude on the glide slope and then fly it down the slope at an exact three-and-a-half degree angle. If, when he arrives over the ramp, he has flown the slope perfectly, his tailhook will cross the ramp fourteen feet above it. If he is more than a few feet too high, his hook will miss the arresting wires, or bounce over them, for what is known as a "bolter." Procedure requires Navy pilots to shove the throttle (or throttles in multi-engine aircraft) to full power the instant the airplane contacts the flight deck. When the plane's tailhook catches an arresting wire, bringing it to an abrupt halt, the pilot immediately retards the throttle, the plane is allowed to roll back a few feet so the tailhook is disengaged from the wire, the hook is raised, and the aircraft is guided away from the active landing area. The arresting gear is then reset for the next approaching plane. Should a pilot experience a bolter and his tailhook fail to catch an arresting wire, his engine is at full-power so he can get airborne and go around for another landing attempt. With every approach, the LSO and his back-up each hold an up-raised "pickle" switch which either of them can use to activate flashing red lights on the Fresnel array, signalling a wave-off to the pilot. The wave-off is not optional.

LSOs grade every landing approach to a carrier. They use a trend analysis form to chart the ongoing record of every pilot's performance. When all landings in a flight operation have been completed, members of the LSO team visit the pilots who have just landed to discuss their grades for the task. Few things in the life of a carrier aviator are more important than these grades. If he cannot consistently and safely bring his airplane aboard the ship, the pilot is all but worthless to the Navy and will be sent to the beach. The grade given by an LSO for a landing approach is nearly always final and not subject to appeal. The grades given range from OK: a good approach with no problems; to FAIR: a performance with slight deviation from the correct approach; to NO GRADE: unacceptable deviation from the correct approach; to WAVE-OFF: the approach was too far from correct, was unsafe and had to be aborted; to BOLTER: try again.

Competition among pilots for good grades is naturally high. When a pilot has done everything well and made a good approach, his tailhook should catch either the number two or number three wire. If the approach was a little high or fast, he may catch the number four wire; if a bit low or slow he may get the number one. Both numbers one and four are less safe than two and three—three being the most desirable.

One of the most dangerous things a human being can do is a "night trap": landing on a carrier at night. Nothing a pilot must do requires greater skill, is more demanding and genuinely frightening. Poor performance in carrier night landings is the biggest cause of naval aviators losing their wings, and some pilots say that even after hundreds of night carrier landings, they never get easier. Some feel that the more night landings they do, the more nervous and uneasy they are about them. "Doing a night trap concentrates the mind wonderfully," comments one F/A-18 pilot. It is the lack of visual cues that creates the problem for pilots on night traps. Landing at night on an airfield offers a whole range of vital cues with which a pilot can judge how he is doing in his approach. Nighttime at sea is black on black. Often there is no horizon, making the experience even more disorienting. Setting up a

Responsible for all flight activity aboard the carrier USS *Coral Sea* in the summer of 1974, the Air Boss shoulders a heavy burden.

Every carrier landing of every naval aviator throughout his or her entire service career is evaluated and graded by landing signal officers; far right: LSO Bob Croman suffered a tragic accident when struck by an errant F8F Bearcat fighter during a landing attempt.

proper approach can be a genuine waking nightmare. However, many people believe that a little fear (in combination with intelligence and a high degree of capability) in such a demanding situation, can be a good thing. It keeps you sharp, focused.

When carrier-based planes have to come to the boat in foul weather, there is a wide spectrum of electronic aids ready to assist them on modern U.S. carriers, from the instrument landing system (ILS), to the tactical air navigation system (TACAN), to the carrier controlled approach (CCA), to the automatic carrier landing system (ACLS). The latter is capable of bringing a plane to touchdown when the pilot has no visual contact with the ship, much less the flight deck. In ACLS, a precise guidance radar on the ship locks on to the automatic pilot in the plane when it is eight miles out from the carrier. Computers on the carrier and in the plane feed position updates to each other and the ACLS sends signals to the plane's autopilot which establishes the approach. With this method, the autopilot can fly the plane to a safe landing on the carrier without the pilot ever having to touch the stick.

On 1 May 1945 several U.S. Marine F4U Corsairs were operating from Kadena Airfield on the island of Okinawa in support of troops there. The carrier USS *Yorktown* received a "May Day" distress call from three patrolling Corsairs that had been blown off course and out to sea by unusual 100-mph winds. The fighter pilots were dangerously low on fuel when they called for help. When the carrier answered their call the Marines reported that none of them had ever landed aboard a carrier before. "Do you have tailhooks?" asked the *Yorktown* officer. "We'll see . . . Yes,"

replied one of the Marine pilots. The carrier's Air Boss then obtained permission from the ship's captain to let the Marines try to land aboard. Crash Two, the secondary landing signal officer, got on the LSO platform and talked the Marines into the landing pattern and up the groove, while the primary LSO, Crash One, signalled them with his paddles. All three pilots landed aboard safely and, as one of them climbed out of his cockpit, he remarked to one of the airplane handlers, "What was that man doing with those paddles back there?" "Brother, he's the landing signal officer and he was giving you a wave-off!"

Robert Croman was an SBD Dauntless dive-bomber pilot in the South Pacific during the Second

World War. In March 1944 he was ordered back to the U.S. to attend Landing Signal Officer school. After graduating, Croman was assigned to Carrier Air Group 19, which was to be the first U.S. Navy unit to fly the Grumman F8F Bearcat fighter.

A heavy fog had suddenly materialized at the U.S. Navy airfield near Santa Rosa, California, and visibility there was less than half a mile. It was 18 July 1945. Bob Croman was LSO for CAG 19 which was practicing field carrier landings for the first time with their new Grumman Bearcats. The pilots of the group were discovering the new plane to be both extremely powerful and utterly unforgiving. Croman was in his position at the end of the runway and with him were an assistant LSO, an ambulance, and its crew.

The hot little Bearcat, with its big Pratt & Whitney engine and enormous propeller, developed a lot of torque. A pilot had to keep "ahead" of the machine or it would get away from him. The first three planes did well and Croman gave them each a "cut" signal to land. The next pilot, though, was clearly losing control of his plane in the approach, coming in too slowly. The LSO gave him the "slow" signal but the Bearcat continued lower and slower in the descent. At that point Croman tried desperately to get the errant pilot back on track, as the fighter roared toward him. The pilot added power, but too late. Torque pulled the plane to the left, toward where the LSO stood. It hit the runway hard, collapsing the left wing and landing gear and twisting the big propeller.

Had this happened aboard a carrier, Bob Croman might have been able to throw himself into the safety net adjacent to the LSO platform. But on this airfield there was no escape for him. The Bearcat slid, screeching toward him; he dove at the area beneath the plane's right wing and felt a heavy thud. He was lying on his stomach, dazed and unable to move. It seemed to him that he had lain there a very long time. The wrecked plane had continued down the runway after hitting him. The pilot got out of it without so much as a scratch.

Croman had been flung like a rag doll on impact with the Bearcat. He lay contorted, with his right leg mangled. The leg was bleeding profusely and he clearly needed urgent treatment. Those at the scene rushed to help him. One person applied a tourniquet and removed Bob's jacket. A medic gave the LSO a shot of morphine. Oddly, to that point Croman had felt no significant pain. The pain arrived and was unbearable. He recalled, "I knew I was not dead. You

can't hurt that bad and be dead."

The doctors at the Santa Rosa base dispensary could do little to help apart from stabilizing Croman. His leg was nearly severed six inches from the ankle, attached only by bits of flesh. Croman was flown to the Oakland Naval Hospital and rushed to an operating room. He lay there, awaiting help from a doctor when the doors opened and in came a Dr. McRae, the same doctor that Croman had met and become friendly with fifteen months earlier in the South Pacific. McRae took charge of the situation and reattached Croman's leg in a surgical procedure lasting more than eight hours.

Bob Croman underwent sixteen additional operations on his leg during the five years after the tragic accident. Both his Navy and flying careers were ended. But, despite the fact that his leg had atrophied preventing the movement of his ankle, he was extremely grateful to the Navy for the treatment he received, and especially thankful to Dr. McRae who somehow arrived at that critical moment.

"A safety net, perhaps ten feet wide, was placed a few feet below and abaft of the LSO. From 'Vulture's Row' I watched LSO Bert Harden signal a plane to take a wave-off because the aircraft was too slow. The airplane responded slowly, and headed directly for Bert, who dived for the safety net. He jumped so vigorously that he completely missed the net and made a perfect swan dive into the sea sixty-five feet below. The destroyer behind *Enterprise* picked him up unharmed."
—Jack Kleiss, former U.S. Navy pilot

Frank Furbish, former U.S. Navy fighter pilot: "The threat is as much the boat as the enemy. Carrier aviation is a very unforgiving occupation. Lives are lost and careers destroyed due

Nicknamed "Paddles," this World War Two landing signal officer is at work guiding a naval aviator to a safe landing aboard their carrier in the Pacific.

to the specialized skill required to land on the boat. There are many excellent pilots who can fly a fighter with incredible skill but can't land on the boat. And the opposite. One study of experienced carrier pilots who had been hooked up to sensors, showed that their heart rates and respiration were actually higher when landing on the ship than in combat. Daytime carrier landings are generally not too difficult if the seas are calm and the weather is tolerable. Night carrier landings are always challenging. Operating on the ship at night is not a soothing experience. It requires complete and total concentration along with a good measure of confidence. Night take-offs and landings during poor weather with a pitching deck and blue water ops with no divert are the ultimate tests of aviation skill. I would question the credibility and sanity of anyone who claimed to be relaxed during night traps.

"Your first carrier landing is an experience you never forget. In my case, the training carrier at the time was the USS *Lexington*, an old World War Two-era small deck carrier that was based at Pensacola, Florida.

"We had a very early brief around 0530. The night before, we had all tried to get to bed early in order to be rested for the day. My roommate was asleep in about fifteen minutes and began a loud and continuous snore. I couldn't relax and got just two hours sleep. When we reported to the brief, the flights were delayed for hours, but we had to 'stand by.' It was going to be a long day.

"Your first carrier landing is solo. An instructor pilot takes out three students on his wing and drops them off in the 'break.' The break is a maneuver that starts parallel to the ship on the starboard side at 800

feet. Once past the bow a hard level turn and descent to 600 feet for the downwind. At this point you are slowing the aircraft and configuring for landing, speed brakes, gear, flaps, and hook. Spacing is critical, not only on the ship, but relative to the aircraft ahead of you. The Air Boss wants forty-five second intervals for landing. The speed in the break is usually around 350 knots. You are on your own from there until you finish your qual. Your first two passes are touch-and-gos. The intent is to put young pilots at ease, knowing they did not have to trap on those first two. We considered it 'practice bleeding.'

"When naval aviators are asked what it is like to land on a carrier, the most common response is that it is 'a cross between having sex and being in a train wreck.' Having accumulated nearly 300 traps, I would say that the day landings are closer to the sex, and the night landings are closer to the train wreck. There is a good reason why you only do day carrier landings prior to wings: retention. Night carrier landings are, without a doubt, the extreme test of aviation skills. All aspects of flight, glide slope, line-up, and angle of attack, must be right on. The hook clearance on the F-14 over the round-down is about fourteen feet. The line-up tolerance is just as critical. If your speed is fast, the hook won't catch (nose low, tail up) and if you are too slow, you risk an in-flight engagement, slamming the aircraft to the deck. Do this all at night, in weather, and with no diverts within a thousand miles, and you not only have a test of skill, but one of character.

"We practiced night after night on a specially lit runway. We used San Clemente Island, a good training site due to the lack of lights from a city or base, and the fact that there was a sixty-foot cliff just short of the

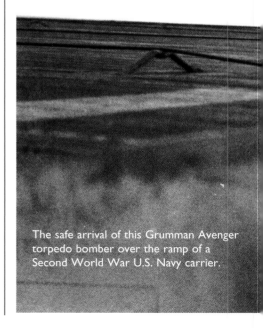

The safe arrival of this Grumman Avenger torpedo bomber over the ramp of a Second World War U.S. Navy carrier.

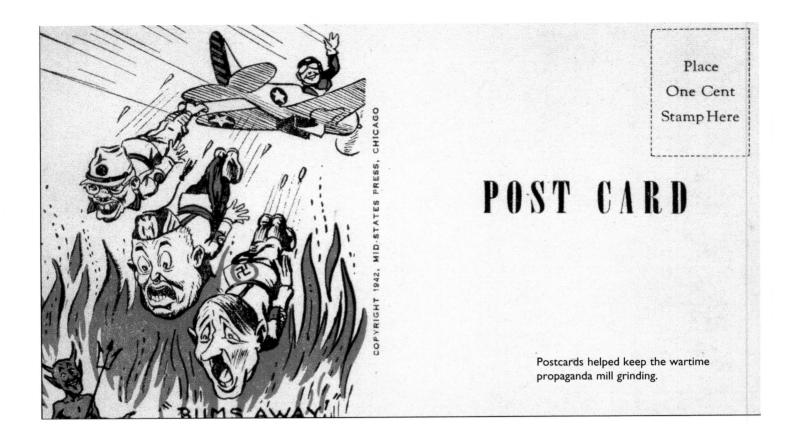

runway. 'Work-ups' didn't end after your initial qual, as landing on the boat is a fleeting skill. The need to stay 'current' is ongoing, and there are various safeguards in place to ensure that pilots stay 'in qual' once on the ship. These rules require day traps prior to night traps, and/or a divert field should a pilot go for more than seven or fourteen days without a carrier landing. While shore-based, we constantly went out of qual and had to work back up to a proficient level prior to deploying. This applied to pilots with 2,000 traps as well as to those with ten. It's not like riding a bike.

"During work-ups and refresher quals I was on the flight deck when a good friend's career came to an end. Bhudda and his RIO (Radar Intercept Officer backseater), Boog, were out on a refresher night qual during work-ups

for a cruise when he pulled off a little too much power for a little too long. The F-14 has a slow 'spool-up' time for the engines, and it was too little too late. He hit the round-down with the tail and the hook of the airplane. He continued down the deck and once again became airborne as I saw a large piece of the nettings steel support rattle by. The back of the plane was engulfed in flame and he was instructed to eject. Luckily, they both got out and were uninjured. They were picked up by the helo within minutes. Bhudda never made it back. He was given all the help he needed, but could never get past the fear of night traps and, eventually, quit the Navy. He had excelled for two years of arduous training, was one of the best in all phases of flight, and yet, due to one mistake, he never made it to the fleet.

"Tom 'Boog' Powell became my best friend during my time in the Navy. Initially, we didn't get along well on the cruise while sharing the junior officers' bunk room. Personalities sometimes clash when nine guys share a small room. Later, though, we did most everything together. We rode bikes, played golf, and went skiing every January while on shore. We even took our bikes on the boat, to ride while on port calls. Boog was a RIO. He had stayed in the Navy Reserves and continued to fly the F-14. He was flying a training mission and his pilot lost control of the plane. The pilot was unable to regain control and they were forced to eject. This was the second time Boog had had to eject, and he was killed when he hit the canopy on the way out. The pilot was uninjured. Carrier aviation is so

KEEP 'EM FLYING!

unforgiving. I miss him.

"Instrument flying is the key to carrier operations, and carrier pilots are the best instrument pilots in the world by necessity. There are no lights in the middle of the ocean, and when the skies are overcast or there is no moon, there is no horizon. More than one pilot has flown into the water at 300 knots, never realizing that he was disoriented. Due to the nature of their operations, Navy pilots must learn to handle vertigo and trust their instruments implicitly. Their lives depend on it.

"Better dead than look bad at the boat. A common phrase among naval aviators. Landing on the boat is what counts. It is a specific skill related to, but not dependent on, a pilot's abilities in other phases of flight. We had one F-14 pilot who would not

take his plane in the vertical during air combat maneuvering Obviously, his 'fighting' skills were preferable to those of a pilot who could outmaneuver the best fighter pilot, but who had trouble getting aboard the boat. Operating on the boat is what it's all about. Hardly anyone sees you shoot down your opponent, hit the bullseye, or fly perfect formation, but they all see you land on the boat. The pilot's, and more importantly, the squadron's reputation is always on the line. There is a camera system that shows a live TV view of the flight deck from several angles, including a camera mounted in the flight deck on the centerline. There are TVs in all of the ready rooms and throughout the ship for anyone to monitor. There is also a requirement for a squadron representative to be with the Air Boss during day ops, and

in PriFly at night, to answer any question that may be raised about a squadron mate's performance. Most of the questions are rhetorical and the red-faced squadron rep makes a logbook entry about which the pilot / guilty party must respond to later.

The hook found a wire, and the trap now led to another under-appreciated challenge: taxing on the flight deck. The interval between landings was typically about forty-five seconds, so it was essential to clean up and get out of the way quickly. Once your aircraft stopped, the cable pulled it back a few feet and released your hook, allowing it to be raised. At the same time, you are retracting the flaps, sweeping the wings, and looking for the signals of the taxi director yellow shirt. Taxiing on the flight deck can sometimes be uncomfortable if the deck has become slippery from oil, fuel, salt spray, etc. Combine a slippery deck with heavy seas and at times your airplane would slide. Usually there was the need to swing the nose out over the side of the deck in order to squeeze all of the aircraft onto the deck. Sitting seventy feet above the water as the deck pitches down, and feeling the wheels bump the scupper, made for a very uneasy feeling. Once out of the airplane, I usually sought the quickest route to the 03 level, just below the flight deck and out of harm's way. The flight deck is a very unsafe place to work. More than one unsuspecting sailor has walked directly into a whirling propeller or been sucked down the intake of a jet. The noise level is so high that you often can't tell where the threat lies."

Alan Leahy, former Royal Navy fighter pilot: "On 10 September 1952, while embarked in HMS *Glory* in the Mediterranean, I was briefed to carry out a take-off using Rocket Assisted Take-Off Gear (RATOG). The brief required the pilot to carry out a full-power take-off firing the RATOG at a specific point in the take-off run. The brief then said that if the RATOG did not fire, there would be room to throttle back and brake to a stop before reaching the bow. The brief should have said, there would be nearly room . . .

"When I pressed the button to fire the RATOG, it didn't. I throttled back and tried to brake to a stop. I did not stop and instead went over the bow at a walking pace.

"Eyes shut, eyes open just as quickly, to find the cockpit full of water and bubbles just the way it was in the USN 'Dilbert Dunker' ditching trainer eight years before. Unstrapping my seat harness and parachute har-

ness, I tried to stand up and clear the cockpit. As I stood up, two spigots in the cockpit canopy, designed to slot into holes on the windscreen, caught the back of my Mae West and I was unable to clear the cockpit because of the water pressure caused by the rate of sink of the aircraft. I had to get back into the cockpit and turn round so that I could get out by covering the spigots with my hands and force myself clear. Once clear I saw the aircraft turn onto its back as it continued to sink on down, but there was no sign of the ship or its propellers, which frightened me somewhat. My first idea was to stay down until the ship passed over me, but then I realized that if I stayed any longer where I was, I would probably drown.

"I was then confused as to which way was up, but that was cleared by inflating my Mae West. I tried to swim up and away from where I thought the side of the ship was. I surfaced about ten yards clear of the ship's side, abeam of the starboard propeller. I immediately took a deep breath and choked as I still had my oxygen mask on and the oxygen tube was under water.

"After unclipping my mask I noticed that my dinghy was still clipped to my backside. It was a work of moments to unclip the dinghy, inflate it, and clamber in. After that, all I had to do was sit there in relative comfort and wait for the seaboat from the plane guard destroyer to come and rescue me."

The following incident occurred on the USS *Constellation* (CVA-64). An F/A-18 pilot, call sign "Oyster," was launched from Cat 1 and fodded (foreign object damage) both of his engines. Most people witnessing the launch thought that the pilot had ejected, but quickly realized that he was still in the plane. Somehow, he

managed to get the Hornet level at about eighty feet and then gradually milk it up to 150 feet. It was 8:45 pm and there were scattered clouds with a ceiling between 1,000 and 1,500 feet. It was quite dark.

One of the Hornet's engines had failed completely, while the other was having massive compressor stalls which were obvious to personnel on the carrier, even at a distance of six miles. The pilot was maintaining his minimal altitude through the use of full afterburner on the one remaining engine, with his landing gear up. He jettisoned his weapons stores and dumped his fuel down to a level of 4.0 in order to maintain level flight. He was unable to climb to 3,000 feet in order to do a wave-off/approach capability check. However, the flight deck was ready to recover him, and the ship decided to let him attempt a normal pass. He began to line up for it, and immediately decided that he could not make it successfully. He came up along the starboard side of the ship, and again, it appeared that he was going to eject. An incredible amount of debris was coming out of the right engine of the Hornet, and by this time the pilot had run his remaining fuel down to near zero. It seemed that he would be able to adequately slow his rate of descent once he began to approach to the carrier, but he clearly would have no bolter capability, and it was decided to erect the net straps barricade to stop his aircraft if necessary. The barricade was rigged quickly, and the LSO platform was cleared except for the landing signal officer and his back-up.

The F/A-18 was high in the approach and, by the time it had begun to correct down, the pilot was getting too far out of the parameters and the LSOs had to "pickle" him (signal a red-light wave-off). The Hornet staggered past the ship, its one engine making a sickening whine and pop as it emitted a salvo of flare-like matter from the tail cone. Clearing the top of the barricade by less than fifteen feet, the plane was now down to .8 on fuel. The pilot was able to climb to just 600 feet for his last approach and the LSO talked to him continuously as he intercepted the glide path at one mile out from the ship. The LSO told the pilot to go ahead and sacrifice a few knots of air speed if necessary, to keep the airplane on the glide slope, as the ship had plenty of natural wind over the deck.

The pilot was having trouble keeping the Hornet aligned in the approach, and drifted left a bit, and then was a little low, but, as the plane neared the ramp, the LSO felt that the pilot was going to clear the round-down, and gave him the cut to land. The plane slammed onto the deck about twenty feet beyond the round-down and went on to engage the barricade on centerline. It was an emotional moment on the LSO platform and around the carrier, with great cheers erupting on the flight deck as Oyster popped the Hornet canopy and emerged safely. His airmanship, guts, and determination in saving his airplane had been heroic.

"The small group of pilots who make up the LSO team must be in constant sync with each other to be certain that the controlling LSO is kept aware of the condition of the flight deck, clear or fouled. Safety is always the primary consideration in all flight deck operations.
The ingenuity on the boat was at

times entertaining. We had an F-14 that lost its snubber pressure. That is a nitrogen pre-charge that puts down pressure on the hook to prevent it from bouncing back up after it hits the deck. 'Mullet,' the pilot, made several passes and on each attempt, the hook skipped over the wires (a bolter).

Then a chief appeared with several rolls of toilet paper which he positioned under the number three wire to raise it higher off the deck. On the next pass, Mullet was aboard."
—Frank Furbish, former U.S. Navy fighter pilot

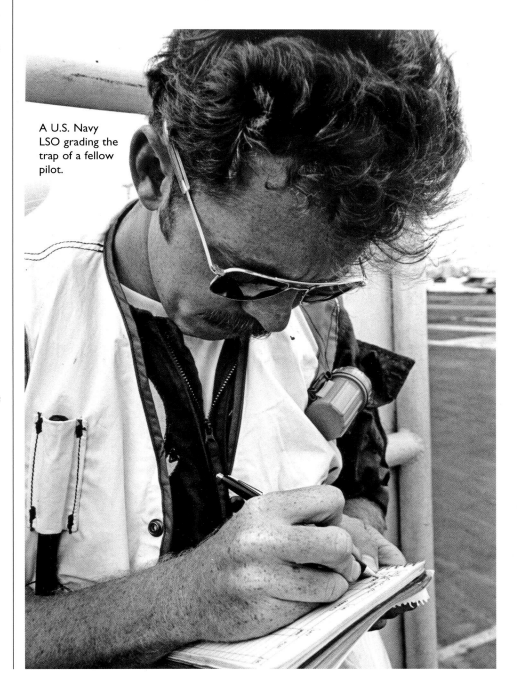

A U.S. Navy LSO grading the trap of a fellow pilot.

A Royal Navy Sea Harrier arriving back aboard the carrier, HMS *Illustrious*.

NAM

An LTV A-7 Corsair II about to be launched from the flight deck of the USS *Lexington*.

REAR ADMIRAL PAUL GILLCRIST, U.S. NAVY (Retired), was Commander Gillcrist in the spring of 1968 when he was flying F-8 Crusaders from the USS Bon Homme Richard (CVA-31) with VF-53: "How could I ever forget him? He did a very courageous thing . . . putting himself in great jeopardy . . . and for me . . . and he did it with such casual grace that, contemplating it now, all these years later, still makes my throat constrict.

"It was a rather pleasant spring day . . . sunny skies, balmy breeze, blue sea and a bluer cloudless heaven. What more could a carrier pilot ask? Then, of course, there were those God-damned sea snakes. As I walked forward on the flight deck towards my airplane, I looked over the starboard catwalk at the surface of the Tonkin Gulf. It almost made me sick. As far as the eye could see there were hundreds of thousands of sea snakes sinuating through the water in clusters of a dozen or so. They ranged in size from about two feet to five feet. Of a yellowish-green color, they swam just below the surface of the water with only their heads sticking out. Our intelligence officer had briefed us on them before we arrived in the Gulf for the first time and told us they were the most poisonous reptiles on the planet. The thought of parachuting into the water filled with thouse hideous things made my stomach turn.

"Our flight headed in-bound to a highly-defended target in the Hanoi area of North Vietnam. The mission was photographic reconnaissance to assess the damage that had been done by a strike just thirty minutes earlier. Since it was such a highly-defended target, I made the decision to go in as photo escort armed with four vice-two Sidewinder air-to-air missiles. Our normal load-out

was two of the deadly missiles, one each mounted on a single pylon on either side of the airplane's fuselage just aft of the cockpit. The reason for this was aircraft weight. Our tired old F-8E Crusaders had grown in weight over the years from structural beef-ups to the addition of electronic warfare equipment and deceptive electronic-countermeasures devices. The weight had become a problem, since each additional pound of gear meant one pound of fuel less with which we were allowed to land back aboard ship.

"At first it didn't seem to matter much . . . nothing more than a minor operational restriction with which we had to abide. But gradually, as the airplane's empty weight increased, we began to realize that our number of landing opportunities was decreasing by one for every 200 pounds increase in empty. At night a landing used up three times as much fuel. So, for every 600 pounds increase in the empty weight of the airplane, one less attempt to land was imposed.

"Back in the Pentagon in 1974, I did a study for my own personal interest. Using the A-4, F-8, F-4, and A-7 as examples, I found that, on average, a Navy tactical carrier airplane grew in empty weight at the rate of one pound per day of operational life. The accuracy of that rule of thumb was startling.

"So it was with careful consideration that I opted for the four-missile configuration because, after all, we were going into MiG country. Who knows? I might need the extra two Sidewinders. As was the standard practice, the photo pilot, flying an RF-8, took the flight lead. I was his escort and his protection should the North Vietnamese decide to send out their MiGs after him. We 'coasted in' about twenty miles south of Haiphong, going

A McDonnell Douglas F-4 Phantom

at 'the speed of heat' as usual, and I found that, because of the drag associated with the extra missiles, I was using a lot more afterburner than the photo plane.

"The target, which was a railroad bridge between Haiphong and the capital city of Hanoi, was heavily defended . . . we already knew that. Nevertheless, the quantity of flak was startling as it always is. They were waiting for us, knowing that it was U.S. policy to get bomb damage assessment after each major raid. I was flying a loose wing on the photo plane, scanning the area for MiGs, of course, but also for flak because I knew that Ed would soon have to bury his head in his photo display shroud for the final few seconds of the run to be sure that the bridge span was properly framed in the camera's field of view. Neither he nor I wanted to mess this run up and have to come back another time. That would be too much. During the actual picture-taking part of the run, when the photo pilot was too occupied to observe flak, I made it a habit to be in a strafing run at the most likely source of flak in the vicinity of the target. It always made me feel better, since just sitting there being shot at is always unpleasant and unnerving.

"Just as Ed settled down for the photo portion of the mission, which took an eternity of about five seconds, I heard a low SAM (surface-to-air missile) warble (radar lock-on), followed immediately by a high warble (SAM launch) and my heartbeat tripled in an instant. I was on Ed's left flank and saw the SAM lift off at about four o'clock and only maybe ten miles away. There was a huge cloud of dust around the base of the missile as it lifted off and levelled almost immediately as it accelerated towards us. There was nothing I could do but call

it out knowing that Ed would have to break off his run at the very last minute. I think the North Vietnamese knew precisely what they were doing. There was no way Ed could stay in his run because the missile was accelerating towards his tail at a startling rate. My mouth was dry as I keyed the microphone.

" 'One from Two. SAM lift-off at four o'clock, ten miles. Break hard right, now!' Ed broke and I did the same, feeling the instant onset of at least nine g's squeezing the g-suit bladders on my legs and abdomen. The SAM roared on by us just as another high warble came on in my headset. This one I didn't see and that really bothered me. 'No joy on the second one,' I shouted into the mike. 'Keep it coming right, Two.' Then I saw it and it scared me badly since it was now off my left wing and coming at us fast. 'Reverse it left and down,' I shouted hoarsely over the radio. Watching it pass to our left and explode about 200 yards away, I saw that we were skimming the treetops and called out to Ed: 'Two, let's get out of here!' I heard two distinct clicks of a microphone and knew that Ed agreed with me. The water was only a few miles away by this time and we were headed straight towards it. The two Crusaders thundered across the beach at perhaps 100 feet in full afterburner and doing in excess of 600 knots.

"About ten miles off the beach, when we knew we were outside the SAM and flak envelopes, we came out of burner and commenced a climb. Ed's voice came over the radio sounding apologetic and sheepish. 'Two from One. I missed it.' We both felt badly. Bomb damage assessment of the bridge from the previous strike (half an hour earlier) was important and we both knew it. Another strike would be launched within the hour

U.S. Navy helicopter crew members aboard their carrier off the Vietnam coast.

to go after it if the bridge span was still standing. As we passed to the seaward side of the northern SAR destroyer, I suggested that we report in to the ship's strike operation center and ask them what they wanted us to do—although I was already fairly sure what the answer would be. We orbited at 15,000 feet over the Gulf as Ed checked in and reported failure, and asked for directions since the strike seemed important to them. Panther Strike told us to wait while they checked with Task Force 77 for further directions. As suspected, after waiting for what seemed like an eternity, they told us to go back and try again. After the photo run had been completed we were directed to return to the ship as fast as we could so that the results could be analyzed and another strike launched if

necessary. At my urging, Ed requested that an airborne tanker be made available for us upon our going feet wet. And they were waiting for us.

"Ed made a similar approach, using a different ingress route, and this time, flak and a SAM warning notwithstanding, we got the pictures. We both overflew the bridge in excess of 600 knots and made the turn towards the Gulf via a pre-planned route that ran on a southerly heading just west of Haiphong and then almost due east to the water over a relatively unpopulated area. Just as we approached the target my low-fuel warning light illuminated and it shocked me. Nonetheless, we continued our egress from the target area as planned and went feet wet low and at high speed.

"I was elated because I was sure it was a successful photo run and

neither of us had been hit. This time there hadn't even been any SAMs launched, just a radar lock-on. Ed had plenty of fuel remaining and began his climb at full power with the intent of hurrying back to Panther. I kissed him off and, looking at a fuel gauge which read only 400 pounds, I headed for a rendezvous with the tanker who had dropped down to 10,000 feet twenty miles southwest of the northern SAR destroyer. My mouth was dry as I began my rendezvous with the tanker. With only 400 pounds of fuel my engine would flame out in just fifteen minutes. This was, I thought ruefully, cutting it too God-damned close. The tanker had been refuelling some A-4s in the air wing and been vectored to the northern SAR destroyer by the ship when we asked for a tanker before going back in for the second run.

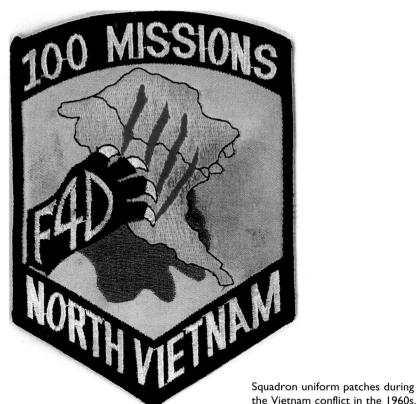

Squadron uniform patches during the Vietnam conflict in the 1960s.

"Naturally, I was extremely happy to see the tanker and was equally anxious to get plugged in. When I told the tanker pilot my fuel state, his voice suddenly sounded a little strange. He was extremely apologetic and explained to me that he had just given away all of the fuel in his buddy store. I was shocked. How could this have happened? Somebody back at the ship had really screwed up by failing to tell him to hold at least 1,500 pounds for me. A cold chill crept over me. There was no way I could get even half way back to the ship with only 400 pounds of fuel.

"It is worth spending a few words of explanation on fuel and what it means to a carrier pilot. In any fleet squadron there is standard operating procedure which dictates landing back aboard a ship with a reasonable fuel reserve to take care of emergencies like a crash on deck, bad weather, malfunctioning recovery systems, or a recovery delay for any of a dozen other reasons. For example, the low-fuel level warning light comes on in the cockpit of an F-8 Crusader at 1,100 pounds remaining. No carrier pilot who wants a long, safe career should ever be caught airborne with that light illuminated. There is a similar light in the A-4 which comes on at about 1,100 pounds. So to find one-self 125 nautical miles from the ship in a Crusader with 400 pounds of fuel is not just critical . . . it is way past crit-ical . . . the stuff of which nightmares are made.

"By now we had joined up and were climbing to cruise altitude for our return to the ship . . . except I was not going to make it. It was a strange feeling . . . one of finality. It was all unreal. And again I thought of those sea snakes. We levelled off at 20,000 feet, and with my fuel gauge now reading 100 pounds I began to prepare myself for ejec-tion. We were flying close together. The lower my fuel reading the clos-er I flew to him. Perhaps proximity to a friendly face made me feel comforted.

"The A-4 tanker pilot throttled way back to match a maximum endurance profile for the Crusader. Since getting back to the ship was out of the question, we were buying some time before I flamed out . . . just a few more minutes . . . but every minute now seemed very precious. The tanker pilot's head, which was only fifty feet away from mine, turned to look at me for what seemed a long time but was probably only twenty seconds. Then I saw him look down in the cockpit. A moment later the propeller on the nose of his tanker buddy store began to windmill in the airstream. This was the driving mechanism which reeled the refuelling basket in and out.

"The buddy store consisted of a fuel tank, a refuelling hose, a take-up reel and an air-driven propeller to deploy and retract the basket. The fuel tank contained 300 gallons (2000 pounds of fuel) when full. The tanker pilot also had the capability of trans-ferring fuel into and out of the tank from his own internal tanks. It was the tanker pilot's responsibility always to retain enough internal fuel to get back safely to the ship. I found it curious that the propeller was turning and then was startled to see the refuelling basket reel out to its full extension. The pilot then looked over at me and transmitted over the radio.

" 'Firefighter Two Zero Four. I have just transferred 500 pounds of fuel into the buddy store. Go get it.' I couldn't believe my ears.

" 'What about you?' I asked, almost afraid to do so.

" 'You'd better take while you can,' he warned ominously, as though he were already having second thoughts. I slid back into position and prepared to tank. Never was my tanking skill so necessary as this moment. There could be no missed attempts. My last glance at the fuel gauge showed 100 pounds. I resolved not to look at it again. The sight made me physically ill.

"The in-flight refuelling probe on a Crusader is high on the port side of the fuselage just aft of the pilot. In actual measurements the tip of the probe is exactly thirty-one inches to the left of the pilot's eye. Therefore the inner rim of the refuelling basket, when the probe is centered in it,

is only about a foot away from the canopy. The basket seems to float around like some wayward, feathery entity whenever one tries to engage it with the probe. In actual fact, the basket, for all its airy movements, is in the tight grasp of a 250-knot gale. The airstream grips it like a vice. Thus it has all the resiliency of a steel rail. If it so much as touches the canopy of a Crusader, the result is an instant and violent implosion and fragmenta-tion of the plexiglas into a thousand tiny shards which end up everywhere inside the cockpit. To say that tanking is a touchy evolution is the under-statement of the year.

"Needless to say, my technique on this particular tanking attempt was flawless and the tip of the probe hit the basket in its dead center with a 'clunk' which resulted in a small sine wave travelling up the hose to the end of the buddy store. It is a com-forting sound and sensation which one can feel in his pants and right hand. It is the next best thing to sex.

"The very act of tanking, of course, uses fuel. It therefore took me about 100 pounds to get the 500 pounds, which left me with a net gain of 400 pounds. Now my fuel gauge read a much more comfortable 500 pounds, leaving me feeling in 'hog heaven.' I disengaged and slid once more out to the right side of the tanker. We looked at each other and there was an unspoken understanding in the tilt of the tanker pilot's head that he had bought me some time . . . perhaps only fifteen minutes, but a very pre-cious increment of life nonetheless. Experiencing no small amount of guilt, I felt compelled to ask him the obvi-ous question.

" 'Can you make it back?' The answer was delayed.

" 'I'm not sure,' he said, but quickly added, 'There's another tanker up

here somewhere. Maybe he's got a few pounds to give.' The tanker pilot then inquired of the ship about the tanker that had been sent north to tank the BARCAP (barrier combat air patrol). The ship came back quickly and informed us that he was indeed returning at maximum speed to ren-dezvous with us. The voice which told

Randy Cunningham and Willy Driscoll were the last two U.S. Navy aviators to achieve 'ace' status in the Vietnam War. Their aircraft was the McDonnell Douglas F-4 Phantom.

us that was more mature and sounded more senior. I suspected immediately that, recognizing that they had screwed up royally, they had put the first team on the problem. On a carrier at sea, everyone is in training for the next higher notch on the ladder.

"We droned along, still at maximum endurance speed, watching our fuel gauges and the distance-measuring device on the TACAN display. It was really simple mathematics, the kind naval aviators learn to do quickly in their heads. My fuel flow gauge told me the engine was burning fuel at the rate of 2,400 pounds per hour (divided by sixty converts to forty pounds per minute). My airspeed indicator told me my speed was 300 knots. Indicated airspeed decreases as altitude increases at the rate of two percent per thousand feet. Therefore, at my altitude of 20,000 feet my true airspeed would actually be forty percent higher than what my airspeed indicator read. Forty percent of 300 equals 120 which, when added to 300, equals 420 knots true airspeed. Divide 420 by sixty and it comes to seven miles per minute. If I am burning forty pounds per minute, then each mile I traverse through the air costs me six pounds of fuel. By cross-checking the distance-measuring equipment reading on my airspeed indicator telling me how far away the carrier is, I corroborate that my groundspeed is roughly what my true airspeed is, meaning little or no wind effect to worry about.

"But, no matter how often I run the numbers through my head, they told me that my airplane would flame out before I got to the ship. Again, I thought of those God-damned sea snakes. Our only hope was that the other tanker had some fuel left to give. Moments later a target appeared on the left side of my radar scope, thirty miles away and converging. A few moments later, my tanker pilot, who had eyes better than mine, called out somewhat excitedly, 'Tally Ho! The tanker, ten o'clock, fifteen miles.' The several minutes it took for us to complete the rendezvous seemed like forever, during which we were informed that there was 1,400 pounds of 'giveaway' fuel available. My tanker pilot said, 'Firefighter, you go first and take 800 pounds and I'll take 600, Okay?' What could I say? My fuel gauge again showed 300 pounds.

"Of course, the ship gave us priority in the landing sequence. We made a straight-in approach with the tanker taking interval on me at about ten miles astern. The sight of the ship steaming into the wind with a ready deck is one of the most beautiful sights in all of my memory. The LSOs seemed to understand our sense of urgency. We both caught the number two wire and taxied forward for shutdown. The arrestment felt great, the feel of the ship under my wheels

felt wonderful. The blast of warm air that filled my cockpit when I opened the canopy tasted like pure oxygen. Life was beautiful at that moment. As I climbed out of the cockpit I felt a sudden and enormous exhaustion. Then I took one last look at the fuel quantity gauge. It read 100 pounds.

"On the way from the airplane to the ready room I took a short detour to the edge of the flight deck and scanned the sea for the snakes. Strangely, there were none to be seen.

"Five minutes later, while finishing filling out the mainenance 'yellow sheet' in my ready room seat, I took a sip of steaming hot coffee and relished the moment. Then I got up, walked over to the duty officer's desk and pressed the lever on the 19MC squawk box. 'Ready room four, this is ready room two, Commander Gillcrist calling. Is the pilot of Four One Four there?' The answer was immediate. 'He's listening,' said a voice.

" 'Young man, you have cojones of brass. I owe you one.' The now-familiar voice of the tanker pilot came right back. 'No problem, skipper. Glad to be of help. I'll collect at the bar in Cubi.'

"I never got to pay off that debt. Three days later, that fine young man was literally blown out of the sky by a direct hit from an 85mm anti-aircraft shell.

"The three salvos from the Marine honor guards' rifles jolted me in much the same way that the violent 85mm explosion must have done when it ended that young man's life. For the first time in my life, as I stood at attention, saluting with the bugler playing taps, the tears coursed down my cheeks. The flight deck was heaving slowly in mute response to a gentle swell. Then the Marine honor guard tilted the catafalque up. The coffin slid out from under the American flag and fell into the sea."

Spread the table and contention will cease.
—English proverb

"Under the ladder to the flight deck, starboard side of the hangar deck, was the gedunk locker. Soft ice cream, candy bars, cigarettes, etc. Sea stores cigarettes were three to six cents a pack. While in flight quarters, we would elect one man to go below and get the gedunks, and hope he got back before we had to man the planes."
—Lynn Forshee, former U.S. Navy radio/gunner, USS *Yorktown*

NAVY PILOTS CALL IT A SLIDER. IT'S A burger, and a slider with cheese is probably the most popular order at the "dirty shirt" wardroom—the canteen on a carrier where pilots and Naval Flight Officers in their flight suits are always welcome.

Kevin Morris joined the Royal Navy in 1977. He went in as a Cook's Mate and made his way steadily through the ranks. He went from Cook to the training to be a Chef. From that he transferred to catering, moving away from the "craft side" to management, including accounting, budgeting, and stock management. In 1993 he attained the rank of Chief Caterer and was selected to go to Dartmouth to the Brittania Royal Naval College to take a commission. As an officer he held positions at the Navy's Cookery School where he was responsible for training cooks and stewards, and another shore position in which he managed contracts and camp catering. By October 1999, he had been aboard the aircraft carrier HMS *Illustrious* for a year, in charge of food services. His responsibilities included anything and everything to do with food, from the menus to hygiene standards, to making sure the ship had enough food on board at all times. He was concerned with anything to do with the galley, the store rooms, the ship's company eating areas, and the dining halls. Nothing to do with food aboard *Illustrious* escaped his attention.

Morris aboard *Illustrious* in 1999: "Several inputs go into the menu planning, including budgetary input. It's no good putting something on the counter that people don't like or won't eat. The menus are constructed on a weekly basis, and we run from a framework of six menus on a rotational basis. Each week we look at the menu that is next in the rotation and make minor adjustments relating to stock remaining on board that we need to turn over. We also look at the ship's program, where the ship is going to be in the world. We don't want to put on a hot, stodgy pudding if we're going to be in the tropics. We also have to consider what the ship is doing. We have to adjust our feeding methods to comply with the ship's program. If we are to be at action stations, we generally have action messing. If there is a RAS (replenishment at sea) going on, we have to look at the style of menu that we put on and the timings of meals because a lot of people can't come down for a meal at normal times. If, for instance, we are taking on fuel, there are a lot of people involved in special duties throughout the ship who have to remain at their duty station and may not be able to get down for a specific meal. We have to make provision to feed them wherever they are stationed, or extend the meal times so they can come through afterwards. After we have looked at the programming side, we try not to be repetitious in our meal planning. But when you are putting four hot choices on for lunch and four hot

SLIDERS

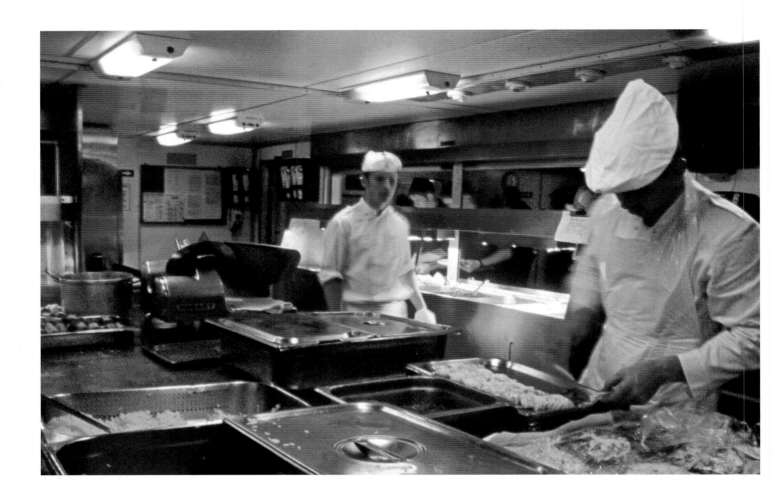

choices on for the evening—eight popular hot choices a day seven days a week—you quickly run out of popular choices. We have to make sure that a dish doesn't come around too often. We have to make the menus as varied as possible.

"Certain trends have been filtering through in recent years. There is a general move away from red meat consumption and towards fish and chicken. Vegetarianism is coming on in a whole range of forms. There are a number of tastes to take into account. We are also getting a lot of ethnic minorities coming through, which provides us with another challenge. Still, many of the dishes that we prepare and serve today are the same ones

that we were serving ten to fifteen years ago.

"The biggest thing on board is morale. Food and morale are very closely linked. You can have the best machines, the best equipment, the best ships, but if you can't feed people well, you're not going anywhere.

"One of my biggest jobs is to make sure we have enough food, and for 1,200 people, that is an awful lot of food, and you run out very quickly. Ideally, we need to replenish every two weeks. We go through sixty to seventy pallets of food a month.

"Certain items are very difficult to get outside of the UK. Sausages are very popular; everyone has them for breakfast, and you just can't get

them anywhere else. We just bought some in Amsterdam because we had run low, but they didn't go down well with the ship's company. It's one of those things."

Waldorf Salad
(yield: 100 portions)
Ingredients
3 tbsp. (¾ oz) milk, non-fat, dry
7/8 cup water, warm
½ cup lemon juice
¼ cup (2 oz) sugar, granulated
1 ¼ qt (2 lb 8 oz) salad dressing
3 qt (4 lb) celery, freshly diced ½ inch
1 qt (1 lb) walnuts, coarsely chopped
2 ½ gallons (9 lb) apples, fresh, eating, unpared, cored, diced, ⅓ inch
4 lb lettuce, fresh trimmed

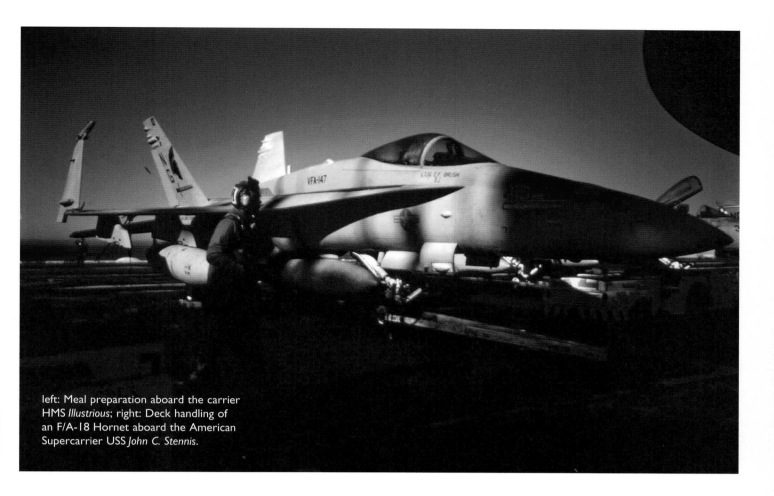

left: Meal preparation aboard the carrier HMS *Illustrious*; right: Deck handling of an F/A-18 Hornet aboard the American Supercarrier USS *John C. Stennis*.

Method
1. Trim, wash, and prepare fruit and vegetables.
2. Reconstitute milk.
3. Combine lemon juice, sugar, and salad dressing. Add to milk. Mix well.
4. Add celery, nuts, and apples to salad dressing mixture. Toss well to coat pieces.
5. Place one lettuce leaf on each serving dish, add salad. Cover, refrigerate until ready to serve.

Benny L. James was serving on the USS *Enterprise* in the autumn of 1944. "My brother came to visit me while we were riding at anchor in Ulithi in the hot Pacific. I was standing watch on gun mount number five when I heard my name called. I turned around and saw my older brother. We had not seen each other in three years. He was stationed on a destroyer, the USS *Halsey Powell*, which was anchored up in the north anchorage. He stayed all night and ate supper with me. We had a good visit and I showed him around the Big E. We talked most of the night and slept while on the gun mount. He was supposed to be back at his ship by 0800 hours. As the time approached for him to go, we could not find anyone who was going in that direction. We asked several coxswain if they would take him to the north anchorage, and they all responded in the same way—they wouldn't take him for a hundred bucks. I said that it was only fifteen minutes up there, and they said they wouldn't do it for two hundred dollars. Finally, in desperation I asked a boatswain mate if he would take a gallon of gedunk (ice cream) for making the trip. He looked at me hungrily and said: 'Make it two gallons and you're on.' I said I would throw in a pint of chocolate syrup and he about went nuts.

"When I went down to get the ice cream, the man who ran the freezer said that no one got any gedunk until after 1100 hours, and then only the flyers and officers. When I explained the situation he relented and slipped me a couple of gallons in a box and said not to tell anyone for at least thirty years. I said, for a pint of topping,

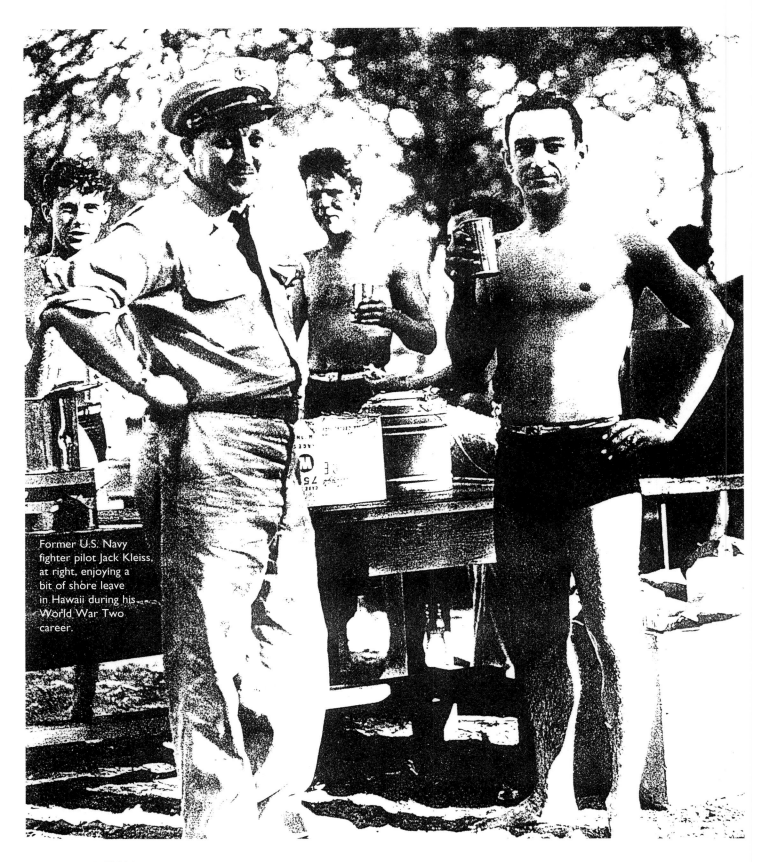

Former U.S. Navy fighter pilot Jack Kleiss, at right, enjoying a bit of shore leave in Hawaii during his World War Two career.

I would clam up for fifty years. When I got back up to the aft port crane they were ready to shove off—without my brother. When I finally got the boatswain mate's attention, and let him know what I had, he motioned my brother to come aboard, ice cream and all. The last I saw of them, they were dipping into the ice cream and heading north at full speed. I later got a letter saying my brother was only fifteen minutes late for muster."

Wardroom menu for dinner, HMS *Illustrious*, Wednesday, 16 June 1999

Crab and prawn salad with warm
　　vinagrette & French bread
Boeuf a la mode
Pork alentago
Vegetarian to order
Risilees potatoes
Macaire potatoes
Red cabbage with bacon
Roasted parsnips with almonds
Brandy crepes & whipped cream
Selection of cheeses and biscuits

HMS *Illustrious* General Mess menu for dinner, Monday, 7 June 1999

Baked gammon with cumberland
　　sauce
Chicken Maryland with sweetcorn
　　fritters
Lamb Madras with plain rice
Swiss cottage pie
Savoury vegetable stew
Roast and boiled potatoes
Straw Carrots, brussel sprouts,
　　creamed swede
Fruit pie with custard sauce
Selection of cold sweets

"Apart from flying, there were three big events of the day: breakfast, lunch, and dinner. Not that the food was that good, just that eating was something to do, a popular diversion. The officers had two messes. One was on the second deck. It was more formal and run by the black shoes (the naval aviators wore brown shoes). It was set up buffet-style and enlisted personnel assisted with the clean-up and beverage refills. There were specific protocols seemingly designed to keep the aircrew out. One was the requirement to wear khakis. Flight jackets were also forbidden. Aircrew wore flight suits, unless prohibited by having to stand watch or some other function. So, having to change uniform in order to eat was not worth the effort. Thus the aircrew ate in the 'dirty shirt' located on the 03 level, just two knee-knockers from our ready room. The dirty shirt was also buffet-style and had a small eating area. There were no waiters. Eating on the ship can be compared with many other facilities that feed thousands, such as hospitals, colleges, and airlines. Most of the food was mediocre. We had names for certain food items. Rollers are hot dogs, and sliders are hamburgers. The reasons for the names become apparent during heavy seas. Trail markers are brussel sprouts, and bug juice is Kool Aid. Auto-dog is not a food, but a machine for dispensing soft ice cream. Most guys would spiral the ice cream on a dinner plate, or lay it down in a straight line, hence the name. Another machine related to eating was the cake dryer, rumored to have sucked all the moisture out of cakes and other baked products.

"Entertainment was difficult on the boat. Fortunately, you were usually busy with flying, collateral duties, watches, etc. The ship had a TV station that played movies, news, and canned videos provided by contractors, relating to ship and aircraft. The most popular show was the thirty-minute workout video shown in the morning, of women doing exercises to music, a tradition that has probably gone the way of the politically correct Navy. The plat (ship's TV) was also constantly on to monitor flight deck operations. VCRs and computers were staples in the staterooms and in the ready room. Personal computers were life savers, not just for work, but also for entertainment. While on cruise, I taught myself how to program in dBase and wrote programs to assist me in my collateral duties. We had a few computer games to pass around. The advantage of email then would have made life seem much less isolated. Playing cards was another favorite diversion. Generally, there was a poker game running within our squadron several nights a week. Each new game was named after the last port call, and the stakes were small and usually friendly.

"The ship provided several diversions. On occasion flight ops would be suspended and there would be a flight deck picnic. Grills were moved to the deck for a meal of steaks and chicken. Some would set up chairs and towels to bask in the sun and just relax. Others would jog. Once my RIO (Radar Intercept Officer) and I were assigned to stand 'Alert 5' during the flight deck picnic. One would expect that the alert would have been cancelled due to the presence of a thousand people on the deck, obviously preventing any launches. Wrong.

"The most legendary tradition on the ship occurred when we crossed the equator. Pollywogs, people who haven't crossed the equator before, become shellbacks and are given a certificate commemorating the event. The entire ship is transformed into a gigantic hazing exercise, with both officers and enlisted men utilizing leftover food, grease, hoses, and water to unpleasant effect. Shellbacks count their 'graduation' certificates among their most prized possessions, in order not to have to do it all again. The best diversion, though, is the next port call.

"Port calls are the light at the end of the tunnel. Morale peaks just prior to a port call and, of course, the end of the cruise. The PAO (Public Affairs Officer) sends in an advanced detachment to set up tours and hotel packages, and squadron officers also go in early to set up the admin and establish hotel accommodations. The admin was usually a suite which was the central meeting place for the squadron officers. It was run and maintained by junior officers who were allowed (required) to stay there and protect the booze locker and the squadron memorabilia (flag, mascot, etc.) Often, the advance det would hand out flyers to any half-attractive females to come to a party held at the admin the first night in port. This never came off quite as well as anticipated. Apparently, spending too much time on the boat obscured and distorted one's vision and perspective on female beauty. Most guys would go to the party, put in their required 'face time' and then go elsewhere. Port time was normally spent in typical tourist activities, sight-seeing, dining, and visiting the 'hot spots.' Booze on the ship was forbidden yet obtainable. There was always someone who had a stash for nights when a little 'medicinal nourishment' was needed. The point was never to overindulge. To get caught with alcohol meant extra duties, less flying, and being placed 'in hack.' This meant that you were to remain aboard the ship during the next port call. After months at sea, the last thing you wanted was to be left on the boat while your squadron mates were on the beach. There was one time when alcohol was allowed, in fact, distributed on the ship. Beer Day came about when the ship had gone more than forty-five days at sea without a

port visit. We had spent more than ninety days, and were rewarded with two beers a piece, distributed under the supervision of the military police, and it had to be consumed on deck."
—Frank Furbish, former U.S. Navy fighter pilot

Life, within doors, has few pleasanter prospects than a neatly arranged and well-provisioned breakfast-table.
—from *The House of the Seven Gables* by Nathaniel Hawthorne

"I remember J.T. 'Boats' Boatwright of the V-5 Division, USS *Enterprise* (CV-6), from Thanksgiving Day in 1942. We were in Noumea, New Caledonia, being repaired by the Seabees after being hit pretty hard in the Battle of Santa Cruz. Our planes were on the beach and 'Boats' and I were sent ashore to repair the synchronizer on one of our SBDs, with orders to stay on the job until the plane was operational. I was Third Class, having just come aboard in Pearl the first part of October. Boats was the old timer at First Class.

"We finished the job and went to an Army mess hall. The Navy didn't have much there at the time. Their cook said they had cleaned him out and he didn't have any food left. After Boats told him our plight he said, 'Wait a minute,' and came back with two bottles of beer and two oranges. We went outside and sat under a coconut tree and had our Thanksgiving dinner. Boats said we could tell our grandkids about it in years to come. It's the only Thanksgiving dinner I remember."
—Wilbur West, formerly with V-5 Division, USS *Enterprise*

"I love the Flora-Bama. Some people say it's a dive, but I think it's great, especially in the winter months when

Galley fires happen occasionally and the cooks have to be able to contend with them. They practice fighting them.

WINES FROM THE WOOD

OUR NAVY   "TAKEN IN TOW"

exceptional, with all the trimmings except flowers on the table. The 'chemist coffee' ensured my life-long aversion to that beverage, and I doubt that anyone ever really adjusted to standing in line so long for meals. Even today I avoid eateries with slow service. Still, many of us carried books to read and others studied for exams, so the time in the lines was not entirely wasted.

"It wasn't all work, by any means. Movies were often shown on the hangar deck, and impromptu shows were staged by talented personnel. The forward deck elevator, lowered about half-way, made a satisfactory stage, and the ship's sixteen-piece band was exceptionally versatile. There was a glee club, a hillbilly band, a ship's radio station with disc jockeys, and a well-stocked library. There were Judo classes, basketball, boxing, and weight-lifting . . . even model airplane building.

"After extended periods on station conducting missions off the coast of Korea, we would enter the harbor at Yokosuka, Japan, for replenishment of supplies, to off-load battle-damaged aircraft, and to spend a few precious days on liberty. The first visit there was a culture shock, as we were not prepared for the food, the language, or even the procedure for buying souvenirs. We quickly adapted and, although we seldom had much spending money, prices there were very low at the time, and we found many items that were useful for shipboard living. There were inexpensive shower shoes which were held on by rubber strips that fit between the first two toes. They felt strange at first, and if one tried to back up they would slide off, and they soon became known as 'go-aheads.' In addition to shopping, we took side trips on the efficient railroads to places such as Tokyo

it's just the locals and the flight students. It's right down there on the beach. Completely tawdry. I love it."
—Shannon Callahan, Naval Flight Officer student, NAS Pensacola

"Beans, beans, and more beans. And sometimes potatoes for breakfast. But Navy food was seldom disappointing

to me. Meals have never been high on my list of priorities. As a 'near vegetarian' I was always popular as a chow buddy, being quite willing to swap my steaks, ham, or pork chops, for desserts. Navy breads and pastries were usually tasty, and even the reconstituted milk wasn't bad if it was cold enough. Holiday meals were truly and Kamakura. During one visit to Yokosuka, a team of Japanese carpenters came aboard to repair flight deck damage caused by a prop plane that had crashed on deck. Our deck had a layer of teak wood on top, chosen because, when hit it would harmlessly 'powder' rather than fragment into dangerous splinters. The ship carried spare teak planks and it was fascinating to watch these skillful workmen in action.

"The *Kearsarge* ported in Hong Kong and we were immediately surrounded by small craft with vendors eagerly shouting up to us about the wares they were selling. We had been alerted about the poverty prevailing, however seeing at first hand the contrast between the high-rise buildings, upscale stores, well-dressed and prosperous people . . . and the wretched people crammed aboard the tiny boats, cramped together in the scummy waterways, was truly depressing. Sailors seldom have much spending money, but we were rich in comparison to these boat people, and it was hard not to feel guilty about our good fortune in having been born Americans.

"A legendary Hong Kong business lady named Mary Soo had organized a group of industrious Chinese to serve as side-cleaners for the U.S. Navy ships. This was among the most miserable chores involved in maintaining an aircraft carrier, yet here were people who were delighted to have work of any sort, eagerly scrubbing away while we were off exploring the wonders of Hong Kong.

"Among our discoveries were store-fronts that were obviously aimed at attracting English-speaking tourists. One such was a shoe shop with the sign NO-SQUEAK JOHNSON. Other stores had tailors who could make low-cost suits, virtually overnight.

There were a lot of wood-carvers too, so some of the crew returned to the ship with garments and large, carved dragons, bragging about their bargains. Imagine their chagrin later when the sleeves came off their hurriedly-made suits, and cracks began to appear in the carved dragons after a few weeks exposure to the sea air.

"The Navy has a policy of rotating work assignments among the men. The reasoning was that there would be enough overlap in qualifications so that all requirements could still be met if part of the crew was on leave ashore. It was inevitable that more than a few people were given jobs for which they were entirely unsuited. Case in point: Algiers had an unsavory reputation, and it surprises me still that we were even allowed to go there. However, we were lectured in advance of our visit about cultural differences and warned about potential concerns, which ranged from unsafe drinking water, to being served dog meat, to encountering pick-pockets. In its wisdom, the Navy decided to send me to the Casbah, of all places, on shore patrol duty. I had no such qualifications, but attended a forty-five minute crash course on becoming an instant policeman, in which it was stressed that we must, at all costs, avoid agitating the natives, and we must not even look at the veiled women. We were told that our main purpose was to keep our sailors, especially the heavy drinkers, in line and out of trouble. I was already apprehensive when they issued us shore patrol armbands and billy clubs, explaining 'We can't give you sidearms because the natives might steal them and use them against you.' Off I was sent, in company with another unqualified sailor, to take the midnight shift. 'Don't worry,' we were told, 'We'll send a resident Casbah policeman along with you in case there might be any language problems.' It turned out that the fellow spoke several tongues, none of them English. We made the rounds of several hot spots and, fortunately, encountered no drunks. We had decided that if we came upon any fights, we would simply let them kill each other. Mercifully, the hours passed uneventfully, and we returned to the ship, grateful to be back aboard.

"Shopping was fun almost everywhere and, except for the French Riviera, we could generally afford at least a few souvenirs. Compensating for the sky-high prices on the Riviera, were the spectacular beaches and the even more spectacular swimming suits. Bikinis were a recent phenomenon that we had only seen in magazines back home, but in France they were everywhere. As a happily-married man, I was not shopping for female companionship, but must admit it was intriguing seeing those totally uninhibited demoiselles, some of them topless."
—Bill Hannan, former U.S. Navy jet engine mechanic

"A couple of months after the [World War Two] started, the Enterprise paymaster asked for the confidential advice of the senior squadron officers. He had noticed that seven enlisted men on the 'Big E' were sending allotments to their wives, all to the same address. It was, however, apparent that only one woman lived at that address. Should the men be told or not? The final consensus was that the matter should be kept secret and the men should not be told as they would be devastated and their essential performance would suffer."
—Jack Kleiss, former U.S. Navy pilot

"Imagine being part of 6,229 men having Thanksgiving together. Now imagine trying to shop for all the food needed to feed these hungry men, not only for Thanksgiving, but for an additional thirteen days. This group was made up of 4,710 soldiers who were headed home after two or more years of fighting the war in Europe, and 1,519 sailors who made up a skeleton crew that was necessary to sail the aircraft carrier Enterprise that was transporting them home.

"The Enterprise had participated in and survived twenty-three Pacific battles in World War Two. She was reported to have been sunk six times by the Japanese, and had seen more action in the Pacific than any other ship. Operation Magic Carpet brought her home to a new assignment in the Atlantic, to bring troops home from Europe.

"I was honored to be part of the crew as we sailed from Pearl Harbor, through the Panama Canal and north along the Atlantic coast to New York. Along the way the Enterprise had her last 'flight quarters' and her planes flew off to land bases. Following a great welcome in New York harbor, and the honoring of the fleet, Enterprise set sail for Boston to be fitted out. The hangar deck had 700 folding bunks five tiers high installed to accommodate 3,500 men. The remaining men were housed below decks. Next came the challenge of feeding our new 'cargo' as well as the crew.

"What and how much food would be needed? I managed to get a copy of the shopping list. A special Thanksgiving menu was planned because we would be in Southampton, England, on that day with our returning soldiers on board. These 4,710 troops were loaded on and assigned to quarters in forty-eight hours. The 500 tons of food loaded on in Boston consisted of 14,000 dozen eggs, thirty tons of cold storage beef, five tons of fresh pork, six tons of butter, three tons of turkey, four tons of ice cream mix, thirty-six tons of potatoes, three tons of tomatoes, four tons of cabbage, fifteen tons of fresh fruit, ten tons of coffee, twenty-five tons of sugar, and fifty tons of flour. We distilled 75,000 gallons of water each day, with 15,000 going into the boilers.

"We arrived in New York on 1 December after a reasonable crossing. Our passengers were quickly unloaded and new supplies were loaded to fill our empty pantry in preparation for our next crossing, scheduled for 8

December. The trip over was uneventful and, again, nearly 5,000 solders were loaded aboard. The plan was to be home a few days before Christmas.

"The Atlantic had other plans for us. We ran into a storm, supposedly the worst in sixty years. Waves crashed over the length of the flight deck, 830 feet long and sixty feet above the water. Life rafts were torn loose, an anchor was ripped off, and water sprayed in on the now seasick soldiers, and a few sailors too. We were actually blown back towards England, and some of *Enterprise*'s old war scars were reopened.

"We did make it home for Christmas. We sailed past Staten Island at 5:30 on Christmas Eve 1945."
—John Dunbar, formerly assigned to the USS *Enterprise*

below: The Royal Navy carrier HMS *Illustrious* is joined at sea by a replenishment vessel.

In the pathway of the sun, in the footsteps of the breeze, where the world and sky are one, he shall ride the silver seas, he shall cut the glittering wave. I shall sit at home, and rock; rise, to heed a neighbour's knock; brew my tea, and snip my thread; bleach the linen for my bed. They will call him brave.
—*Penelope* by Dorothy Parker

ON 2 APRIL 1982, WHEN THE BRITISH government directed that a Royal Navy task force be sent to the South Atlantic to recapture the Falkland Islands from the Argentinian occupation forces of General Leopoldo Galtieri, world opinion was generally opposed. In Britain the more interesting debate for many was military rather than political. How could a relative handful of Sea Harriers, a weapons system not without its detractors at the time, stand up to a force of nearly 200 Argentianian Mirages, Skyhawks, Etendards, and more, in a part of the world where operating conditions, never mind the odds, were truly terrible?

Twenty years before the Falklands campaign, Canadian-born Nigel David "Sharkey" Ward was an Officer Cadet at the Britannia Royal Naval College, Dartmouth, England. In his naval career he went on to become a qualified Air Warfare instructor. Ward trained on and flew Hunters, Sea Vixens, and F-4K Phantoms. In 1981 he became commander of 801 Naval Air Squadron in HMS *Invincible*. In July of that year he was given the opportunity, and the challenge, of proving the capability of the Sea Harrier and its radar and weapons system under operational conditions. He and his squadron had to find out just how good the airplane was and how suitable it was for its job. Ward's years of

experience with the Sea Harrier, his determined efforts to get the airplane operational, and his part in the fight to keep the fast jet Fleet Air Arm alive and airborne, earned him the title "Mr. Sea Harrier." In extracts from his book, *Sea Harrier Over the Falklands*, Commander Ward offers a fascinating look at the air campaign of the 1982 conflict.

"The 801 Squadron recommendations for high-level bombing against Port Stanley airfield had been accepted somewhat reluctantly by the Flag. This reluctance was not really surprising, bearing in mind that the attack relied completely on the capabilities of the [Blue Fox] radar and Navhars [Sea Harrier Navigation Heading Attitude Reference System] for its success—bearing in mind, too, what the Flag thought of such things.

"In reply to our recommendations and after due deliberation, SAVO [Staff Aviation Officer: a member of an Admiral's staff specially appointed to advise the Admiral on all operational and training aviation matters] put forward several fully anticipated questions: how were the pilots going to ensure that they missed the town with their bombs? Would the line of attack take them over the town? And so on. Finally, realizing that my team had no intention whatsoever of risking the lives of the Falkland Island community, and after having been briefed in detail about the profile to be flown by attacking aircraft, the Staff agreed to the proposal. But 801, having generated and recommended the new delivery, were not the first to be tasked with trying it out. That didn't matter very much to me. The main thing was that now we could do our bit to keep the enemy awake and on the alert; the less rest the Argentines ashore

got before our amphibious troops landed, the better.

"To that end—denying the enemy some sleep—we decided in *Invincible* to set up a mission that would give the opposition more than a little to think about in the middle of the night. There were two major detachments and airstrips away from Stanley. On East Falkland there was Goose Green, close to the settlement of Darwin. On West Falkland there was Fox Bay. With the Task Group well to the east, the distance to Fox Bay was about 225 nautical miles as the crow flies. The plan was very simple. I was to get airborne on my own in the small hours of the night and deliver a Lepus flare [a six-million-candlepower flare, dropped or tossed from fast jets to illuminate targets for reconnaissance or night-attack purposes] attack against each defended airstrip. It was hoped that this would give the troops on the ground the false impression that a task force landing was under way—the flares apparently providing illumination prior to an assault.

"The mission was very straightforward. All I needed to do was enter the attack coordinates for each target into my navigation computer, follow the resultant HUD [Head-up Display] directions to the target areas, check the accuracy of the navigation using my radar, and drop the flares. Outbound to the targets I would fly direct to Goose Green from the climb-out point which would take me close to Stanley. On the return leg I would approach the Carrier Group from 240°, that is, well clear of the islands, let down to low level and then run in to *Invincible* for recovery on board.

"JJ, Captain J.J. Black, skipper of *Invincible*, was pleased with the idea of the planned mission: 'Anything we have missed, Sharkey? You know that the weather isn't too brilliant out

SHARKEY

Nigel "Sharkey" Ward made the last Sea Harrier kill of the Falklands War.

The Falklands War lasted ten weeks in 1982. It stemmed from an invasion of the Falkland Islands, known by the Argentines as the Malvinas, in which the Argentines attempted to establish the sovereignty that they had long claimed over the islands. British naval, air, and ground forces took part and the conflict ended on 14 June with surrender by the Argentines. Royal Navy Sea Harriers from the carriers *Invincible* and *Hermes* played a major role in the action.

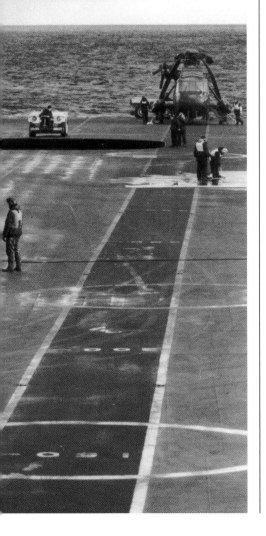

there?' The weather round the Task Group was certainly not very sharp, with high winds, towering cumulo-nimbus and snow showers. But over the islands the forecast was for much fairer conditions. The mission would therefore present no problems and it hurt my pride even to think that I might have a problem getting back on board. I shut my mind to snow showers and thought only of dropping the flares.

" 'No thanks, sir. I'm very happy with all that. Can we just make sure that the Flag lets all our surface units know exactly what's going on? One lone aircraft approaching the force at night from the southwest is just asking for a 'blue on blue' [one's own forces shooting down own aircraft].

" 'Don't worry, we'll ensure that they let all units know.'

"There was practically no self-brief-ing required for the mission. It was a question of kicking the tyres, lighting the fires, and getting airborne.

"I arrested my rate of climb after launch at 500 feet, settled the air-craft down to a height of 200 feet above the waves, set 420 knots and departed the ship on a north-westerly heading for seventy miles. As my eyes became fully attuned to the darkness the sea surface became visible, with the healthy wind kicking up a lot of spray and phosphorescence and clouds towering around and ahead of me like huge cliffs. Inside the cockpit I had dimmed the lighting almost to extinction, including the geometrical patterns on the HUD. Arming missiles and guns, just in case. I reached the climb-out point and headed for the stars, turning to port as I did so to get on track for the first destination.

"The aircraft climbed at a cool 30° nose up for the first 15,000 feet and very quickly I was throttling back at Mach 0.85 and 35,000 feet, enjoying

the view. Under the black, star-speck-led sky and towards East Falkland, the cloud thinned and dissipated. Although it was the middle of the night, Stanley was well-lit and could easily be seen from the top of the climb.

"Dick Goodenough, the 801 Squadron Air Engineer Officer, had given me the jet with the most sought-after radar and Navhars—004. The engineers kept full records of the performance accuracy and reliability of each radar and Navhars system. This attention to detail, which includ-ed comprehensive post-flight briefs, paid excellent dividends. But although all the aircraft performed well, 004 seemed to be the pick of the bunch. The avionics were functioning per-fectly. Before passing just to the south of Stanley, I checked the navigation system accuracy with my radar and, until commencing descent for Goose Green, used the radar in its air-to-air mode to check the skies to the west for enemy fighters. There were none, nor did I expect any. I was enjoying being alone and thought of my lads back at home—they would have given anything to have been on this flight.

"I chose to run into Goose Green up Choiseul Sound and had an excel-lent surface radar picture to confirm the accuracy of my desired flare-drop position. Having checked the Lepus selector switches and pylon, I mon-itored the Navhars readout, which was telling me time-to-go to release, and the HUD, which was guiding me unerringly to the target. Pickling the bomb button, I felt the flare body leave the aircraft, applied power and commenced the second climb of the night to high level.

"After about twenty seconds I rolled the Sea jet inverted in order to see the flare ignite. Goose Green lies on a narrow isthmus of land which separates Choiseul Sound from Grantham Sound. When the flare went off it seemed to be in the right place—right on target. Now for Fox Bay.

"The second target was well-covered in thick cloud, but that made no difference to the attack profile. My radar confirmed what the Navhars and I had no doubt at all when I pickled the bomb-release button that the Lepus was again bang on target. It was as easy as riding a bike. Having seen the glow from the flare through the cloud, I turned to the east in the climb and set off on the long dog-leg home.

"At 140 miles to go to the deck, I was suddenly illuminated with fire-control radar from a ship below. The relative silence of the cockpit was shattered by the radar warning receiver alarm. I had detected a vessel on radar earlier and had presumed it was on detachment from the Task Group.

"Thoughts of the Argentine Navy firing Sea Dart at me flashed through my mind. I broke hard to starboard and descended to the southeast, away from the contact which was only twenty miles to the north. But I was still locked-up by the fire-control radar, and having taken initial avoiding action I started to analyze the threat. It certainly wasn't Sea Dart—the noise in my earphones didn't have the right characteristics—and so I was pretty safe now, thirty miles south. I turned port onto east, arresting my descent as I did so, and climbed back up to 30,000 feet. I would circumnavigate the ship that had shown such an unhealthy interest in me. At the same time I would interrogate it on radio.

"I found the culprit on the pre-briefed Task Group surface / air frequency. 'Warship illuminating lone Sea Harrier, come in.'

"The warship had obviously not been briefed on the SHAR [Sea Harrier] mission and was unwilling to believe I was who I said I was. Being now a little short of fuel after three and a half climbs to high level, I left my personal signature encoded in terms of four-letter words and bid them goodnight. If I had been on a slightly different track and hadn't had my radar information to tell me where to evade to, I could have been engaged by my own forces. So much for the promise to pass information to all ships.

"By the time I began my final descent towards the Carrier Group I was back amongst the clouds. They were massive and very turbulent. After I had descended to low level and was running in to the expected position of the ship via the safety lane, I callled, '004 on the way in. Estimating 280°, twenty-five miles. Over.' Tony, the Direction Officer of Invincible, was immediately on the air. 'Roger, 004. Read you loud and clear. I have no contact on you, repeat no contact. Clutter from snow clouds too intense.' He was concerned. Good old Tony; there's a man you can really trust. He'd do anything to get his pilots down safely.

" 'Roger, I'll conduct my own approach and call out my ranges to go.' I was feeling confident thanks to two important facts. Firstly, when Invincible gave a ship's estimated position for the recovery aircraft, you could bet your pension on her being in that position when you returned from your flight; especially in bad weather. So I was very sure in my mind that I could find the deck using my Navhars information. The second fact was that I had practiced self-homing to the deck on many occasions, and we had also carried out the trials on the software for self-homing when ashore in the Trials Unit. It was no higher work load for the pilot than following instructions from the ship's precision approach controller.

A Royal Navy Sea Harrier departs from the ski ramp of HMS Illustrious.

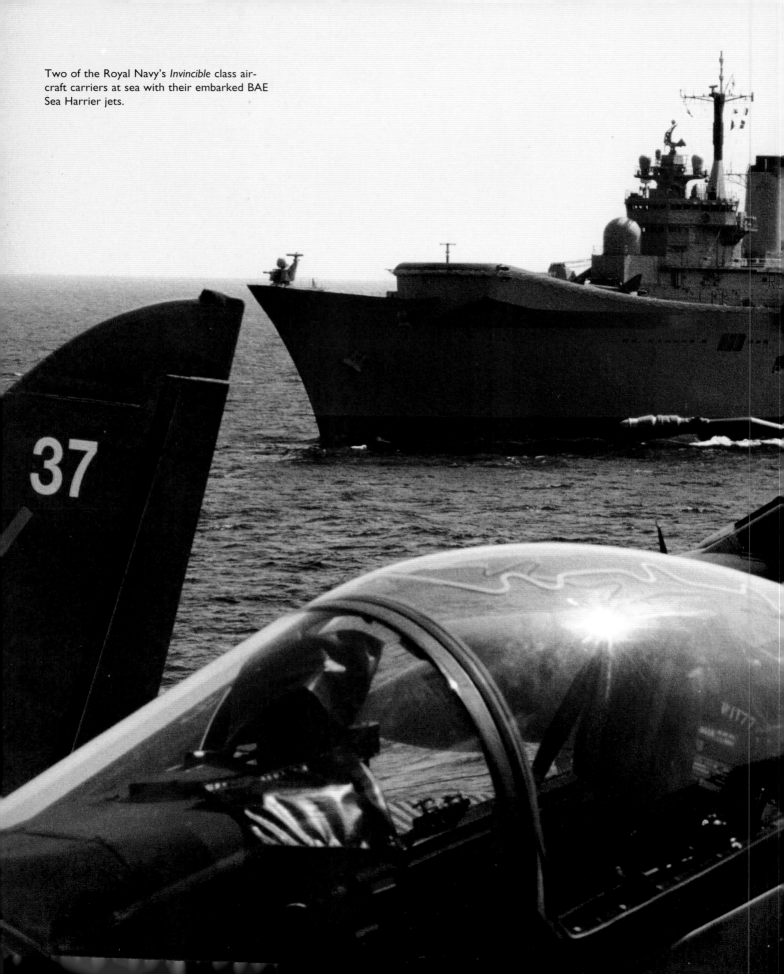

Two of the Royal Navy's *Invincible* class air-craft carriers at sea with their embarked BAE Sea Harrier jets.

"On my radar screen, the *Invincible* 'position destination marker' that I had selected on my nav computer sat less than two miles from one of the ship contacts in view. I had already programmed the 'marker' with the ship's pre-briefed recovery course and speed and was happy to see it was holding good formation on the contact nearest to it. That had got to be *Invincible*—I hadn't enough fuel left to make mistakes. There was enough for one approach only.

"It was a simple matter to update the radar 'marker's' position by fixing the radar onto the contact. The Self-Controlled Approach programme in the Navhars computer software was provided so that pilots could safely carry out their own precision approach to a chosen destination. My chosen destination was the ship, and as I lined up five miles astern of what I thought was *Invincible*, I selected the precision approach mode on the HUD. I also locked the radar onto the ship to keep the 'destination' infor-mation as accurate as possible. Now I was all prepared for recovery to the ship.

" 'Five miles on the approach,' I called.

" 'Roger, still no contact.' Tony must be sweating buckets down there.

"I was at 800 feet and the world outside was black. Approaching three miles I prepared to commence descent. The radar was firmly locked on to the contact ahead.

" 'Three miles.'

" 'Still no contact.'

"Was I on the right ship? I began to wonder as I started down the slope. My jet was being tossed around a bit by turbulence from heavy clouds, which would certainly account for the clutter Tony had mentioned. There was no other course but to wait and see. I cleared the doubts from my mind.

" 'Have you now at one and a half miles. On the glide slope.' Tony sounded relieved. I was relieved. Tony continued with his calls all the way to half a mile. He had passed the wind over the deck as forty knots gusting fifty. It felt like it in the cockpit too. The buffeting increased as I got lower.

" 'Half a mile.' My head-up information said the same. I delayed selecting 'hover-stop' for a few seconds because of the strong head-wind, then, nozzles down, power going on. At a quarter of a mile I called 'Lights,' and there, behind the radar cross in the HUD, appeared the ship's island. As usual the cross was just about on Flyco. Radar off and concentrate on controlling the jet. As I was moving sideways over the deck from alongside, the wind backed through 30°. I ruddered the nose into it before setting onto the deck with an uncharacteristic thud.

"That's my excitement over for the night', I thought. It was 0400 hours, and a long day lay ahead.

A Westland Sea King / Sikorsky helicopter operating from HMS *Illustrious* in 2000; right: Harrier jets during the Falklands War.

"By the time June arrived we had grown well-used to operating in the unpredictable South Atlantic weather, and to our routine air transits from the islands for combat air patrol. Combat opportunities against the Argentine Air Force and Navy pilots were becoming less and less frequent. But there was never a moment to relax vigilance on CAP because the enemy had not given up. On the contrary, they still held all the strategic points on the islands, and although Land Forces Deputy Jeremy Moore's men had landed, they were not yet in a position to displace the occupation forces.

"Intelligence gleaned from various sources indicated that Port Stanley was still being supplied by air on a nightly basis by AAF Hercules aircraft, and the same aircraft were making regular use of the landing strip at Fox Bay to support their logistic resupply efforts. Without a radar look-down-over-land capability, there was little that we could do to intercept these night resupply flights, especially with the Task Group positioned between 200 and 230 nautical miles to the east of San Carlos Water. The majority of the Sea Harrier effort by day continued to be spent on maintaining CAP stations around the beachhead and, at that range from the carriers, our on-task time had come down to about twenty-five minutes over the Sound, and that was pushing it. It was, nevertheless, effort well spent, and the SHAR's continuous presence to the west of the amphibious operating area continued to deter and disrupt enemy air attacks.

"On 1 June my section had launched after daybreak and we had carried out our CAP duty over Falkland Sound without any sign of trade. Everything appeared quiet in the skies to the east as our two jets commenced the climb-out to the north of San Carlos en route to the ship. Our home transit would be at 35,000 feet and, in the climb, Steve [Thomas] kept his Sea jet in neat battle formation on my starboard beam.

"HMS *Minerva* was the Local Area Control Ship and we had not yet switched from her radio frequency. The craggy north coast of East Falkland Island was well below us when my helmet headphones crackled as *Minerva* called us up.

" 'I just had a pop-up contact to the northwest of you at forty miles. Only had three sweeps on the contact and it has now disappeared. Do you wish to investigate? Over.' I could tell from the controller's voice that he really felt he had something but didn't want us to waste our time if he was wrong. After all, forty nautical miles was a long way in the wrong direction when our aircraft could be running low on fuel.

"He needn't have worried; neither I nor Steve would dream of turning down the slimmest chance of engaging the enemy. Before he had finished his call I had already started a hard turn to port with Steve in my wake. I was flying aircraft side number 006 and its radar was on top line.

"In the turn and using the radar hand-controller thumb-wheel, I wound the radar antenna down to just below the horizon, and as we steadied on a north-westerly heading, there was the target. The green radar blip stood out as bold as brass in the centre of my screen at just less than forty miles. 'Judy! Contact at thirty-eight miles. Investigating.' This was a chance we couldn't miss.

"I decided to try to lock the radar to the target to get some accurate height information on it. The radar locked easily, telling me as it did so that the target had to be a large one at that range, and gave me what I wanted to know, a height difference of 4,000 feet. I was at 12,000; that made the target at 8,000. I broke the lock so as not to alert the target. He would be listening out on his radar warning receiver. I wound our speed up to 500 knots in a shallow descent. Target range decreased rapidly to thirty-four miles, thirty miles—then it seemed to hold. There was only one possible reason for that.

" 'Steve, I think he's turning away. He's now at right 10° at twenty-eight miles. 4,000 below.'

" 'Roger. Contact.' Good! Steve also had contact. I locked the radar again. Still about 4,000 feet below, but we had already come down to 10,000 in descent.

" 'He's definitely turned away and he's descending. Must have seen us.' The shore control radars of the Argentine forces must have monitored the start of our intercept and then passed the information to the target. It was now a race against time and fuel. *Invincible* was over 200 miles away and we should have been heading home. But there was an easy alternative. I called *Minerva* on the radio.

" 'We may be too short of fuel to get back to Mother after this. Can you ask the assault ships to prepare to take us on board in San Carlos?' A short pause before *Minerva* came back. 'We have decks ready to take you if you need it.'

" 'Roger. Please check that weapons will be 'tight' in the missile zone if we pay you a visit.' I knew it wasn't necessary to remind *Minerva* of that, but it was better to be safe than sorry.

"Roger. No problem.' The shipbome controller then settled down to monitor the chase—if we destroyed the target it would all be as a result of his sharp radar pick-up and concentration.

"Having sorted the fuel problem out in my mind, I could give my full attention to tracking the target, which was now heading west and had descended to low level below the cloud. We were still cracking along above the cloud in brilliant sunshine. I checked my missile and gun switches; safety flaps were up and everything was live and ready to go.

"The sea state was markedly rough and as we continued to close on the fleeing target from above, I wished

that the Flag and all his Staff could have been in the cockpit with me to witness the radar's performance in these look-down conditions. The radar was holding contact with the target on every sweep.

"We were now approaching the cloud-tops at 6,000 feet and catching the fleeing aircraft fast. To stand any chance at all of survival, the slower target ahead would need to stay in the cloud layer and try to evade us with hard maneuvering. But there was little chance of that being successful either, since I had had a lot of practice against large evading targets by day and night.

"Steve, you'd better stay above the cloud until I am visual with the target below.' If he popped up through the cloud layer, Steve would get him.

"Roger. Still good contact at nine miles.

"I descended steeply into the cloud layer, breaking through the bottoms at 1,800 feet. I still had the enemy on my radar screen; a fat blip at six miles and closing fast. I looked up from the radar and flight instruments and there it was at 20° left, a Hercules heading for the mainland as fast as it could go. It was at a height of about 300 feet above the waves.

"Tally-Ho, one Herky-bird! Come and join me down here, Steve.'

"I closed on the four-engined transport fairly quickly and when I felt I was just within missile range and had a good growl from the seeker-head, I fired my first Sidewinder. As usual, it seemed an eternity before it came off the rails and sped towards the target. I had locked the missile to the left-hand pair of engines. The thick white smoke trail terminated after motor burn-out and the missile continued to track towards the Hercules' left wing. I was sure it was going to get there, but at the last minute it hung tantalisingly short and low on its target and fell away, proximity-fusing on the sea surface below.

"There was no mistake with the second missile. I locked up the Sidewinder on the target's starboard engines, listened to its growling acquisition tone, and fired from well under one and a quarter miles. It left the rails with its characteristic muffled roar and tracked inevitably towards the right wing of the Hercules, impacting between the engines. Immediately, both engines and the wing surface between them burst into flames.

"Our fuel state was now getting marginal, to say the least. The job had to be finished, and quickly. Otherwise the Argentine aircraft might still limp home and escape. I knew the Hercules had an excellent fire suppression system in the wings and we couldn't let it escape now.

"I still had more than 100 knots overtake as I closed to guns range and pulled the trigger. My hot-line aiming point was the rear door and tailplane and all of the 240 rounds of 30mm high-explosive ammunition hit their mark. There were no splashes in the sea below. As I finished firing, and with its elevator and rudder controls shot away, the large transport aircraft banked gradually to the right and nose-dived into the sea. There could have been no survivors.

"Pulling off the target hard to port, I called *Minerva*. 'Splash one Hercules! Well done on spotting it!'

"As the controller's excited voice came back on the air, I could hear the cheers of the Ops Room staff in the background. They also knew that the Hercules force had been running supplies into Stanley on a daily basis, usually at night and always at very low level. To our ground forces they were a high-priority target. This Hercules had shown some complacency by popping up to 8,000 feet, and had paid the price.

" 'Nice one.' It was the *Minerva* controller. 'Do you wish to land in San Carlos? We'd all like to see you both.

" 'Roger. Wait. Steve, check fuel.'

" '2100,' came the reply.

"I had a couple of hundred less and the ship was 230 miles away. We couldn't rearm my aircraft on board the assault ships and as I thought we could just squeeze home to *Invincible*, I decided to turn down *Minerva*'s kind invitation.

"Sorry, we can just make it back to Mother, so we'd better do that. Thanks anyway for standing by.

"We were already in the climb and in less than half an hour were touching down on deck. There had been a tailwind so we ended up with about 400 pounds of gas in the tanks—more than I had expected.

"During the preceding weeks there had been much talk in our crew room about knocking down a Hercules or similar large transport. Given the chance, everyone favoured flying up alongside the cockpit and signalling to the crew to jump out. We felt no animosity towards the Argentine pilots; they were just doing what they had to do, and if their lives could be spared, then they would be. Sadly, there had been no time for such chivalry on this occasion. The choice was chivalry, thus possibly giving the enemy aircraft the opportunity to survive and maybe running our Sea jets out of fuel, or a quick kill. Circumstances and, in particular, fuel states dictated that it had to be the latter choice. I didn't lose any sleep over it, but wished that we had had more time to play with.

"The Hercules intercept turned out to be the last kill of the air war in which the Sea Harrier weapon system was able to play its full part."

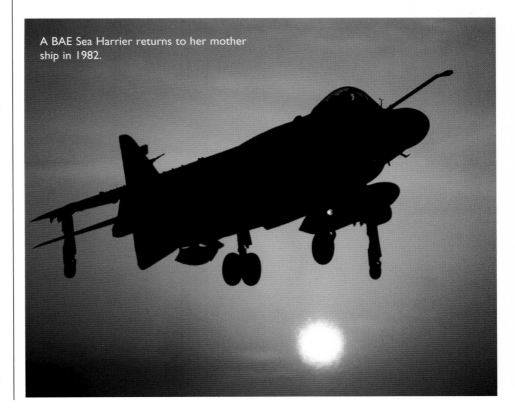

A BAE Sea Harrier returns to her mother ship in 1982.

The safe return of a Sea Harrier to her ship.

ALL BRANCHES OF THE MILITARY HAVE their problems, but in peacetime, navies suffer more in one way than the other services. No matter how dedicated a person may be, or how much he likes his job, nothing can take the place of being with the ones he loves, or make up for the prolonged periods away from them. It's a hard fact. Every navy has its requirements and commitments which have to be met. They have to take precedence over all other considerations. Lengthy work-ups prior to lengthy deployments are just part of the deal, and that isn't likely to change.

What looks like fun, excitement, challenge, and adventure to a twenty-three-year-old naval aviator fresh from the Fleet Replacement Squadron may look very different to a mid-grade aviator officer who has experienced two or three work-up cycles and deployments which, cumulatively, have taken him away from his wife and kids for half of the six years he has been in the service. Never mind the benefits, the travel, adventure, security, the satisfaction in serving his country, even the thrill of flying military aircraft which drew him to the Navy in the first place and which he has wanted to do all his life more than anything . . . even that may no longer seem quite so essential. Nature has kicked in and he's only human. And not incidentally, just how much understanding can one expect from a wife or girlfriend?

What is a navy to do? How is it supposed to retain the guy who has taken the training, served his obligation faithfully and efficiently, and must soon decide whether to stay in or leave this service that he has been part of for several years? It can't hope to match the salary he can get on the outside. He'd be of no use to the fleet if the Navy were to let him stay ashore permanently—navies go to sea and that's what he was trained to do. If even the flying has lost some of its lustre for him, at least compared to quality time with the family, where is the incentive for him to re-up? And what about that seat with the airline that may be waiting for him? Economics have a way of changing, and that seat may not be there the next time he looks. What should he do? Stay in? Get out?

Danny Vincent, USS *John C. Stennis:* "The hard part of navy life is leaving your family for six months. Everyone will say that, but it's equally hard to

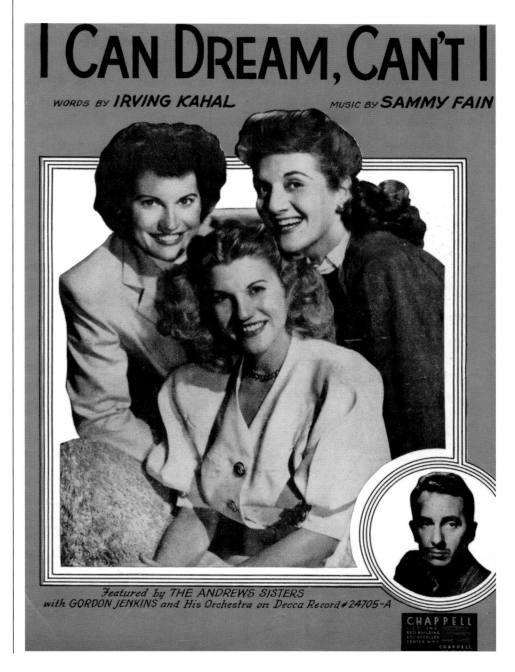

I CAN DREAM, CAN'T I

WORDS BY IRVING KAHAL   MUSIC BY SAMMY FAIN

Featured by THE ANDREWS SISTERS
with GORDON JENKINS and His Orchestra on Decca Record # 24705-A

CHAPPELL
CO. INC.
RKO BUILDING
ROCKEFELLER
CENTER N·Y·C
CHAPPELL

do the work-up process that we go through. We go out for two or three weeks at a time; we're in port for maybe three weeks and then it's out for ten. It just disrupts the family life.

"I like email. I want to know if my son fell and hurt his head. I would want to know it right away. I would be concerned the whole time until I got that email saying he was OK. With email you feel like you stay connected with all the stuff that's going on. For special occasions like Christmas and some holidays, they sometimes do a real-time video thing and now there are a lot of satellite phones too.

"The introduction of women on the ships was a huge thing. There were growing pains associated with it and it was a topic of discussion with just about everybody for a long time. But we've all seen that women can integrate into the environment and it's not a big deal. We still have some old salts, people who have been in the Navy for a long time who are gonna resist. But the Navy is evolving and changing, and those people are being asked to leave after they've fulfilled their twenty years. The new airman who checks in on board, who only knows a navy with women on the ships, it's nothing to him. The ship's company, including the air wing, is about 6,000 people now, of which about ten to twelve percent are women.

"You're always gonna have people that complain, but the way you combat morale problems is, you keep people busy. If they are involved in doing their jobs, they may not be happy that they're away from home, but they're gonna be content doing what they're doing as long as they know there is a goal. I think morale on the ship is fine. We have movies, satellite TV, email, computers, satellite phones, video games, workout facil-

ities—it all contributes to improving morale. We all made a conscious choice to be here."

"I'm looking forward to the six-month deployment. I don't mind being out at sea. I'm young. It's not that I have nothing to look forward to if I were to stay on shore, but I think the cruise is a chance for me to get out and see things. I'm not married. It's a chance for me to save money, and a lot of time to think, so I don't mind it. The foreign ports are great. In the Gulf we hit Dubai and Bahrain. On our transit we'll most likely hit Perth, Hobart, Hong Kong, Singapore, and Hawaii."
—Aaron Zizzo, USS *John C. Stennis*

"Separation and how to deal with it was an individual dilemma. At times, the feeling of isolation was enormous. I assume that the problem has been diluted with the advent of email. During my time, the C-2 Cod (Carrier Onboard Delivery aircraft), lovingly called Miss Piggy, was our infrequent connection to home. It would deliver the mail, which was obviously not timely but was always received with much anticipation. It was a gloomy day when you didn't get a single piece of mail or a 'care package' from home. Care packages were boxes containing stale cookies or other treats. Besides the contents, these packages commonly contained portions of hometown newspapers used to wrap the food items and these papers would be distributed around the ready room. It was the simple things that were missed.

"Separation from family was the hardest aspect of ship life for most. Several members of the squadron came home from a cruise to be introduced to a new child. Then there were those who came home from a

The key multi-role fighter of the U.S. Navy into the twenty-first century, the Boeing F/A-18 Hornet.

cruise to an empty house. I remember counselling an enlisted man who had just received a letter from his wife. It was a common practice to sign a power of attorney allowing a spouse the authority to run the household. In this case, the lady had used the power of attorney to sell his house and wipe out his finances. She then moved in with a friend of his. We had only been gone for three weeks. Life on the ship can be tough. There were others who revelled in the separation—an extended break from a bad marriage or a timely excuse to end a relationship. Most immersed themselves in their work, wrote and received loving letters, and returned to rebuild their relationships with their families."

—Frank Furbish, former U.S Navy fighter pilot

"My girlfriend was very supportive actually. She has always been very supportive and she knew that I wanted to fly when we first started going out together. She's never tried to say it's too dangerous and why do I want to do it? She's always put up with me being away a lot and only seeing me at weekends, and now, of course, she's putting up with me being away for longer periods on the ship and certainly next year in the Gulf, for quite a long time. I think she's very

The joys of a long-awaited homecoming.

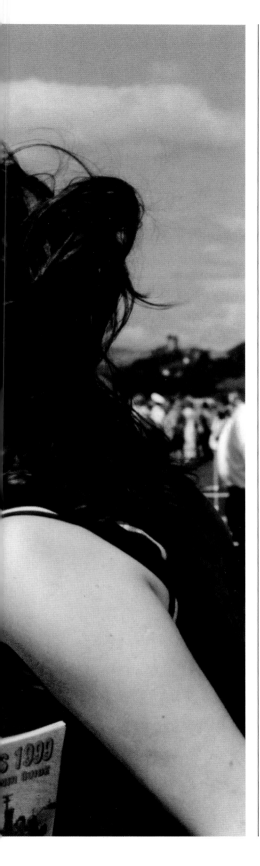

pleased that I'm doing what I want to do and I'm very lucky to have someone who thinks that way. Email has made a big difference, although the number of emails you can send is limited. I think it's five or six a week sent to a private address. It's a fantastic way of keeping in touch and really, in this modern world, there's no reason why we shouldn't have it available. But even though we have got email, receiving and writing letters I still find very important, and often receiving a letter is more personal. Someone has actually taken the time to do it and it's nice to receive. I actually do write home quite a lot on snail mail as well."
—Nick Walker, HMS *Illustrious*

"The six-month deployment for me is both interesting and kind of scary. I have a wife at home with a pre-existing medical condition, so I have that in the back of my mind. If I was single or had a wife in healthy condition, I'd be looking forward to it. For her sake, if I had a choice, I wouldn't go on the deployment. We do keep in touch by email and my division are aware of what I'm dealing with at home. Once in a while they'll allow me to call home just to double-check on her and make sure everything is going OK. My job is very good and very rewarding. My father was an E-8 in the Navy, and from watching him in his career, taking on board a lot of the stuff that he did, I learned from him. Being in the Navy has taught me about responsibility. I grew up real fast."
—Parnell Chapell, USS *John C. Stennis*

Letter from a sailor's girlfriend: "Dear John, I couldn't wait any longer, so I married your dad. Love, Mom"

"There were always one or two members of the squadron who were on the 'wild side' on shore leave, but most were the best guys in the world. You flew their wing in formation, or they yours. This took trust. You flew with your team daily, lived with them, lifetime friendships were formed. All my squadron friends who survived the war later married and raised families."
—Richard May, former U.S. Navy fighter pilot

Admiral Mark Stanhope, former commanding officer, HMS *Illustrious*: "We are recognizing now that one of the most important requirements to continue the good will and motivation of our people is to ensure that they can talk to their home. The old letter is still an important mechanism, but it's somewhat dated in this day and age of instant communications, and while we're around the UK, everybody wants to use their cell phones. We have a system on board here on daily orders. It says Mobile Phone State Green which means that they can use their mobile phones should they wish to. There are about 700 mobile phones on board this ship. Most people have standard mobile phones that you can use around the UK, but there are some phones on board, 'anywhere in the world' phones, and they like that sort of access. Away from home, we have to look at other mechanisms to keep them all in touch. Email is a great facility on board, and they are allowed to send up to five letter-page emails a week.

"We have an operational requirement to have phone connectivity with headquarters, the Ministry of Defence and such like, which carries with it, on a ship of this size, about nine or ten different telephone lines. During the working day these are being utilized by various officers to do their business, but in the evening we take three, sometimes four of these lines and pass them through a phone box

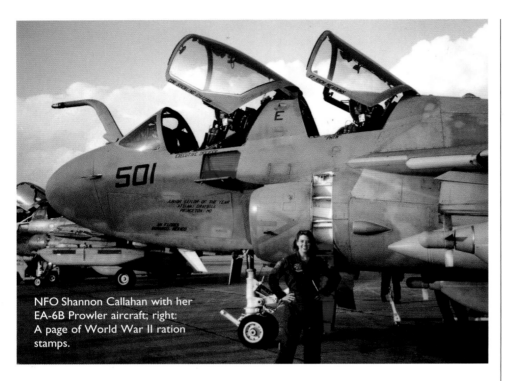

NFO Shannon Callahan with her EA-6B Prowler aircraft; right: A page of World War II ration stamps.

down below. The ship's company can go into this phone box and ring a number that gives them access to any net that they want to use to phone home. This costs, I think, about thirty-three pence a minute. Quite expensive. In my time in submarines, we went away for eight weeks and didn't speak once to family. Here they have it available to them at cost. It carries with it a burden. I can't deny that. The burden is that it has changed communications. The average sailor on board suffers the ups and downs of home life . . . little Johnny is sick or the wife has just smashed the car up, or mother is ill, and so all the woes that we were, frankly, cocooned from in the past, as you go away and leave your wife to sort out all the problems, go home at the end of a trip and help her sort them out . . . now its on a daily basis. So, lots of information gets fed to people that they want to do something about but can't.

"We have something called the Naval Families Services System, which is an organization where, if there is a problem at home, an illness or a bereavement, or a marital problem, or anything, the wife can get hold of this organization, which can then go and see the wife and find out just how serious the problem really is. They will then signal me with their recommendation. They will tell me what the problem is and maybe give me a recommendation that, in their opinion, it's important that we give this sailor three weeks leave to go home and sort out the problem, or support the family, or look after the children while the wife is ill, and I would normally react to them positively. It would only be an operational expedient that would cause me to say 'I'm sorry. I understand the situation, but I cannot spare this man.' That's finally my judgement. In and around the UK we would make that judgement fairly easily. You can

get people on and off. What we can't do abroad is get them backwards and forwards very easily. When we go to the Gulf, for instance, it's easy for me to reduce the number of people on board this ship when we're doing an exercise. I'm not quite so free and easy about giving up one of my two radar maintainers when radar is critical to our operational capability. So that becomes slightly more demanding. How do I ensure that the ship's company can appreciate the difference? How can I make sure that when we get out to the Gulf they are clear that this isn't quite the free and easy time that they've had before, and that I'm going to be a bit more restrictive in dealing with them? My answer to that was that I think you've got to be as open as you can with the ship's company about the business in the first place. Set it up. 'Put the money in the bank.' That is, in circumstances when it is quite possible to let the people go, let them go. Then, when you can't let them go, at least you can say, 'Look, I've got a track record here of letting people go as best I can when the circumstances permit. Right now, the circumstances do not permit. I'm sorry. Sod's Law says it happens to you when we were operational, and it happened to Jimmy Smith over there when we weren't operational.' I think that's really the only way you can do it. They did join the Navy and the Queen pays them, and therefore, in the end, you've got to take the Queen's shilling, as they say, and do the business.

"I think it is essential today to provide our people with instantaneous communiction. I'd go further. I know in the American Navy, on deployment, they sometimes even offer to the ship's company video links with home so they can see little Johnny growing up.

"People don't like being separated and you can't show the stiff upper lip in true grit British style and go away for two-and-a-half years. It wasn't so long ago, not in my time in the Navy, but certainly in my lifetime, that the Navy used to go away for two-and-a-half years. You'd sail from Portsmouth, leaving your wife and kids on the jetty. Now we have formal limits on how long these ships can be deployed. We have harmony rules on how long the ship's got to sit in its own dockyard port. Theoretically, the planners should look at keeping these ships in dockyard ports, which is Portsmouth for *Illustrious*, for something like forty-three percent of the year. You aggregate your time over two or three years to compensate for the fact that some years you're gonna be away more than others. That's what we're working too. We don't allow ships to go away for longer than six months. If they do, someone's got to explain why that is, and if that's the case, then allowances are made for a foreign visit, to support the wives going out for that foreign visit, or provide interest-free loan support to wives going out for that visit. This is very much part of the way we are doing our business now and the more we can make the lifestyle of these people acceptable, the easier it is to recruit them. Much of what I'm suggesting does cost money; there's no two ways about it, but it can be leeched onto the side of the operational requirement anyway. TV! It seems small beer, but the government in one of their last defence reviews, are trying to fit satellite television to all ships. It's quite difficult to do, actually. This big platform is a challenge in itself. I can switch on the TV and get CNN because of its operational importance. In the Gulf, in the ops room in my command seat, I can convert the screen to present to me an intelligence picture, flight deck cameras, or

CNN, and in the Gulf CNN was an important mechanism because they pick it up so much quicker than most. We're looking at putting satellite televisions on all ships."

You love us when we're heroes, home on leave, or wounded in a mentionable place. You worship decorations, you believe, that chivalry redeems the war's disgrace. You make us shells. You listen with delight, by tales of dirt and danger fondly thrilled. You crown our distant ardours while we fight, and mourn our laurelled memories when we're killed.
—from *Glory of Women* by Siegfried Sassoon

Frank Furbish: "One of the most valued possessions I took away from my stint in the Navy was the camaraderie built with my squadron mates. Your squadron becomes your family while on the boat. The bunk room member's problems become your problems and an individual's joy becomes a collective joy. Things didn't always run smoothly in that small room housing the nine of us, but overall we got along well. I still keep in touch with several of my fellow squadron mates. Along with the camaraderie, serving aboard the boat builds a sense of duty and pride in your country. Most folks don't take in 'the big picture' and just go out and do their job while serving aboard the ship. Defending the rights of your country and developing pride in a job well done is a reward in itself.

"Perhaps the greatest morale booster for most of us was receiving mail. Those with sweethearts or wives and family really needed reassurance that everything was OK at home. Even the act of writing was therapeutic and stabilizing, and helped offset our loneliness and feelings of futility. It was sad to realize that some crew members never received mail or packages, and those of us who did, often tried to share as best we could. While being away from home for such lengthy periods strengthened personal bonds for some, it undermined them for others."

When a carrier returns to its home port after a long deployment half a world away, the final few hours before the great ship can be maneuvered to her berth, tied up, and connected to the quay by gangplanks, can be the longest hours of the cruise. Thousands of wives, children, girlfriends, parents, relatives, and friends anxiously press forward on the quay, straining to pick out their particular sailor amid the ranks of officers and ratings lining the edge of the flight deck.

As the ship is finally secured, there are shouts of sailor's names, and hundreds of waving arms and hands holding up homemade signs: HEY BOBBY, CAN'T WAIT, IT'S A BOY! and WELCOME HOME. The restless, expectant crowd has been waiting six months for the return of this vessel and now the final moments of waiting are almost agony. By Navy tradition, the men of the ship's company who are the fathers of babies born while the carrier has been on deployment, are entitled to disembark before all the others. The first moments of the homecoming, tearful and happy, are treasured.

A rare non-operational day aboard a Royal Navy carrier at sea. The flight deck is made available to the crew for a picnic and other activities.

There's still no letter . . . in my troubled mind I seek a reason, and quickly reasons find. Indeed, they tumble in, to be discarded, each as it comes . . . it could be that you're very busy; missed the evening post; or else it's held up in the mail. A host of explanations . . . yet that gnawing fear o'errides them, still keeps dunning at me that you just don't want to write. And vainly I attempt to thrust aside the thought; deny it with your last note, and the one before. But no. I must resign myself to wait until tomorrow, or the next day and a day. Surely then I see your handwriting and envelope. And life is sweet, until a week or so, when . . . still no letter.
—*Still No Letter* by John Wedge

IN THE GULF

A Grumman F-14 Tomcat taxiing out for take-off at NAS Miramar near San Diego. Introduced into fleet service in September 1974, the F-14s were finally retired from U.S. Navy operational work in 2006.

YOU START OFF WITH A BIG BAG OF LUCK and an empty bag of experience. The trick is to fill the bag of experience before you empty the bag of luck.

It was all set to be the first daylight strike of the Gulf War, the Allied Coalition effort to force the invading Iraqis back from their incursion into neighboring Kuwait. F/A-18C Hornets from the U.S. Navy carriers *John F. Kennedy* (CV-67) and *Saratoga* (CV-60) were to launch the daylight phase of an ongoing strike series to be conducted round the clock. The night before, 16 January 1991, the black sky over Baghdad was rent with streaks and dotted lines of neon-like anti-aircraft artillery fire. The triple-A was in response to a massive first strike by several coalition aircraft, on airfields and other facilities around the city. Iraqi surface-to-air missiles flew at the attackers, and a few interceptors of Saddam Hussein's air force rose to the occasion. In the evening's action, three Iraqi MiG-29s and Mirage F1s fell to the weaponry of U.S. Air Force F-15C Eagles. The flak and SAMs accounted for some Allied aircraft losses; the interceptors remained but a threat.

The next day the Navy continued the activity. Lieutenant Commander Mark Fox was flying from the *Saratoga* in one of the spare aircraft, airborne in case any of the other Hornets on the raid should develop a problem and have to abort. In fact, three squadron aircraft had to return to the carrier, unable to complete their assignment, and Fox moved into the line-abreast formation to join the mission.

The four F/A-18s proceeded on course toward their airfield target, H3 in western Iraq. They were heavy, each of them loaded with four Mk 84 2,000-pound bombs. The Hornets were being monitored from above by an AWACS E-3B Sentry aircraft from the King Khalid air base near Riyadh, and an E-2C Hawkeye of VAW-125 from the *Saratoga*.

Mark Fox had prepared well for the attack he was running in on. He had set and checked the required switches for the drop. As the *Saratoga* Hornets approached the target from the south, Fox began hearing radio calls from aircraft of the *Kennedy* strike force Hornet pilots who had sighted a few Iraqi MiG-29 Fulcrums following them as they left the target area after releasing their ordnance. In seconds, two U.S.A.F. F-15C Eagles appeared from a higher flight level and fell upon the MiGs, disposing of them and their potential threat to the heavily loaded Hornets.

Now the Hornets were less than thirty-five miles from the bomb-release point, when the Hawkeye called them with a "bandit alert." More MiGs were in the area and were believed to be heading for the Hornet flight as it continued toward H3. The situation became serious when the Hornets received a second call from the Hawkeye, telling them that the MiGs were fifteen miles dead ahead. At that moment, both Lt. Cdr Fox, and Lt. Nick Mongillo in a nearby Hornet, elected to reset their weapons systems to "missiles" for possible air-to-air engagement. When the four Navy pilots drew within ten miles of the bandits, three of them got "missile-lock" on the two enemy aircraft which were MiG-21 Fishbed fighters. Fox had the MiG on the right; Mongillo took the other. Radar missile-lock was then also achieved by the other Hornet pilots.

The MiG fighters approached the Hornets head-on at supersonic speed and did not waiver. Fox was the first to fire, sending a Sidewinder toward his MiG. For good measure, he also fired a Sparrow missile at his target. The MiG became a fireball, absorbing both missiles, but it was the Sidewinder that had destroyed it. Within seconds of Fox's kill, Mongillo loosed a Sparrow at the MiG in his lock, splashing it as well. Though heavily loaded with bombs and not ideally set up for aerial combat, the two Hornets had made their kills and now joined up with the other two for the bomb run. They attacked the airfield target and turned south again on a heading for the Gulf and their carrier. Two towering columns of black smoke marked the locations on the desert floor where their MiGs had impacted.

The incident may have been the first when fighter/attack airplanes carrying 8,000 pounds of bombs engaged and shot down two other fighters, and then were able to continue on and complete the bombing attack. Lt. Cdr Fox knew, however, that if the MiGs had been able to get behind his flight, the Hornets would have been compelled to jettison their bombs in order to take on their adversaries. In the only confirmed U.S. Navy air-to-air victories over Iraqi fixed-wing aircraft in the Gulf War, the Hornet proved the really special plane most Navy pilots had long believed it to be.

This is the transcript of a radio conversation between a United States Navy ship and Canadian authorities off the coast of Newfoundland in October 1995. It was released by the U.S. Chief of Naval Operations, 10 October 1995.

Canadians: Please divert your course fifteen degrees to the south to avoid a collision.
Americans: Recommend you divert your course fifteen degrees to the north.

Canadians: Negative. You will have to divert your course fifteen degrees to the south to avoid a collision.
Americans: This is the Captain of a U.S. Navy ship. I say again, divert YOUR course.
Canadians: No. I say again, you divert YOUR course.
Americans: This is the aircraft carrier USS *Abraham Lincoln*, the second largest ship in the United States Atlantic Fleet. We are accompanied by three destroyers, three cruisers, and numerous support vessels. I demand that you change your course fifteen degrees north. I say again, that's one-five degrees north, or counter-measures will be undertaken to ensure the safety of this ship.
Canadians: We are a lighthouse. Your call.

Learn from the mistakes of others. You won't live long enough to make them all yourself.

"Flight operations consisted of various missions for each specific tactical aircraft. Fighter missions varied, from the boring grid search looking for submarines, to actual combat. Obviously, missions are dependent on the world political picture—news we rarely knew.

"Standing 'alerts' is part of carrier life. We fighter pilots had three alert stages: thirty, fifteen, and five minutes. The status refers to the amount of time required to be airborne and ready for combat. Alert Thirty required us to stay within 1,000 feet of the aircraft. In other words, don't leave the boat. Alert Fifteen meant being in full flight gear, sitting in the ready room. Alert Five was 'stood' sitting in the aircraft, strapped in and ready to go. At times the aircraft was even hooked up to the catapult. The

watches were stood in succession: Thirty, then Fifteen, then Five, with each stage two hours long. At night Alert Thirty was stood in your rack; Alert Fifteen in the ready room watching a video of anything even remotely entertaining, or sleeping in a chair. Alert Five at night was 'stood' in the aircraft, either sleeping or reading a book. There was a friendly competition between the two sister squadrons to be the first off the deck, and in one dramatic incident a RIO, in order to be the first off, took a bad INS alignment. The crew were stationed on a combat air patrol a few hundred miles from the carrier, outside of radio range of the ship. In the course of their flight, they lost their alignment and bearings, and could not relocate the ship and were not close enough to contact the ship by radio. Eventually, they ran out of fuel and were forced to eject. Luckily, they were picked up by another ship after spending a very long night in their life raft."
—Frank Furbish, former Navy fighter pilot

When Kelly Kinsella was a high school student in the Washington DC area, she was interested in attending a college that had a good competitive swimming program. In the middle of her senior year, she received a call from the swim coach at the United States Naval Academy, recruiting her to swim there. Her grandfather had been a Class of 1935 Academy graduate, but that had been the extent of her involvement with the institution. Intrigued by the possibility of being accepted for enrollment in the Naval Academy, she applied and did very well there, so well that by the second semester of her senior year, she was entitled to select her choice of Navy career assignment areas; she chose aviation.

At left, the light aircraft carrier HMS *Illustrious*, at right, the 102,000-ton USS *John C. Stennis*.

Following her 1993 graduation, Kelly reported to NAS Pensacola for API and Primary training. From there she selected the E-2/C-2 pipeline. Although at that point jets were open to women aviators in the Navy, she preferred the C-2 Greyhound or COD (carrier onboard delivery) community and has never regretted her decision. "I really enjoy my job and think that I get more out of flying people to and from the carrier than I would dropping bombs. My job may not be as glamorous as a fighter pilot's, or seem as important to an outsider, but I wouldn't trade the C-2 community for any other.

"The final test for the E-2/C-2 pipeline is to carrier qualify in the T-2 Buckeye. The first time one lands on a carrier is one of the greatest days in your life. It is an amazing experience to fly solo, in a four-plane formation with one instructor in the lead plane and two of your close friends rounding out the flight, out to a carrier. Circling overhead, you ask yourself if you are really supposed to land on that small ship down there.

"After winging, I went to the Fleet Replacement Squadron (FRS), which is responsible for training newly-winged aviators in the aircraft that he or she will fly in the fleet. Again, qualifying at the carrier is the final check at the FRS, only this time you get to go at night as well. Night carrier aviation is what sets naval aviators apart from all other pilots. I am now in my second Westpac deployment, doing night landings. It takes a long time to become confident at night. To say that one ever becomes comfortable at night would be a bit misleading.

"During my time in this squadron [VRC-30], I will have done two Westpac deployments to the Arabian Gulf and numerous evolutions off the

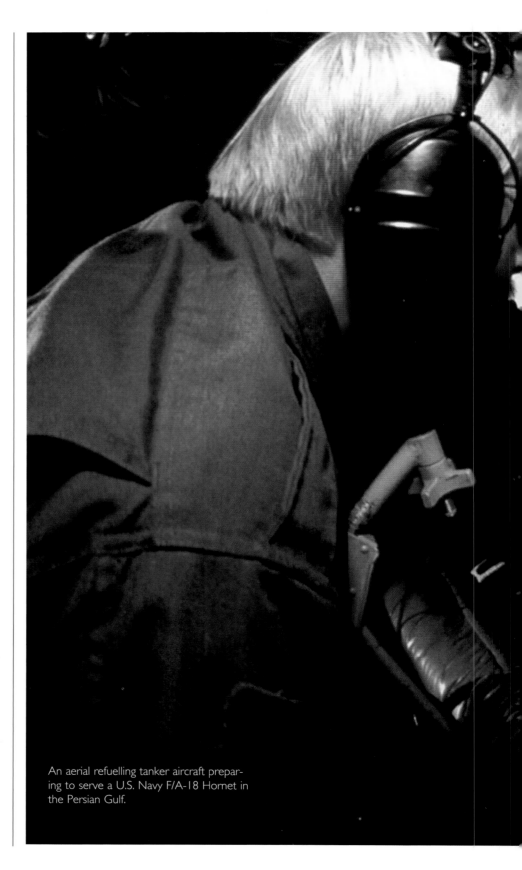

An aerial refuelling tanker aircraft preparing to serve a U.S. Navy F/A-18 Hornet in the Persian Gulf.

POWER RUDDEVATOR

CIRCUIT BREAKERS

An F/A-18 Hornet strike figher secured
for the night aboard the supercarrier
USS *John C. Stennis*.

coast of southern California. One of
the nice parts of being a COD pilot
is that we are always supporting one
carrier or another. There have been
very few months at the squadron
when I did not go out to the ship to
get some traps. I have flown all sorts
of folks out to see the ship and that
is what makes the job so much fun.
I have met Cabinet members, foreign dignitaries, Hollywood stars, and
famous athletes. Famous or not, to
see the look on anyone's face as they
get ready to fly out to the ship, or
when they have just had their first cat
shot, reminds me that I have a rare
job indeed. We sometimes get run a
bit ragged, flying back and forth several times a day, but the enthusiasm
of the people we take to the carrier
is contagious and really makes the job
enjoyable.

"I have obviously not known any
different than the Navy of today,
where women fly any and all aircraft.
The COD has been flown by women
longer than any other carrier aircraft
because it is not considered a com-
batant aircraft. There have been many
times when I have found myself to be
the only woman in a room, but that
can happen in almost any traditionally male-dominated job. I have been
trained exactly like every other aviator,
past and present, to do a job. The
women who paved the way in carrier
aviation did a remarkable thing and
made it easier for my age group to follow. The men I work with who are my
age have always worked with women,
so it is not an issue. Some of the older
generation are still getting used to
having women in the squadrons, but
so long as we are doing the job well,

there's nothing they can say anymore
about our presence. We are here and
we are doing well.

"Being on a carrier with almost
5,000 men, I would be lying if I said I
didn't receive any different attention
for being a woman. You stand out
and that's just a fact. But again, the
most important thing is getting the
job done. I feel very fortunate that on
this carrier [the USS *John C. Stennis*]
there are several female aviators. My
last Air Wing only had two female
pilots—myself and my roommate, an
E-2 pilot. We felt we were under the
spotlight quite a bit, but that comes
with being the only two women. This
Air Wing has women in every type of
aircraft. My roommate is a helicopter
pilot, also on her second cruise. The
two women next door to me were
naval aviators before combatants

A Boeing McDonnell Douglas F/A-18 Hornet photographed from an aerial refuelling tanker aircraft.

opened up to women, flying A-4s in the Philippines and Puerto Rico. One is now an F/A-18 Hornet pilot and the other is an EA-6B Prowler pilot. They both have flown combat missions and are respected for their abilities as much as any pilot in the squadrons.

"Having two senior aviators like them on board also helps set the standard for the new women checking into squadrons. Their professionalism and talent set the tone for the Air Wing. There are also two F-14 RIOs, two E-2 Naval Flight Officers, two S-3 pilots, and two other helicopter pilots (in addition to my roommate). So, we are well represented. The best part about being with all of these women is that they are typical women who just happen to also be naval aviators. We are not here to prove anything or to be 'one of the guys'; we get along great with our fellow aviators and are all doing the job the Navy has trained us to do. We are all good friends, and having the support of one another makes life at sea much more enjoyable.

"Following this cruise, I have chosen to take non-flying orders. The decision to not fly for the next three years was a difficult one, but at this point it is the right one for me. I am going back to the Naval Academy to work in the swimming department. I look forward to sharing everything I have learned with the future aviators, especially the women. It's a level playing field now and hopefully they are ready to take advantage of that. I am ready to move on and have a family—my fiancé will still be flying for the Navy and I want to be home enough to start having children. I know I will eventually go back to flying, perhaps civilian flying or in the reserves. I don't think anyone can completely walk away from flying—it's too amazing. My dream is to fly seaplanes, either in the northwest or in the Caribbean, depending on my family. I hope my kids will be proud to say that their mom was a carrier aviator who flew all over the world and met many fascinating people. How many people can tell their children they have done what I have been fortunate enough to experience? At times I look back and wonder how this all happened. I never set out to do anything so great, but I sure have had a ball."

Somebody said that carrier pilots were the best in the world, and they must be or there wouldn't be any of them left alive.
—Ernie Pyle, war correspondent

GALLERY

A Vought F-8 Crusader ends its days in the
airplane graveyard near Davis-Monthan AFB,
Tucscon, Arizona.

McDonnell Douglas F-4 Phantoms
in "finger four" formation.

U.S. Navy attack aircraft gathered at an air
base in the Persian Gulf in 1991.

A U.S. Marine Corps AV-8B Harrier II jet, an improved version of the British VSTOL ground attack aircraft.

The Northrop Grumman EA-6B electronic warfare / attack aircraft was developed from the Grumman A-6 Intruder. The last deployment of the Prowler was scheduled for November 2014. It is being replaced by the Boeing EA-18G Growler which entered Navy service in late 2009.

The flight deck of an aircraft carrier is among the most dangerous of working environments.

AN AIRCRAFT CARRIER GLOSSARY

Ace: Fighter pilot credited with five or more aerial kills.

ACLS: Automatic Carrier Landing System.

ACM: Air Combat Maneuvering.

AEW: Airborne Early Warning.

Air Boss: Officer responsible for carrier flight operations.

Air Wing: The complement of aircraft on a carrier.

Angle of attack: The angle of the wing of an aircraft to the flight path of the aircraft.

ASW: Anti-Submarine Warfare.

AV-8B: Boeing McDonnell-Douglas version of the BAE Sea Harrier V/STOL jet fighter.

Avenger: Grumman TBF / TBM torpedo bomber.

Ball: Primary optical landing aid on a carrier.

Bandit: Identified enemy aircraft.

Barrier net or Rig: Nylon webbing arrangement that can be set up to halt an aircraft whose arresting hook has malfunctioned.

Bat turn: Extreme sharp turn.

Bear a hand: Help out.

Bearcat: Grumman F8F fighter aircraft.

Belay that!: Cancel the previous message or order.

Bingo Field: A land runway where an aircraft can be diverted if the pilot is unable to land on a carrier.

Bird Farm: Nickname for an aircraft carrier.

Blue Angels: U.S. Navy flight demonstration team.

Blue shirts: Flight deck personnel who handle chocks and chains, drive tractors, and operate the elevators.

Blue Water Ops: Flight operations flown beyond the reach of a Bingo airfield.

Boat, the: Aviator reference to the aircraft carrier.

Bolter: A failed landing on a carrier, when the arresting hook does not engage any of the four arresting cables on the flight deck.

Box: The channel on a catapult entry in which an aircraft nosewheel is positioned to facilitate the hook-up and launch.

Brown shirt: The airplane captain responsible for the care and readiness of the aircraft.

Buccaneer: British Aerospace/Blackburn strike aircraft.

Burner: The afterburner unit on an aircraft jet engine; used to provide maximum thrust or power.

CAG: Carrier Air Group; also Carrier Air Group commander.

Call Sign: Pilot's nickname.

CAP: Combat Air Patrol.

Catapult: Steam-powered system utilized to launch aircraft to flying speed from a carrier flight deck.

CATCC: Carrier Air Traffic Control Center.

Cat grip: Grab handle on canopy jamb of F/A-18 Hornet and F-14 aircraft; also known at the "towel rack."

CCA: Carrier Controlled Approach in which a pilot is talked down the approach to the flight deck by a radar controller in the ship.

CDC: Combat Direction Center on a carrier, where all tactical information is displayed and analysed.

Chock: A frame that is placed around an aircraft tire to prevent the plane rolling.

Chopper: Helicopter.

Chow: Food; a meal.

CO: Commanding Officer.

COD: Carrier Onboard Delivery, a twin-engined aircraft used to ferry cargo or passengers to an from an aircraft carrier.

Corsair: Chance-Vought F4U fighter aircraft.

Corsair II: Vought A7 fighter aircraft.

Coupled approach: A landing approach in which the autopilot of the aircraft is linked to radio navigation aids.

Cranial: The safety helmet worn by aircraft carrier flight deck personnel.

Cross-deck pendant: The segment of the arresting cable which is stretched across the flight deck and is engaged by the tailhook of an aircraft.

Crusader: Chance-Vought F-8 fighter aircraft.

Cut, the: Landing Signal Officer signal for a pilot to land.

CV: U.S. Navy designation for a conventionally-powered aircraft carrier.

CVE: U.S. Navy designation for an escort aircraft carrier.

CVL: U.S. Navy designation for a light aircraft carrier.

CVN: U.S. Navy designation for a nuclear-powered aircraft carrier.

Cyclic Ops: Aircraft launches and recoveries from a carrier at one or two-hour intervals.

Dauntless: Douglas SBD dive-bomber aircraft.

Dilbert Dunker: A device for teaching emergency escape from an aircraft downed in the sea.

Dropline: A series of orange lights down the stern centerline of an aircraft carrier, used by a pilot on landing approach to gauge the corrections he makes in his approach.

ECM: Electronic Counter-measures; a system used for jamming enemy detection, weapons and communications.

Eject: Emergency escape from an aircraft by means of an explosive-charged seat.

Elevator: An ascending and descending section of the flight deck of an aircraft carrier, used to transport aircraft between the hangar deck and the flight deck.

Etendard: Dassault Breguet strike fighter aircraft; also Super Etendard.

EWO: Electronics Warfare Officer.

FDO: Fighter Director Officer.

Fish: Torpedo.

Flag Plot: Admiral's working spaces.

Flak: See Triple A.

Flanker: Sukhoi Su-27 jet fighter aircraft.

Flattop: Aircraft carrier.

Flight deck: The platform exposed surface of an aircraft carrier where aircraft are launched and recovered.

Float coat: Inflatable vest worn by flight deck personnel.

FLOLS: The Fresnel Lens Optical Landing System employed as the primary landing aid on an aircraft carrier; also called the Ball.

Fly-by-wire: Control surfaces of an aircraft that are operated by electronic rather than mechanical means.

FOD: Foreign Object Damage resulting when an aircraft engine injests debris from the flight deck of an aircraft carrier.

FOD Walk-down: Carried out before every flight event; in which many personnel form a line across the flight deck, to walk its length in search of any objects that might foul aircraft engines or injure people if blown around by taxiing aircraft.

Fouled deck: When the flight deck of a carrier is not, for any reason, in a condition to receive recovering aircraft.

FRS: Fleet Replacement Squadron; see RAG.

Fulcrum: MiG-29 jet fighter aircraft.

Galley: Where chow is prepared.

Gannet: Fairey ASW/AEW aircraft.

Gedunk: Ship's store where candy and junk food is sold.

Glidepath: Approach course of an aircraft that is descending and recovering to the flight deck of a carrier.

Glideslope: An optical or electronic beam that marks the approach glidepath of a recovering aircraft.

GQ: General Quarters.

Green shirts: Flight deck crewmen who secure aircraft to catapults for the launch to flying speed.

Greyhound: See COD.

G-Suit: Flight suit that brings compressed air pressure to reduce effects of gravity load forces on an airman's lower body.

Handler: Person responsible for positioning, moving and arranging aircraft on the flight and hangar decks of a carrier.

Hangar deck: The area of a carrier, under the flight deck, where aircraft are stored and maintained.

Hawkeye: Grumman E-2 airborne early-warning aircraft.

Helix: Kamov Ka-31 helicopter.

Hellcat: Grumman F6F fighter aircraft.

Helldiver: Curtiss SB2C dive-bomber.

Helo Dunker: Device for teaching emergency escape technique from a helicopter down in water.

Holdback: A breakable link device that restrains an aircraft on the catapult until the instant of the launch.

Hook: The arresting tailhook of an aircraft, located beneath the tail and utilized to engage an arresting cable on the flight deck of a carrier.

Hornet: Boeing Northrop Grumman F/A-18 jet multi-role fighter aircraft and aircraft family.

Hot-pumping: Refuelling an aircraft with its engine(s) running.

HUD: Head-up display, where the instrument data are projected onto a transparent screen between the pilot and the windshield.

ILS: Instrument Landing System.

INS: Inertial Navigation System.

Intruder: Grumman A-6 attack aircraft.

Island: A superstructure on the right side of the flight deck of a carrier, housing the bridge, PriFly, and other personnel.

Jet blast deflector: A metal rectangular barrier that is raised behind an aircraft on the catapult awaiting launch; used to protect deck personnel.

Jinking: Evasive aircraft manouver.

Joy stick: Aircraft control column; often includes firing switches and other controls.

Kamikaze: World War Two Japanese suicide pilot, attack, or aircraft.

Knee-knocker: Oval-shaped doorway through a bulkhead on a carrier.

Launch: When a catapult flings an aircraft from the flight deck of a carrier.

Liberty: Shore leave.

LLD: Landing light device; the Ball on a carrier Fresnel Lens Landing System.

LSO: The Landing Signal Officer, responsible for guiding the recovery of aircraft to the flight deck of a carrier. The LSO judges and comments on aircraft approaches, assisting the pilots, giving grades and critiques of all landings; also called "Paddles."

MAD: Magnetic Anomaly Detector; device utilized to locate submerged enemy submarines.

Mae West: Inflatable life vest.

Main deck: On a carrier, it is the hangar deck; the deck from which the numbering of all other decks begins.

Marshal: Or Marshalling Stack; a holding pattern located behind the carrier, for aircraft prior to their approach abnd recovery.

Meatball: See Ball.

Military power: Maximum aircraft engine power.

Mouse: Self-contained two-way radio headphones for the use of certain flight deck personnel.

MOVLAS: Manually Operated Visual Landing System, used as a back-up for the FLOLS on a carrier.

Mule: A small tractor used for moving aircraft on the flight and hangar decks.

NAS: Naval Air Station.

NFO: Naval Flight Officer.

Nose tow: A tow bar that extends from the nose wheel of a carrier aircraft, which secures to the catapult for launching.

Now hear this!: Listen up.

Nugget: Neophyte pilot.

O Club: Officers' Club.

Old Salt: Experienced sailor.

Panther: Grumman F9F fighter aircraft.

Phantom: McDonnell-Douglas F-4 fighter-bomber.

Pickle: A hand-held switch device by which an LSO can illuminate a row of red lights on the Ball to wave off an approaching pilot.

Port: The left side of a ship; also a harbor or docking place.

Precision Approach Radar: Shows the altitude and position of an aircraft that is approaching the carrier for a landing recovery.

PriFly: Primary flying control station in the island.

Prowler: Grumman EA-6 attack-early warning aircraft.

Purple shirts: Deck crews responsible for refuelling of aircraft; also called "Grapes."

Qual: Pilot's aircraft carrier qualification flights.

Rack: Enlisted man's bed; a three-high bunkbed.

RAG: Replacement Air Group; see FRS.

Ramp: The aft edge of the flight deck of a carrier.

Ready Room: Briefing and lounge space for a squadron.

Red shirts: Deck crews who handle ordnance, load bombs and ammunition; they also handle fire equipment.

Rig for: Set up or prepare.

RIO: Radar Intercept Officer; rides the back seat of F-4 Phantom, F-14 Tomcat, and F/A-18F Super Hornet aircraft, performing navigation and weapons system functions.

Roof: Slang for flight deck of a carrier.

Rounddown: The ramp or aft end of the flight deck.

SA: Situational awareness.

SAR: Search and rescue.

Scuttlebutt: Rumors.

Seafire: Supermarine fighter aircraft.

Sea Fury: Hawker fighter aircraft.

Sea Hawk: Hawker fighter-bomber aircraft.

Seahawk: Sikorsky UH-60 helicopter.

Sea King: Westland/Sikorsky helicopter.

Shuttle: Device on catapult which protrudes above the flight deck; the aircraft nose tow is attached to the shuttle prior to launch.

Sick bay: Ship's hospital.

Silver suits: Personnel who handle crashes and fires.

Skyhawk: Douglas A-4 attack aircraft.

Skyraider: Douglas AD attack aircraft.

Slider: A hamburger.

SNJ: North American Aviation trainer aircraft.

Sortie: One mission flight by one aircraft.

Spool up: Running up the power of a jet engine.

Squawk box: A ship's intercom system.

Starboard: The right-hand side of a ship.

Strafe: To fire an aircraft's guns at a surface target.

Swordfish: Fairey multi-role biplane.

TACAN: Measures bearing and distance between the carrier and an aircraft.

Tail-end Charlie: The last aircraft in a formation.

Tomcat: Grumman F-14 jet multi-role fighter aircraft.

Torpecker: Torpedo bomber.

Tracer: Visible fired ammunition.

Trap: An arrested landing of an aircraft on a carrier flight deck.

Triple A: Anti-aircraft artillery; also called ack-ack or flak.

Turbo-Mentor: Beechcraft T-34 primary trainer aircraft.

Val: Aichi D3A dive-bomber.

VFR: Visual Flight Rules; operating procedures for use in good weather.

Viking: Lockheed S3B ASW aircraft.

VSTOL: Vertical Short Take-off and Landing.

Vulture's Row: Observation area located high on the island structure.

Wave-off: Aborted landing approach; an order from the LSO to a pilot to abort his landing approach.

White shirts: Deck crewmen responsible for inspecting at the catapult prior to launch.

Wildcat: Grumman F4F fighter aircraft.

XO: Executive Officer.

Yellow shirt: Crewman who directs the movement of aircraft on the flight deck of a carrier.

Zero-Sen: Mitsubishi A6M fighter aircraft.

PICTURE CREDITS: Photos from the collection of the author are credited AC; photos by the author: PK; U.S. National Archives: NARA; U.S. Navy: USN; Tailhook Association: TA; Imperial War Museum: IWM; HMS *Illustrious*: ILLUS. P3 top-ILLUS, left-AC, right-AC, P5-ILLUS, P6-AC, P9-NARA, P10-ILLUS, P13 top-AC, bottom-IWM, P14-ILLUS, P16-NARA, P18-AC, P21-PK, P22-NARA, P24-PK, P26-NARA, P29-ILLUS, P30-AC, P31 top-AC, bottom-NARA, P32-ILLUS, P34-PK, P35-PK, P36-AC, P39 all-AC, P40-PK, P42-AC, P44-AC, P45 both-AC, P46-NARA, P48-AC, P49-NARA, P50-NARA, P51-PK, P52 top-NARA, bottom-USN, P53-USN, P54-NARA, P56-USN, P59-NARA, P61-NARA, P63-AC, P64-AC, P67-AC, P68-AC, P71-AC, P72-AC, P75-NARA, P76-AC, P77-AC, P78-NARA, P80-AC, P83-AC, P84-AC, P88-AC, P90-ILLUS, P92-AC, P94-ILLUS, P96-ILLUS, P97-ILLUS, P99-AC, P100-PK, P101-ILLUS, P103-AC, P104-AC, P106-PK, P108-PK, P109-PK, P110-NARA, P112-BILL HANNAN, P115-PK, P116-PK, P117 both-PK, P118-NARA, P120-PK, P123-PK, P124-PK, P127-courtesy of BRUCE PORTER, P128-USN, P130-PK, P131-PK, P132-PK, P134 both-PK, P135-PK, PP136-137 all-PK, P138 left-PK, right-AC, P140-USN, P143-USN, P145-PK, P146-AC, P149-PK, P150-PK, P151-AC, P152-NARA, P154-NARA, P156-AC, P157-AC, P159-PK, P160-ILLUS, P162-NARA, P164-AC, P167-AC, PP168-169-AC, P17-courtesy of Randy Cunningham, P173-AC, P174-ILLUS, P176-PK, P177-USN, P178-AC, P181-ILLUS, P182-AC, P183-AC, P185-ILLUS, P187-courtesy Nigel Ward, P188-AC, P191-ILLUS, P192-ILLUS, P194-ILLUS, P195-AC, P196-AC, P199-ILLUS, P200-ILLUS, P202-USN, P203-AC, P205-USN, P206-ILLUS, P208-courtesy Shannon Callahan, P209-AC, P210-ILLUS, P212-ILLUS, P214-PK, P217-ILLUS, P218-AC, P220-USN, P221-NARA, P222-PK, P224-AC, P226-USAF ACADEMY LIBRARY, P228-USAF ACADEMY LIBRARY, P230-AC, P232-ILLUS,

ACKNOWLEDGMENTS: The author is grateful to the following for their kind help in the development of this book: Bill Barr, Malcolm Bates, George Blair, John Bolt, Jennifer Brattle, Eric Brown, Piers Burnett, James Cain, Shannon Callahan, Larry Cauble, Parnell Chapell, Bill Ciazza, M.S. Cochran, Ed Copeland, Jack Crascall, Robert Croman, Frank Cronin, Tracy Curtis-Taylor, Dale Dean, Claire Donegan, John Dunbar, Dewey Durnford, Robert Elder, Lynn Forshee, Mark Fox, Oz Freire, Frank Furbish, Richard K. Gallagher, George Gay, Tess Gay, Paul Gillcrist, Jack Glass, Hill Goodspeed, Stephen Grey, Mark Hanna, Bill Hannan, Thomas Harris, Susan Henson, Tony Holmes, Chris Hurst, Jan Jacobs, Benny L. James, Dave Jones, Hargita Kaplan, Margaret L. Kaplan, Neal B. Kaplan, Kelly Kinsella, Jack Kleiss, Craig Kodera, Thomas LaGrange, Casey Law, Alan J. Leahy, Jack Leaming, Elvin Lindsay, Bruce Lindsay, Paul Ludwig, Mike Machat, Richard H. May, John McCrarrie, Judith A. McCutcheon, Richard "Mac" McCutcheon, Rick McCutcheon, Dale McGhee, Hamilton McWhorter, Don McMillan, Neil Mercer, Steve Millikan, Nick Mongillo, Morris Montgomery, H.B. Moranville, Kevin Morris, Jeff Mulkey, Patrick J. Nichols, Steve Nichols, David B. Oates, Michael O'Leary, Merle Olmsted, Arnold W. Olson, Brian O'Rourke, Bruce Porter, Henry Sakaida, Doug Siegfried, Wayne Skaggs, David Smith, David Soper, Mark Stanhope, Danny Stembridge, John Strane, Nagel Sullivan, David Tarry, Hannah Tausz, Mark Thistlethwaite, Ed Toner, Stanley Vejtasa, Danny Vincent, Michelle Vorce, Alex Vraciu, Nick Walker, George Wallace, Nigel 'Sharkey' Ward, Sky Webb, Wilbur Webb, Pat Weiland, John Wellham, Wilbur West, Scott Whelpley, Andy Withers, Dennis Wrynn, Aaron Zizzo. My thanks to the following for the use of their previously published material: Airlife Publishing Ltd—excerpts from *Wings of the Navy*, by Captain Eric Brown, reprinted by permission of the author; Arms and Armour Press—excerpts from *Kamikaze*, by Raymond Lamont-Brown, reprinted by permission; Causley, Charles—for the use of his poem HMS *Glory*; Dell Division of Random House—excerpt from *Air Warriors*, by Douglas C. Waller; Fitz Roy, Olivia—for the use of her poem *Fleet Fighter*; Gay, Tess (Mrs George Gay)—excerpts from *Sole Survivor*, by Ensign George Gay, published by Midway Publishers and reprinted by permission of Tess Gay; Hutchinson Publishing Group—excerpt from *War In A Stringbag*, by Charles Lamb; Larteguy, Jean, and Blond, George—excerpts from Larteguy's edited version of Blond's description of a kamikaze attack, in Larteguy's *The Sun Goes Down*; McGraw-Hill—excerpt from *Daybreak For Our Carrier*, by Lieutenant Max Miller; Naval Institute Press—excerpt from *The Divine Wind*, by Captain Rikihei Inoguichi and Commander Tadashi Nakajima, with Roger Pineau; Turner Publishing Company—excerpts from *USS Enterprise (CV-6)*; Ward, Nigel—excerpts from *Sea Harrier Over The Falklands*, published by Orion, reprinted by permission of the author; Wedge, John—for the use of his poem *Still No Letter*.

BIBLIOGRAPHY: Bennett, Christopher, *Supercarrier*, Motorbooks International, 1996; Bowman, Martin W., *Shades of Blue*, Airlife Publishing Ltd, 1999; Brown, David, *Kamikaze*, Brompton Books Corp., 1990; Brown, Captain Eric, *Wings of the Navy*, Airlife Publishing Ltd., 1987; Burgess, Lieutenant Commander Richard R., *The Naval Aviation Guide*, Naval Institute Press, 1996; Caidin, Martin, *Golden Wings*, Bramhall House, 1960; Chant, Christopher, *Warships of the 20th Century*, Tiger Books International, 1996; Chesneau, Roger, *Aircraft Carriers of the World-1914 to the Present*, Arms and Armour Press, 1992; Chinnery, Philip, *Desert Airforce*, Airlife Publishing Ltd., 1989; Clancy, Tom, *Carrier*, Berkley Books, 1999; Congdon, Don, *Combat WWII Pacific Theater of Operations*, Arbor House, 1958; Costello, John, *Love, Sex & War*, Collins, 1985; Eliot-Morris, Samuel, *The Two-Ocean War*, Atlantic-Little Brown, 1963; Farmer, James H., *Celluloid Wings*, Tab Books, 1984; Garrison, Peter, and Hall, George, *Carrier Aviation*, Presidio Press, 1980; Goldstein, Donald M., Dillon, Katherine V., and Wenger, J. Michael, *Pearl Harbor-The Way It Was*, Brassey's, 1995; Harrison, W.A., *Swordfish Special*, Ian Allen, 1977; Holder, Bill, and Wallace, Mike, *F/A-18 Hornet A Photo Chronicle*, Schiffer, 1997; Holmes, Tony, *Combat Carriers*, Motorbooks International, 1998; Holmes, Tony, *Seventh Fleet Supercarriers*, Osprey Publishing Ltd, 1987; Horsley, Lt Cdr Terence, *Find, Fix and Strike*, Eyre & Spottiswoode, 1945; Humble, Richard. *Aircraft Carriers*, Michael Joseph Ltd, 1982; Ireland, Bernard, *The Rise and Fall of the Aircraft Carrier*, Marshall Cavendish, 1979; Isby, David C., *Jane's How to Fly and Fight in the F/A-18 Hornet*, Harper Collins Publishers, 1997; Jackson, Robert, *Air War Over Korea*, Airlife Publishing Ltd, 1998; Johnsen, Frederick A., *Douglas A-1 Skyraider*, Schiffer, 1994; Johnston, Stanley, *Queen of the Flattops*, E.P. Dutton & Co., 1942; Johnstone-Bryden, Richard, *HMS Ark Royal IV*, Sutton Publishing Ltd, 1999; Keeney, Douglas, and Butler, William, *No Easy Days*, BKF, 1995; Kelly, Orr, *Hornet*, Airlife Publishing Ltd, 1990; Lake, Jon, *Grumman F-14 Tomcat*, Aerospace Publishing, 1998; Lamont-Brown, Raymond, *Kamikaze*, Arms and Armour Press, 1997; Lawson, Robert, and Tillman, Barrett, *Carrier Airwar*, Motorbooks International, 1996; Loomis, Robert D., *Great American Fighter Pilots of World War II*, Random House, 1961; Lowry, Thomas P., and Wellham, John W.G., *The Attack on Taranto*, Stackpole Books, 1995; McManners, Hugh, *Top Guns*, Network Books, 1996; Melhorn, Charles M., *Two-Block Fox*, Naval Institute Press, 1974; Mercer, Neil, *The Sharp End*, Airlife Publishing Ltd, 1995; Miller, Lt Max, *Daybreak For Our Carrier*, McGraw-Hill, 1944; Monbazet, Jean-Pierre, *Super Carriers*, Osprey Publishing Ltd, 1989; Musciano, Walter A., *Warbirds of the Sea*, Schiffer, 1994; O'Leary, Michael, *United States Naval Fighters of World War II in Action*, Blandford Press, 1980; Poolman, Kenneth, *Escort Carrier 1941-1945*, Ian Allen, 1972; Porter, Col. R. Bruce, with Hammel, Eric, *Ace!*, Pacifica Press, 1985; Preston, Antony, *Aircraft Carriers*, Bison Books Ltd, 1982; Reynolds, Clark G., *The Fast Carriers*, McGraw-Hill, 1968; Reynolds, Clark G., *The Fighting Lady*, Pictorial Histories Publishing, 1986; Ross, Al, *The Escort Carrier Gambier Bay*, Conway Maritime Press, 1993; Shores, Christopher, *Air Aces*, Bison Books Ltd, 1983; Silverston, Paul, *US Navy 1945 to the Present*, Arms and Armour Press, 1991; Smith, John T., *The Linebacker Raids*, Arms and Armour Press, 1998; Smithers, A.J., *Taranto 1940*, Leo Cooper, 1995; Spick, Mike, *McDonnell Douglas F/A-18 Hornet*, Salamander Books Ltd, 1991; Steichen, Edward, *U.S. Navy War Photographs Pearl Harbor to Tokyo Bay*, Bonanza Books, 1956; Sweetman, Bill, *Joint Strike Fighter*, MBI Publishing Company, 1999; Taylor, Michael, *Naval Air Power*, Hamlyn Publishing, 1986; Watts, Anthony J., *The Royal Navy*, Arms and Armour, 1999; Weiland, Charles Patrick, *Above & Beyond*, Pacifica Press, 1997; Wellham, John, *With Naval Wings*, Spellmount, 1995; Wolff, Brian R., and Alexander, John, *From The Sea*, Reed International Books, 1997; Wragg, David, *Carrier Combat*, Sutton Publishing, 1997; Wragg, David, *Wings Over The Sea*, David & Charles, 1979; Wrynn, V. Dennis, *Forge of Freedom*, Motorbooks International, 1996.